SIMULATION STUDIES IN ARCHAEOLOGY

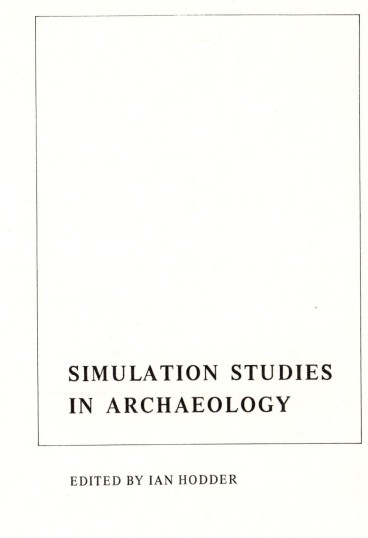

SIMULATION STUDIES IN ARCHAEOLOGY

EDITED BY IAN HODDER

CAMBRIDGE UNIVERSITY PRESS

CAMBRIDGE

LONDON – NEW YORK – MELBOURNE

Published by the Syndics of the Cambridge University Press
The Pitt Building, Trumpington Street, Cambridge CB2 1RP
Bentley House, 200 Euston Road, London NW1 2DB
32 East 57th Street, New York, NY 10022, USA
296 Beaconsfield Parade, Middle Park, Melbourne 3206, Australia

First published 1978

Printed in Great Britain at the
University Press, Cambridge

Library of Congress cataloguing in publication data

Main entry under title:
Simulation studies in archaeology.

(New directions in archaeology)
1. Archaeology – Simulation methods – Addresses,
essays, lectures. I. Hodder, Ian. II. Series.
CC75.7.S55   930'.1'028   78-51670

ISBN 0 521 22025 4

CONTENTS

For Christophe

CONTRIBUTORS

A.J. Ammerman, Program in Human Biology, Stanford University,
      California, USA.
S. Black, Department of Anthropology, University of Auckland,
      Auckland, New Zealand.
A.J. Chadwick, 52 Gough Way, Cambridge.
K.P. Donnelly, Statistical Laboratory, 16 Mill Lane, Cambridge.
K. Elliott, Department of Management Science, Imperial College,
      University of London, London.
D. Ellman, Department of Computer Science, The University, Leeds.
D.P. Gifford, Anthropology Studies Board, Merrill College, University
      of California, Santa Cruz.
F.W. Hamond, Clare College, Cambridge.
J.W. Harbaugh, Department of Applied Earth Sciences, Stanford
      University, California.
I. Hodder, Department of Archaeology, University of Cambridge,
      Cambridge.
D. Moore, Department of Computer and Information Science, The
      Ohio State University, Columbus, Ohio.
E. Okell, Department of Mathematical Sciences, Plymouth Polytechnic,
      Plymouth, Devon.
J.M. O'Shea, Department of Archaeology, University of Cambridge,
      Cambridge.
A. Voorrips, Albert Eggis von Giffen Institute for Pre- and Protohistory,
      University of Amsterdam.
L.J. Zimmerman, Department of Social Behaviour, University of South
      Dakota, Vermillion, USA.
E.B.W. Zubrow, Department of Anthropology, Stanford University,
      California.

PREFACE

Like many archaeologists, I was introduced to computer simulation by Jim Doran's (1970) article in *World Archaeology*, although Clarke (1968, p. 472) had already noted the potential for stochastic simulation in archaeology. Doran's article contained views such as that the 'history' generated by a simulation might well be both surprising and illuminating (p. 297), that the computer can construct and test a simulation of some complex system evolving in time as the practical equivalent to systems theory (p. 296), that computer simulations 'will certainly encourage that clarity, precision and objectivity of thought which so many are seeking' (p. 298), and I remember being excited reading his paper.

Simulation is used in many disciplines, such as sociology, anthropology, geography, economics, transport studies. Yet, after Doran's article nothing much seemed to happen in this respect in archaeology. Then, gradually, simulation studies began to appear such as those by Thomas (1972) and Wobst (1974), and already in 1975 Doran and Hodson could review a number of applications. But their conclusion was still disappointing. They agreed (p. 306) that simulation techniques 'have archaeological potential. But it must be admitted that there is virtually no direct evidence in support of this suggestion.'

Since that time the increase in experimental work which Doran and Hodson demanded has been considerable. In North America especially, a rash of studies using simulation has appeared. At the same time, more traditional statistical and quantitative analyses of archaeological data seemed to have reached a stage where it was impossible to interpret the results of complex analyses. Computer simulation offered an exciting and rewarding new line of enquiry — a way out.

Many of the applications of simulation in archaeology are concerned with trying to mimic some set of data. Thus a map of archaeological sites may have been obtained and one can try to simulate different processes in order to produce a similar map. The actual data might, on the other hand, be the fall-off curve of an artifact type away from its source. Here some hypothetical exchange process would be simulated, and fall-off curves would be produced and compared with the actual data. The aim in such studies is to show that particular theoretical processes *could* have produced the archaeological data. The effects of changing the parameters which control the simulation can be seen, and the variation in results due to any random or stochastic component in the model can be monitored. Simulation is used, then, to experiment with hypotheses which could have produced a set of archaeological data and to examine the behaviour of systems and processes. It involves modelling a process by a similar process which is usually simplified so that the functioning of the process or system being studied can be more easily understood. The nature of simulation and the reasons for using it are further discussed in chapter 1.

Simulation can be done by hand. But simulating complex processes in this way may be very time-consuming if large numbers of variables and events are involved. So computers are usually used simply as an aid, to speed things up. Although it can work very quickly, the computer can do nothing which the archaeologist cannot do himself. The computer can process information and carry out simple orders, but these orders need to be explained to it in special languages. Of the many languages which the larger computers can understand, FORTRAN is one of the most widely used (for example by Ammerman, Gifford and Voorrips in this volume). Introductions to programming in FORTRAN are provided by Calderbank (1969) and McCracken (1965). However, FORTRAN is relatively primitive and was not designed specifically for simulation. Languages more suitable for complex simulations are discussed in chapter 2.

The first two introductory chapters thus provide a basis for understanding the rest of the book where simulation is applied to settlement, population and exchange processes. Simulation can also be useful in examining the characteristics and performance of particular statistics and techniques, and this is shown in chapters 8 to 11. The overall role of computer simulation in archaeology, and the advantages and problems, are discussed in the concluding chapter. The editor's introductions at the beginning of each section place the chapters in the context of already published work in the same field.

This book, then, is intended to examine the role of computer simulation in archaeology. It provides an optimistic yet critical appraisal. Simulation is not the answer to every archaeologist's interpretative problems since it brings difficulties with it. But it does offer the chance of taking the interpretation of archaeological remains onto a level where clear thinking and precise procedures are encouraged, yet where the archaeologist's 'imagination' also plays an important role.

I should like to thank Jim Doran of Essex University for his useful comments, Brian Hartley of Leeds University for putting up with my strange attraction to large machines, and Françoise for refusing to take it too seriously.

References

Calderbank, V.J. (1969) *A course on programming in FORTRAN IV*, Chapman & Hall, London

Clarke, D.L. (1968) *Analytical Archaeology*, Methuen, London

Doran, J. (1970) 'Systems theory, computer simulations and archaeology', *World Archaeology* 1: 289–98

Doran, J. & Hodson, F.R. (1975) *Mathematics and Computers in Archaeology*, Edinburgh University Press

McCracken, D.D. (1965) *A Guide to FORTRAN IV Programming*, Wiley, New York

Thomas, D.H. (1972) 'A computer simulation model of Great Basin Shoshonean subsistence and settlement patterns' in D.L. Clarke (ed.), *Models in Archaeology*, Methuen, London

Wobst, H.M. (1974) 'Boundary conditions for Palaeolithic social systems: a simulation approach', *American Antiquity* 39: 147–78

PART ONE

Introduction:
Simulating the past

Chapter 1

**The contribution of simulation
to the study of
archaeological processes**
F. W. Hamond

Introduction

Archaeology possesses the unique ability to perceive human behaviour over a timespan considerably longer than is possible in other behavioural disciplines. Such behaviour is by no means random, and its regularities are often manifest in recurrent associations in the structure of artifacts associated with this behaviour. Such recurrences are termed patterns, and their successional development over time is known as a process (Harvey 1969, p. 419). Through an analysis of artifact patterns and processes, it may thus be possible to explain how and why such processes occurred and thus gain an understanding of human behaviour over a considerable timespan.

The exceedingly complex nature of archaeological phenomena necessitates the use of models in their understanding. All models act as simplifying devices, containing certain properties whose behaviour is analogous to reality. These properties are not totally equivalent to the properties of reality, but are a subset of them (Clarke 1972). Through the examination of these analogous properties, reality may be comprehended more clearly. The term simulation is sometimes used as if it were synonomous with modelling (e.g. Churchman 1963, p. 1), or with specific types of modelling (e.g. mathematical modelling, Bourelly 1972, p. 188).

However 'simulation' may also be used in a more restricted sense, as the modelling of a process by a process (Schultz & Sullivan 1972, p. 7). It is in this sense that the term will be used in this article, though Doran and Hodson (1975, p. 298) restrict it further, to the operating of stochastic process models. Thus the properties of a simulation model resemble, in form, some of the processual properties of the real-world situation under examination.

General introductions to simulation are to be found in Schultz and Sullivan (1972), and Shannon (1975). Simulation is widely used in the natural, social and behavioural sciences. In geography for instance, it has been applied to a wide range of topics, such as drainage networks (Haggett & Chorley 1969, pp. 286–93), transportation networks (ibid., pp. 294–302), diffusion studies (notably by Hägerstrand; Harvey 1967, pp. 589–92), and settlement development. This led Doran and Hodson (1975, p. 306) to remark: 'The established value of computer simulation techniques in other fields, together with the complexity of many archaeological problems, suggest that such techniques have archaeological potential. But it must be admitted that there is virtually no direct evidence in support of the suggestion.'

Certainly from a theoretical viewpoint, this would appear to remain the case, as there is little substantive literature on the theoretical and methodological applications of simulation to archaeological problems (e.g. Bourelly 1972; Doran & Hodson 1975). Moreover what does exist tends to be in the form of generalised statements on simulation's potential, rather than a rigorous development of its theory and methodology as applied to archaeological problems.

As is usual with innovations however, the lack of a developed theoretical framework has not hindered the increasing practical application of simulation in archaeology in recent years (cf. Whallon 1972, p. 39). These applications will be reviewed in the introduction to each part of this book.

I shall highlight the necessity of the use of simulation, particularly in the analysis of settlement processes, and develop a framework within which to evaluate the contribution simulation has already made to archaeology, its potential, and problems inherent in its usage.

Why simulate?

The analysis of settlement processes, that is the development of settlement across the landscape through time, is illustrative of the many limitations of the conventional approach to processual studies in general.

Conventional approaches to settlement processes

Conventionally sites are classified according to their function and date of use. The resultant settlement distribution encompasses a complex array of spatial patterns between sites of similar and dissimilar function, and between sites and features of their natural environment. Various analytical techniques are applied to these distributions in order to highlight their patterning. By comparing these patterns, the stability and change in the settlement process may be assessed, and various explanations of its development inferred (fig. 1).

In the analysis of their spatial form, sites can usually be conceived as points lying on a surface. Essentially then, such techniques measure point–point, and point–area relationships. The most basic point–point analytical techniques merely describe certain properties of distributions in the form of summary statistics. Central tendency and dispersion measures (Cole & King 1968, pp. 210–17), for instance, have been used by Sumner (1972) to describe changing prehistoric settlement patterns in southern Iran.

At a higher level of analysis, the distribution's summary statistic is statistically compared with those of distributions whose form is already known. Thus mean-variance, quadrat, nearest-neighbour, Thiessen polygon, entropy and pattern-searching techniques (Rogers 1974; Kershaw 1964) yield particular statistics, which are then compared with comparable statistics of other distributions, most commonly clustered, random and regular distributions. Whallon (1973; 1974) discusses quadrat and nearest-neighbour analyses in the context of spatial archaeology.

At the highest level of analysis, a distribution's summary statistic is compared with those of distributions whose *causative* process is known. Most commonly such a process is random, such that every point within an area has an equal and independent chance of being settled, and the position of any site in no way influences another. Such a process results in a Poisson or binomial distribution, depending on its operating conditions, though processes having also a clustering component give rise to such forms as the negative binomial and Neyman Type A, and those having a regular component, to the negative Poisson and negative generalised double Poisson (McConnell 1966; Rogers 1974). Hodder (1977, pp. 244–54) has used such techniques in an analysis of Neolithic settlement development in Little Poland.

Fig. 1. Patterns and processes seen at three times (T_1, T_2, T_3).

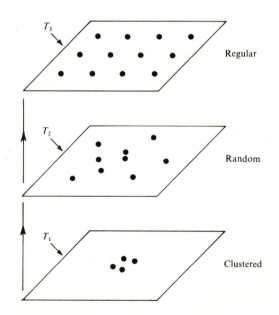

Spatial property

As with point—point techniques, the most basic point—area analytical techniques merely describe sites in relation to one or several features of their surrounding natural environment (e.g. Vita-Finzi & Higgs 1970; Sielmann 1972). However at higher levels of analysis, such patterns are compared with those of known form, and with random patterns, whose causative process is stochastic (e.g. Dohrn-Ihmig 1974).

Limitations in this approach

If meaningful conclusions are to be reached on the basis of these patterns, it must be assumed that the data from which they are derived fully represent the true picture of settlement in space and time.

Archaeological time however can only be measured to a low level of precision. Artifact type-fossils are commonly used to assign sites to a particular time period. However because of the nature of artifact development in space and time (cf. Clarke 1968, figs. 37, 38) such artifacts may also occur, albeit less frequently, in other time periods which are characterised by other type-fossils.

Apart from dendrochronology, the application of which is restricted by a lack of material, carbon-14 dating is the most precise absolute dating method available. However if one accepts that such dates should be interpreted as having a 95% probability of lying within a ± 2 standard deviation range of the mean date quoted, rather than actually being the date quoted (which has a probability of occurrence usually less than 1%), on calibration, such a date has a 4 standard deviation range of uncertainty varying from 180 years in recent periods, to over 500 years in the 5th millenium BC (Clark 1975, table 7). Such imprecision limits the archaeologist's ability to measure the degree of contemporaneity between sites, the duration and absolute chronology of their occupation, and the duration of the time period which is being analysed.

Thus the grouping and description of sites in the context of such time periods may conceal interesting developments within and between these times (fig. 2).

The spatial techniques outlined above have for the most part been developed in fields, such as geography and plant ecology, where the nature of the data is known exactly. However the transformation of a map of prehistoric settlement to an archaeological distribution map is influenced by many biasing factors. I have shown elsewhere (Hamond 1978) that subsequent settlement, natural processes of deposition and erosion, present-day land-use and the variable extent and quality of archaeological fieldwork (fig. 3) can make an archaeological map far from complete. Consequently such biases also occur in any patterns measured.

The techniques themselves may also influence the patterns measured. Area delineation, grid size and placement problems in point—point analyses, and the assumption of no spatial autocorrelation between sites in the use of the chi-squared test in point—area analyses are but a few examples of such limitations.

How meaningful are the patterns measured, even allowing for data and technical limitations? A basic assumption in the inference of process from pattern is that there is a causative relationship between two or more variables which correlate (e.g. sites and soils). However such correlation may not be so significant if the first variable correlated with a third, which also happened to correlate with the second.

Such inference is also usually restricted to either point—point, or point—area relationships, but seldom both. This unrealistic modelling of settlement systems, together with the analysis of one, or at most a few factors in each of these relations, severely restricts the power of processual explanations.

Lastly, but perhaps most important of all, is the problem

Fig. 2. Alternative developments of archaeological form seen at three times (T₁, T₂, T₃).

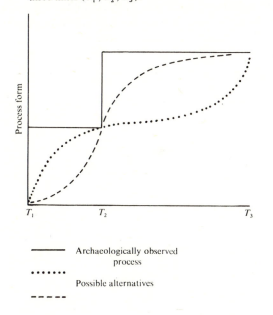

Process form

T₁   T₂   T₃

—————— Archaeologically observed process

········· Possible alternatives

– – – –

Fig. 3. Spatial biases in distribution maps.

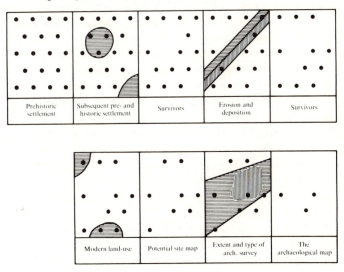

| Prehistoric settlement | Subsequent pre- and historic settlement | Survivors | Erosion and deposition | Survivors |

| Modern land-use | Potential site map | Extent and type of arch. survey | The archaeological map |

of inferring process *from* form. It is unusual for more than one processual explanation to be inferred from the same data. However a pattern may be derived in a large number of different ways (Harvey 1968).

It is for these reasons that a fundamentally new approach to the analysis of processes is needed.

Simulation methodology

There are four basic stages in the use of simulation: hypothesis conceptualisation, model construction, computer implementation, and hypothesis validation. In the first stage the nature of the hypothesis, relevant explanatory factors, its spatial and temporal dimensions, and the scale of analysis involved are specified. In the model construction stage these concepts are synthesised into a precisely stated processual model, in which its components and operation over time are specified. In the third stage, the model is translated into a computer program which is then run on the computer in order to simulate the behaviour of the model through time. In the final interpretation stage, computer-derived outcomes of different models are compared with one another, and with the observed data, to assess the validity of the explanatory hypotheses, by the degree of resemblance between the predictions of the hypothetical process and the outcome of the actual process.

Hypothesis conceptualisation

A realistic explanation of a process should encompass a complex set of quantitatively specified, interacting factors which operate through time. A realistic hypothesis regarding settlement relocation processes, for example, might incorporate features of both the 'natural' and 'social' environments, as well as post-depositional factors.

Though a model should not be simplistic, it ought not to be overcomplicated and unclear. Pareto's principle states that 'In terms of performance and effectiveness [of the simulation model], there are a few significant factors and many insignificant ones' (Shannon 1975, p. 153). Walker's (1972) application of the LIFE game to settlement development shows that quite complicated patterns might be explicable in terms of fairly simple models. However, as Morrill (1965) and Chadwick (1977) demonstrate, it may be necessary to utilise simplistic models initially in the formulation of realistic models.

It is also necessary to consider the nature of the variables in the hypothesis. The non-deterministic nature of human behaviour may be modelled by stochastic variables, such that though individual and short-term behaviour cannot be exactly described, group behaviour in the long term can be predicted. The behaviour of these variables over time should also be considered. Morrill (1965) for example has developed a model which itself changes over time.

The temporal and spatial dimensions of the analysis should also be explicitly specified at this stage, and the scale of analysis, so as to ensure that the correct levels of explanatory variables are built into the hypothesis: 'The scale of the study determines the level of model appropriate for its rep-

resentation and the process appropriate for its explanation' (Clarke 1972, p. 23). This is exemplified in those analyses of the colonisation of Europe, which, at the continental–millenium scale, can be envisaged as a uniform colonising movement across the loess 'tramlines' of Europe, whereas, at a local level, over short time periods, may be seen as a series of short-term random local migrations. The results of large-scale analyses (over small areas and timespans) are easily transformed into interpretations at small scales (e.g. Ammerman & Cavalli-Sforza 1973b), though the reverse procedure is impossible (e.g. Rowe *et al.* 1974). Finally, the temporal and spatial components of the model should be specified simultaneously within it (e.g. Ammerman & Cavalli-Sforza 1973a; Thomas 1972; 1973a).

Model construction

A model is a precise and explicit representation of a processual hypothesis and is directly deduced from it. A systematic framework perhaps offers the best viewpoint for the understanding of the components of a processual model. A process may be thought of as an outcome, O, of a mechanism made up of a system S, subjected to certain inputs I, operating under certain conditions, C, through time (fig. 4). The system itself is composed of elements, each one having a certain value, or parameter, at any moment in time. On the basis of an (incomplete) knowledge of O, the other components must be reconstructed. A simple example of such a system could be the process of population increase, the outcome of a system having the element 'population growth', value 3% per annum, operating under logistic growth conditions, with no in- or out-migration.

Suppose N_i to be the total number of inputs that might possibly be associated with a particular model. Let N_c be its total number of possible operating conditions. Further suppose it to have n possible elements, $E_1, \ldots, E_n$, each of which can have a number of possible parameters, such that element E_1 has $P_{E1}, \ldots,$ element E_n has P_{En} possible parameters. Also suppose each model contains certain stochastic elements which require it to be run R times (see below). Then the total possible number of different models, N, that would need to be compared with one another is:

$$N = (N_i).(N_c).(P_{E1}).(P_{E2}). \ldots .(P_{En}),$$

Fig. 4. The components and feedback mechanisms of a processual model.

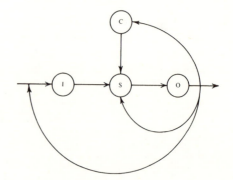

and the total number of outcomes, O, to be compared would be:

$$O = R.N.$$

As an example suppose a model were developed which had 2 possible input conditions ($N_i = 2$), 3 possible operating conditions ($N_c = 3$), each of its 3 elements ($n = 3$) having 2 possible values ($P_{E1} = P_{E2} = P_{E3} = 2$), each model requiring 10 runs. Then

$$O = 10.2.3.2.2.2 = 480.$$

Ammerman and Cavalli-Sforza's (1973*b*) BAND 2 simulation model employs 6 variables (having from 2 to 4 values each), and 3 operating conditions, resulting in 576 possible submodels to be evaluated.

Thus to develop adequately any particular hypothesis, a large amount of costly computer time is required, not only to run the different models, but also to aid the interpretation of the vast amount of output. Hence great importance is attached to this stage of the overall procedure.

Not only must the model's components be specified adequately, but also their behaviour over time considered. Feedback mechanisms in particular must be considered. These mechanisms act so that the output from the system may affect its input, the conditions under which it operates, or the system itself (Von Bertalanffy 1971). Some, or all, of the output may be fed back, each of I, C and S being simultaneously affected totally, partially or not at all (fig. 4). Many published examples demonstrate the use of these feedback mechanisms (Ammerman & Cavalli-Sforza 1973*a*; 1973*b*; Chadwick 1977; Aldskogius 1969; Zubrow 1971; Morrill 1965).

In specifying these feedback mechanisms it is thus necessary to define the nature of the boundary conditions operative on the process, and also to distinguish endogenous variables, which change as the system operates, from exogenous ones which are unaffected (Doran & Hodson 1975, p. 300; Brown & Albaum 1971).

In conclusion then, a simulation model should be composed of a number of exogenous and endogenous factors, of constant and variable values, whose behaviour through time is governed by a complex set of feedback mechanisms. Not surprisingly this ideal is difficult to achieve in practice, and it may be necessary to simplify the model in order to construct, translate, operate and interpret it. In the extreme case one could consider only a few factors, operating within a closed system, behaving in a deterministic and invariant fashion through time (e.g. Zubrow 1971). Feedback mechanisms may also be ignored (e.g. Bylund 1960) or the operating conditions of the system held constant (e.g. Rowe *et al.* 1974).

Computer implementation

Manual operation of stochastic process models is both complicated and time consuming owing to the large number and complex interactions of their components. Moreover each model, having no unique outcome, must be repeatedly run in order to sample representatively all its possible outcomes. The use of a computer speeds up these operations considerably.

The use of a computer necessitates the translation of the verbally described model into a language acceptable to the machine. Such translation is by no means straightforward, and may even be more time consuming than the rest of the study. In the long term though, the computer has considerable advantages in its ability to handle a large number of related models, its repetitiveness and speed. Such advantages must be balanced against the short-term difficulties of its implementation.

The three main steps in this implementation phase are: model translation into a machine-readable language, the verification of this program's correct translation and operation, and, finally, the actual operation of the program model by the computer.

Model translation involves the construction of flow charts and the choice of a computer language. A flow diagram is a schematic two-dimensional representation of the time-ordered series of steps through which the model proceeds (Shannon 1975, p. 53). Such diagrams allow one easily to comprehend the main stages in the model's operation (cf. Brown & Albaum 1971), and the detailed sequence of all possible stages of the process (Thomas 1972, fig. 17.3; Levison, Ward & Webb 1973, fig. 9).

Though such diagrams clearly show the passage of time over which the model operates, the use of digital computers to mimic this operation often imposes a restriction on how time is treated. Processes which continuously change over time may be represented as sequential changes over discrete time periods. Thus simultaneous events are not directly modelled. An artificial ordering of the sequence of occurrence of such events is specified beforehand by the programmer, or randomly selected by the computer. Time itself is often only represented in discrete blocks, of seconds, years, or centuries. Continuous time can be approximately modelled if the behaviour of the model is updated after the passage of only a short time period. However, shortening this time period increases the number of cycles over which the model must operate, for a given process to occur. So a balance must be struck between more detailed temporal information, and increased operating costs. The effects of different orderings of simultaneous events, and choice of time cycle may be gauged by experimentation.

Having explicitly specified the stages in its operation, the model must be translated into a language acceptable to the computer. Both general-purpose languages and those developed specifically for simulation are available. Their relative merits and applicability are discussed by Shannon (1975, p. 98). A general-purpose language, FORTRAN (McCracken 1965), is perhaps preferable to a simulation language as it is easily understood and learnt, widely used, and thus recognisable, repeatable and adaptable by others, and is machine independent (but see chapter 2 for an alternative view).

The program is then written, closely following the modular form and flow of the charted sequence, though it should be sufficiently flexible to be easily modified should the need arise. Such flexibility necessitates some complexity in the writing of the program which must be balanced against its remaining comprehensible. These translation procedures inevitably result in some errors being made. Thus it must be ascertained that the program behaves in accordance with the model from which it is derived. This 'debugging' procedure involves running the program under a set of conditions whose outcome is known beforehand. Discrepancies between the expected and generated outputs are then indicative of programming errors.

Once the verbal model is correctly translated into a computer model, it can then be run through a number of cycles which represent, in a greatly compressed form, the true passage of time. A series of outputs are produced, the interpretation of which may be aided by the further use of the computer.

Hypothesis validation

Only by the actual running of a simulation model can the validity of its associated hypothesis be evaluated. This validation procedure involves the derivation of the model's outcomes, and their comparison with the archaeologically observed data.

The successive temporal outcomes, and their cumulative result, of a particular simulation run can be established both in terms of specific distributions and summary statistics of these distributions, using the techniques outlined earlier in this chapter.

However, because of the model's stochastic nature, none of its outcomes will be unique. The technique of Monte-Carlo sampling (Harvey 1967, p. 582) must therefore be employed to ascertain the range and modal behaviour of the stochastic model's outcomes. If the model is run many times, the cumulative average of its outcomes at each successive time period rapidly converges towards the model's most probable outcome. By this method one can also establish the range of possible distributions, and their properties.

In comparing a real and theoretical distribution a variety of properties should be compared; a spurious similarity may arise from the comparison of only a few properties. The data compared should be compatable both spatially *and* temporally, otherwise similar patterns occurring at different times may be erroneously equated.

Unfortunately there is, as yet, no entirely satisfactory method of comparing spatial distributions. Though visual inspection may distinguish significantly different distributions, it is subjective and cannot distinguish small differences (e.g. Hodder 1977). Most of the statistical techniques outlined earlier in this chapter are however aspatial in character. Thus the derivation of a summary statistic is at the expense of spatial information. Using such techniques, a distribution would be described by the same statistic as its inversion or reflection. Spatial techniques, which compare distributions as a whole are, however, relatively underdeveloped. One possible means of comparison measures the spatial autocorrelation of the differences between the observed and predicted pattern (Cliff & Ord 1973 and see Chadwick, chapter 5 below).

An added difficulty is the fact that the observed archaeological process, being the product of a stochastic development, is but one of many possible outcomes that could have occurred. Thus it must be established whether the actual observed outcome could be a member of the set of theoretical outcomes possible under a particular hypothetical development.

Perhaps the most serious drawback to the comparison of theoretical and observed distributions is the fact that though the former are complete, the latter are not (see p. 3 above). Because it is often uncertain whether the absence of sites in an area is real, or the result of some biasing factor, distributions can only be compared in those areas where archaeological sites exist. If a similarity is indicated, then those areas where sites are not, and are predicted (negative evidence being as important as supporting evidence), can be sampled for sites to see whether this similarity remains.

The contribution of simulation to archaeological theory and practice

Despite the difficulty in the construction and testing of processual hypotheses, simulation is nevertheless potentially useful in the development of archaeological theory and practice.

Hypothesis development

Hypothesis development involves the construction and refining of a realistic hypothesis concerning processual phenomena. At a conceptual level, Clarke (1972) and Zubrow (1971) demonstrate that even the simplest of non-operational hypotheses may have a certain resemblence to reality, and perhaps even highlight facets of the data not previously recognised. The mere recognition of these facets may accelerate the development of more refined recovery techniques in data gathering. Such simple models may also yield sufficiently encouraging results to justify the construction of more complex and realistic hypotheses (e.g. Morrill 1965; Chadwick 1977).

However the full benefit of the use of simulation only comes with the derivation of operational models from these conceptual hypotheses. Doran (1970, p. 297) has remarked: 'The attempt to create computer simulations will certainly encourage that clarity, precision and objectivity of thought which so many are seeking.' The construction of a processual model thus necessitates a rigorous formulation of its associated hypothesis (e.g. Levison *et al.* 1973).

Not only does this procedure necessitate clear thinking, but it also exposes to close scrutiny the assumptions inherent in the construction and operation of the model. Thus many of the spatial relocation rules and operating conditions of the reviewed models may be unjustifiable in human behavioural terms (e.g. Rowe *et al.* 1974; Walker 1972 respectively).

Such explicitness may also highlight potential weaknesses in a hypothesis. For example. Ammerman and Cavalli-Sforza (1973*a*) assume that settlement migration distributions have the form of a Gaussian (Normal) curve, though no justification is presented; Hodder and Orton (1976, p. 144) and Morrill (1965, p. 33) discuss alternative, more likely, descriptions of such migration.

Explicitness also highlights the narrowness of certain hypotheses. Thus Ammerman and Cavalli-Sforza (1973*b*) suggest the swidden system of agriculture to be a causative element in Bandkeramik settlement relocation, though in fact it seems probable that sites were continually occupied over considerable periods of time (Modderman 1971).

More elusive weaknesses are also highlighted, in particular when the data to be explained are themselves used as an explanation. Thus Clarke (1972) simulates, or rather mimics, the regularity of Körös settlement spacing by incorporating into the relocation component of his model the observed regularity of site spacing. Some *a posteriori* justification is given for this however. Thus the components of a processual model should have an *a priori* theoretical justification, if they are not only to explain adequately the particular process under review, but also have a more general applicability to other situations. Such explicitness in the formulation of a processual model thus forces one to consider the variables involved in the process, the nature of the data used in its validation, and the level of explanation invoked.

Some would argue that the benefit of simulation comes not from the running of the model and interpretation of the results, but from its explicit modelling: 'Researchers who do use simulation . . . feel that much of the value of a simulation model lies in the development of explicit statements of the internal relationships in the model rather than in its operation and manipulation' (Marble 1972, p. 385). However it is only by operating such models that the assumptions are tested and errors and ambiguities in the construction emerge.

Such shortcomings may be manifest in contradictions which emerge during the operation of the model, and may be caused by mismanagement in the operation, or more likely, by erroneous model formulation. For example Ammerman and Cavalli-Sforza (1973*a*) permit settlement migration in all directions, which thus makes it possible for settlements to relocate simultaneously at the same place, or in extreme proximity. Relocation can also occur in areas already saturated with people. Both these possibilities contradict the assumptions on which the model is built. Thus all the components of the model must be stated explicitly to minimise ambiguities (cf. Everson & Fitzgerald 1969), and the model constructed so as to be testable.

As has already been pointed out, the operation of a simulation model also generates hypothetical data for the testing of hypotheses and may reveal aspects of the data not previously thought to be of interest (e.g. Thomas 1973*b*). Through operating a model one can establish those factors which are necessary and sufficient to explain the observed process. By the partial omission of these factors, their effects on the model's outcome may be assessed, and those elements that have a significant influence distinguished from those that do not. Though these latter factors may well have operated within

the process, they can be regarded as constants in its operation, and thus be ignored in the explanatory hypothesis. Hodder, for example, (Hodder & Orton 1976, p. 137) demonstrates the insignificant effect that semi-permeable barriers have on exchange mechanisms, though Ammerman and Cavalli-Sforza show (1973*b*) that quite minor modifications to a model may significantly affect its outcome.

In addition to being able adequately to assess the importance of particular processual factors, simulation also allows one to evaluate the sensitivity of models to changes in the parameters of particular variables. Thus a small change in the parameter of a particular element may result in a considerable change in the model's output, though other changes may have little effect. Thus Hodder found artifact fall-off curves to be sensitive to changes in the mean of a negative exponentially distributed step length (Hodder & Orton 1976, fig. 5.28 curves 1,5; 2,6), though relatively insensitive to changes in the number of steps (ibid., fig. 5.28 curves 1–4; 5,6). A more detailed analysis of the data might then be necessary if the actual parameters involved in the process were to be determined, though Hodder and Orton (1976) show that useful generalisations may be made despite the insensitivity of certain of their models. Likewise, despite Wobst's (1974) lack of knowledge of the particular parameters of his model, its equifinal results enabled him to reach productive conclusions.

Theory development

Simulation is an essential tool in the *explicit* testing of *specific* processual hypotheses, and thus in the development of archaeological theories (cf. Thomas 1973*b*; Levison *et al.* 1973).

If it can be established that a model does not adequately explain the data, the hypothesis from which it is derived may be modified, remodelled and retested. However if a high degree of correspondence is found between the archaeological and predicted data, it is usual to accept the validity of the hypothesis, which then assumes the status of a theory. However, Levison *et al.* (1973, p. 12) remark that such a hypothesis has 'no validity other than that which is built into the model'.

Thus one should bear in mind the simplified nature of the model before finally accepting the hypothesis. However, even then, such a hypothesis is only a demonstrable possibility, in that it could have, but might not have, occurred. Hence it is important to construct multiple working hypotheses in order to ascertain the most likely explanations of an actual process. Even if they cannot be tested against the data, they can at least be compared with each other to highlight their key differences. Three different, yet broadly similar hypotheses regarding the spread of farming have already been cited (Clarke 1972; Ammerman & Cavalli-Sforza 1973*a*; Rowe *et al.* 1974). However Bylund (1960) has indicated the need to construct radically different hypotheses in the explanation of any process.

Not only should a variety of models be examined, but each should incorporate a variety of factors in its operation. For example one might consider the factors of population growth, settlement duration, *perception* of a range of environ-

mental features (modified by distance), a distance-dependent
migration component, and the influence of other sites in a
realistic settlement process model (Hamond, in preparation).

However given the many technical inadequacies in data
recovery and interpretation, several hypotheses may equally
explain the data. Despite the continued development of more
refined techniques, there may ultimately prove to be a level of
explanation beyond which we cannot go, as certain processes
may not be distinguishable using the data. As yet though, we
have only just begun to explore the possibilities of simulation.

Acknowledgements

I am grateful to Dr A.G. Sherratt, Ashmolean Museum,
Oxford for his comments on this chapter.

References

Aldskogius, H. (1969) 'Modelling the evolution of settlement patterns:
two studies in vacation house settlement', *Geografiska Region-
studier* 6: 43–108

Ammerman, A.J. & Cavalli-Sforza, L.L. (1973a) 'A population model
for the diffusion of early farming in Europe' in C. Renfrew (ed.)
The Explanation of Cultural Change: Models in Prehistory,
Duckworth, London

Ammerman, A.J. & Cavalli-Sforza, L.L. (1973b) 'Bandkeramik simulation models: a preliminary report'. Unpublished MS

Bourelly, L. (1972) 'Quelques aspects de la notion moderne de simulation' in M. Borillo (ed.) *Les Méthods Mathématiques de
l'Archéologie*, Centre d'Analyse Documentaire pour l'Archéologie, Marseille

Brown, L.A. & Albaum, M. (1971) 'On rural settlement in Israel and
model strategy' in H. McConnell & D.W. Yassen (eds.) *Perspectives in Geography*, Illinois University Press

Bylund, E. (1960) 'Theoretical considerations regarding the distribution
of settlement in inner north Sweden', *Geografiska Annaler* 42:
225–31

Chadwick, A. (1977) 'Computer simulation of settlement development
in Bronze Age Messenia' in J. Bintliff (ed.) *Myceanean Geography:
Proceedings of the Cambridge Colloquium, September 1976*,
Cambridge University Library

Churchman, C.W. (1963) 'The analysis of the concept of simulation' in
A.C. Hoggatt & F.E. Balderston (eds.) *Symposium on Simulation
Models: methodology and application to the Behavioural
Sciences*, E. Arnold, London

Clark, R.M. (1975) 'A calibration curve for radiocarbon dates',
Antiquity 49: 251–66

Clarke, D.L. (1968) *Analytical Archaeology*, Methuen, London

Clarke, D.L. (1972) 'Models and paradigms in contemporary Archaeology' in D.L. Clarke (ed.) *Models in Archaeology*, Methuen,
London

Cliff, A.D. & Ord, J.K. (1973) *Spatial Autocorrelation*, Pion, London

Cole, J.P. & King, C.A.M. (1968) *Quantitative Geography*, Wiley,
London

Dohrn-Ihmig, M. (1974) 'Untersuchungen zur Bandkeramik im Rhein-
land', *Rheinische Ausgrabungen* 15: 51–142

Doran, J. (1970) 'Systems theory, computer simulations and archaeology', *World Archaeology* 1: 289–98

Doran, J. & Hodson, F.R. (1975) *Mathematics and Computers in
Archaeology*, Edinburgh University Press

Everson, J.A. & Fitzgerald, B.P. (1969) *Settlement Patterns* (Concepts
in Geography No. 1), Longman, London

Haggett, P. & Chorley, R.J. (1969) *Network Analysis in Geography*,
E. Arnold, London.

Hamond, F.W. (1978) 'The interpretation of archaeological distribution
maps: biases inherent in archaeological fieldwork', *Archaeo-
Physika* (in press)

Hamond, F.W. (in preparation) 'New approaches to settlement archaeology: the simulation of Bandkeramik settlement development
in the Lower Rhine Basin'. Ph.D. thesis, Cambridge University

Harvey, D.W. (1967) 'Models of the evolution of spatial patterns in
human geography' in R. Chorley & P. Haggett (eds.) *Models in
Geography*, Methuen, London

Harvey, D.W. (1968) 'Some methodological problems in the use of
Neyman Type A and negative binomial distributions for the
analysis of spatial point patterns', *Transactions of the Institute
of British Geographers* 44: 85–95.

Harvey, D.W. (1969) *Explanation in Geography*, E. Arnold, London

Hodder, I. (1977) 'Some new directions in spatial analysis', in D.L.
Clarke (ed.) *Spatial Archaeology*, Academic Press, London

Hodder, I. & Orton, C. (1976) *Spatial Analysis in Archaeology*,
Cambridge University Press

Kershaw, K.A. (1964) *Quantitative and Dynamic Plant Ecology*,
E. Arnold, London

Levison, M., Ward, R.G. & Webb, J.W. (1973) *The Settlement of
Polynesia: a computer simulation*, University of Minnesota Press,
Minneapolis

McConnell, H. (1966) *Quadrat Methods in Map Analysis* (Department
of Geography Discussion paper 3), Iowa University

McCracken, D.D. (1965) *A Guide to FORTRAN IV Programming*,
Wiley, New York

Marble, D.F. (1972) 'Human geography simulations' in H. Guetzkow,
P. Kotler & R.C. Schultz (eds.) *Simulation in Social and Administrative Science*, Prentice-Hall, Englewood Cliffs, New Jersey

Modderman, P.J.R. (1971) 'Bandkeramiker und Wanderbauertum',
Archäologisches Korrespondenzblatt 1: 7–9

Morrill, R.L. (1965) *Migration and the Spread and Growth of Urban
Settlement. Lund Studies in Geography*, Series B, No. 26

Rogers, A. (1974) *Statistical Analysis of Spatial Dispersion: the Quadrat Method*, Pion, London

Rowe, C., Rolfe, J., Dearden, R., Kent, A. & Grenyer, N. (1974) 'The
Neolithic game' in *Oxford Geography Project, 2: European
Patterns*, Oxford University Press

Schultz, R.L. & Sullivan, E.M. (1972) 'Developments in simulation in
social and administrative science' in H. Guetzkow, P. Katler &
R.L. Schultz (eds.) *Simulation in Social and Administrative
Science*, Prentice-Hall, Englewood Cliffs, New Jersey

Shannon, R.E. (1975) *Systems Simulation: the art and the science*,
Prentice-Hall, Englewood Cliffs, New Jersey

Sielmann, B. (1972) 'Die Frühneolithische Besiedlung Mitteleuropa', in
H. Schwabedissen (ed.) *Die Anfänge des Neolithikums vom
Orient bis Nordeuropa. Fundamenta*, series A, vol. 3, part Va

Sumner, W.M. (1972) 'Cultural development in the Kur river basin, Iran:
an archaeological analysis of settlement patterns'. Ph.D. thesis,
Pennsylvania University

Thomas, D.H. (1972) 'A computer simulation model of Great Basin
Shoshonean subsistence and settlement patterns' in D.L. Clarke
(ed.) *Models in Archaeology*, Methuen, London

Thomas, D.H. (1973a) 'An empirical test of Steward's model of Great
Basin settlement patterns', *American Antiquity* 38: 155–76

Thomas, D.H. (1973b) 'Notions to numbers: Great Basin settlements
as polythetic sets' in C.L. Redman (ed.) *Research and Theory in
Current Archaeology*, Wiley, New York

Vita-Finzi, C. & Higgs, E. (1970) 'Prehistoric economy in the Mount
Carmel area of Palestine: site catchment analysis', *Proceedings
of the Prehistoric Society* 36: 1–37

Von Bertalanffy, L. (1971) *System Theory*, Penguin, Harmondsworth

Walker, G. (1972) 'Two settlement simulations' in W.P. Adams & F.M. Helleiner (eds.) *International Geography 1972: papers submitted to the 22nd International Geographical Congress, Canada.* University of Toronto Press.

Whallon, R. (1972) 'The Computer in archaeology: a critical survey', *Computers and the Humanities* 7: 29–45

Whallon, R. (1973) 'Spatial analysis of occupation floors I: the application of dimensional analysis of variance', *American Antiquity* 38: 266–78

Whallon, R. (1974) 'Spatial analysis of occupation floors II: the application of nearest-neighbour analysis', *American Antiquity* 39: 16–34

Wobst, H.M. (1974) 'Boundary conditions for Palaeolithic social systems: a simulation approach' *American Antiquity* 39: 147–78

Zubrow, E.B.W. (1971) 'Carrying capacity and dynamic equilibrium in the prehistoric Southwest', *American Antiquity* 36: 127–38

Chapter 2

Simulation languages for archaeologists
Dan Moore

Introduction

The widely held concept of a computer, by which we will mean a modern, high speed electronic digital computer, as a fast and accurate calculating device is misleading. In fact most computers spend very little time performing arithmetic calculations. Computer professionals refer to computers more accurately as information processing devices. Simulation modelling using computers relies heavily upon this information processing capability, because program models, when used for experimentation (Doran 1972, pp. 428—9), are sets of instructions to a computer detailing how it is to process information about the modelled entities.

While there are many languages available for expressing these instructions, the only languages of any real utility to the general computer user are the *compiler languages* because they are problem oriented rather than machine oriented. A recent roster of compiler languages in use in the United States (Sammet 1976, pp. 655—56) lists 167 languages, some 20 of which are general-purpose languages suitable for expressing program models, and some nine of which are specifically designed for simulation. However, only three general-purpose and three special-purpose languages are of any real importance to the archaeologist who is interested in modelling. This article explores some of the important criteria used to decide which language is most suitable for a specific application. The two most useful languages are studied in detail, and a complete, annotated program modelling a process of technological change is supplied for each.

Available languages

The design of compiler languages has changed remarkably since they first became available in the late 1950s. The first general-purpose language to become widely used was FORTRAN. Owing much to its availability on almost all computers and the fact that it is known by more people than any other general-purpose language, FORTRAN is widely used today for simulation modelling, notwithstanding the fact that it is very primitive in comparison to more modern languages. It is intended for numerical computations and lacks the powerful information handling features useful in sophisticated applications like modelling. ALGOL is an improved language that exists in two versions. ALGOL 60, while still intended for numeric computation, has some features that make it more suitable for other tasks. It is available on many computers and is widely known. ALGOL 68 is a true multipurpose language that is quite useful for the task at hand. However it is not widely available. In competition with it is PL/I which combines the most significant concepts of previous languages and is intended to serve most potential computer users. Whereas ALGOL 68 is a lean language carefully designed to have all the potential a multipurpose language should have, PL/I is a huge language with almost all the features anyone could ask for.

Even the richest general-purpose languages are not very suitable for simulation modelling. They lack built-in features to control timing of events and to manipulate the entities that constitute a model. Thus, while any such model can be expressed in all of the above languages, the programs would have many statements concerned not with the model itself, but rather with making the language suitable for the modelling task. SIMSCRIPT is a language designed specifically for such tasks. It is based upon FORTRAN and by modern standards is somewhat cumbersome. Its designers, however, have created a version called SIMSCRIPT II.5 which has most of the features needed for simulation programs. SIMULA, a language based upon ALGOL and thus more aesthetically pleasing to the modern user, is intended as a general-purpose language with special emphasis on simulation. As such it has fewer special features intended only for simulation work. SIMSCRIPT is widely available in the United States, and SIMULA is not. The opposite is true in Europe. Our example problem is written in both these languages. GPSS is a language based upon a block-diagram approach. While it is the language of choice in many situations, it is not suitable for the task considered here. Models expressed in SIMSCRIPT are fairly comprehensible to the reader not familiar with the language; those in SIMULA are somewhat less so; and those in GPSS are totally incomprehensible to the uninitiated.

Choosing a language

We are concerned here with discrete change simulation and how to choose a language for expressing the models. The guidance given to concept articulation, the programming convenience, and the explanatory value to others are important criteria for making the choice, and under each criterion the languages designed especially for simulation fare much better than the general-purpose languages. As we shall see the very structure of the simulation languages requires of the user a clarity of thought about the model being designed, and provides a vocabulary and syntax in which to perform the thinking, whereas the general-purpose language requires him to reinvent the concept of a simulation model before he can proceed. When using a simulation language he does not have to write program segments to handle the description of entities and processes, their properties, relationships to each other and the environment, and their classification. Also, simulation language programs are very like natural language, unlike programs in general-purpose languages. For these reasons it is better for the archaeologist to use simulation languages if possible.

Emshoff and Sisson (1970) list some features that differentiate simulation languages from others. They provide for the creation of random numbers and random variates. They provide a mechanism to advance time. They provide statistical analysis procedures. They provide a means of defining the classes of entities in the system, and of differentiating between entities of the same class by characteristics or properties. They provide means of adjusting the number of entities as conditions vary within the system. All of these features are needed in a simulation undertaking of any size.

What then are the specific criteria for choosing from among the simulation languages? The most important is availability. Clearly there must be available to the modeller the appropriate language compiler on the local computer system. Less obvious but still of paramount importance is the availability of a well-written user's manual and other documentation, and of knowledgeable and helpful consultants. The modeller will find that a lot of time is spent developing, correcting or debugging, changing, and experimenting with his model. All of these activities require extensive use of the computer. Thus it is not easy, or even possible, to do this work when the proper facilities are not at hand. Proper facilities include both instructional and reference manuals. Language reference manuals are as useless for learning a computer language as dictionaries are for learning a new natural language. Instructional manuals satisfy this need. Reference manuals are as useful as dictionaries for answering specific questions about the language. Hence both kinds of manual are required. Finally, it is expedient to have the help of a person who is an expert in the computer language and either speaks the arcane dialect of the archaeologist or is willing to work at communicating with him. For the archaeologist to learn the language himself is a painful and time-consuming process whose rewards are slight compared to the cost. He will find that there are computer professionals with an abiding interest in making exotic use of the tools of their trade.

Another criterion involves the uses to which the model

will be put. If the program is to be mainly used to communicate the details of the model, then the chosen language must admit of programs readable by interested persons who might not have detailed knowledge of the language. If the program model is to be used by many others for experimentation, then the availability of the compiler on other systems is important.

The costs of the modelling must be considered. These include the cost in personal time invested in model construction and debugging, which can often be excessive. The costs for computer services during the development stage are another factor. Using a language suited to the problem is important in controlling these costs. Using a language with informative error diagnostic messages is also important. Finally, the cost of running the program model is to be considered. Archaeological simulations often run for hundreds of years of simulated time, and include thousands of entities. The computer cost of one experiment with such a model can be several hundred dollars. A careful consideration of all of these costs is needed before language selection is made.

Finally, characteristics of the specific problem must be considered. There must be agreement between the problem conceptualisation and the world view of the language. Are the principle components of the problem events or entities? Do single events have instantaneous occurrences in simulated time? Or are events grouped together into a process that is an ongoing dynamic component of the problem? There are languages whose world views reflect these considerations. Shannon (1975, pp. 108–34) discusses in great detail the variety of languages available and the particular kinds of problem to which they are suited.

Two simulation languages

SIMSCRIPT II.5 and SIMULA are the two languages that best meet these criteria. As the example programs show, they are fairly comprehensible even to the reader unfamiliar with them, SIMSCRIPT rating higher than SIMULA. They are both fairly widely available, SIMSCRIPT more so in the United States, and SIMULA in Europe, which reflects the availability of the parent languages, FORTRAN and ALGOL respectively. Instructional documentation is available on both: Kiviat *et al.* (1973) for SIMSCRIPT, and Dahl *et al.* (1968) and Birtwistle *et al.* (1973) for SIMULA. Reference manuals for compilers on specific machines are also available. It takes longer to learn SIMSCRIPT than SIMULA. This is because SIMSCRIPT is a language much richer in simulation tools than SIMULA. It is also idiosyncratic, being unrelated to its parent language. SIMULA, on the other hand is much like its parent language. Both languages provide good error diagnostics, but are fairly expensive to use for large simulations.

Shannon (1975, pp. 138–40) reports on a survey made of users' opinions of discrete simulation languages. The original survey results are from Kleine (1971), and were later reanalysed by Shannon and Wyatt (1973). Users were asked to rate the languages, and their own familiarity or level of expertise. Kleine's method of analysis used the ratings as additive car-

dinal utility scales. Shannon and Wyatt used both a simple majority rule and a majority rule weighted by level of expertise. The results were as follows, where 'A > B' means 'A was preferred to B' and 'A = B' means 'there is no difference between A and B'.

Capability of language
Kleine: SIMSCRIPT II > SIMULA > GPSS > PL/I > FORTRAN
Same for majority and weighted majority.

Ease of use of language
Kleine: GPSS > SIMSCRIPT II > PL/I > SIMULA
Majority: GPSS > SIMSCRIPT II > SIMULA > PL/I > FORTRAN
Weighted majority same as majority.

Preferred language
Kleine: GPSS > SIMSCRIPT II > FORTRAN > SIMULA
Majority: GPSS = SIMULA = SIMSCRIPT II = FORTRAN > PL/I
Weighted: SIMSCRIPT II > SIMULA > GPSS > PL/I > FORTRAN

SIMSCRIPT II is called an event oriented language. The activity in the system is located in the events, which represent instantaneous occurrences in simulated time. Typical events that might occur in an archaeological model are the loss, and thus deposit, of an artifact, the birth, or death of a person, or the selection of a lodge site. A separate program (routine) is written for each event. In a simulation experiment an event might be caused to occur (and thus its program to execute) at some instant in simulation time as the result of some external cause or as the result of the execution of some other event program. Thus a lodge site selection event routine might schedule the occurrence, a year in the future, of an event routine for the deposit of pottery fragments.

The other important elements are entities, which have attributes, belong to things, own other things and may appear and disappear during the course of simulated time. Thus a person, a lodge, a projectile point, a pot could be entities. The attributes of a lodge might be the date it was built, its size, and location. It might belong to a village, and have inhabitants. It might be created centuries after the start of simulated time, and be discarded from the system (destroyed) before the end of simulated time.

The language provides all the mechanisms for defining the entities, keeping track of their attributes, and maintaining records of set ownership and membership. It provides for the creation and destruction of entities, automatically managing the use of computer memory for storage of this information. A timing routine is provided which keeps a record of the order of occurrence of events, and causes execution of the appropriate next event routine when the previous routine stops. The language also provides streams of random numbers, a choice of random variates, and mechanisms for gathering statistics about the system.

SIMULA is called a process oriented language. A set of related events can be grouped together into a process. This process can execute for a while, cause itself to be interrupted for a time or until it is activated from elsewhere, resume activity, and have subprocesses. A system may contain several processes. Typical processes might be a lodge (or the activity associated with one), a projectile point, a person. A lodge process might first become active when the site is claimed, become dormant while the lodge is being built, and then become active to cyclically produce people who activate new lodges. Thus we see that the events associated with a single entity in a SIMSCRIPT simulation are grouped together into one process in a SIMULA model. This feature is very obvious in the sample programs.

The language provides a selection of features, similar to those of SIMSCRIPT, for scheduling processes, providing random variates, collecting statistics, etc.

An artifact deposition problem

When the edge angle of a projectile point is larger than about 20° it is not useful for cutting. When the angle is too small the point is so thin that it shatters and is again not very useful. It can be asked how the optimum edge angle for a projectile point is arrived at. Is a rational optimisation strategy used? Are empirical studies made? Or is a more random approach taken?

Pred (1967, 1969) views such processes as adaptive— adoptive. Initially a random decision is made. If the outcome is satisfactory, the next time a decision is made the same or a similar strategy is adopted. If the outcome is not satisfactory, another random decision is made, and the process continues. In this case the decision maker is said to adapt to the outcome.

The edge angles produced under rational optimisation strategy can be expected to deviate only slightly from the chosen angle, whereas those produced under an adaptive— adoptive process should vary much more. The example programs constitute two versions of a simulation model for Pred's thesis in this context. The result of an experiment with the model is a set of edge angles, and associated statistical measures. These can be compared with statistical measures of projectile point artifacts. A similar test of a settlement pattern model was carried out by Thomas (1972, 1973).

In the model, individual projectile points are created, exist for a time, then disappear from the system. Among the model parameters are two functions which describe attributes of each point as a function of the edge angle. One function describes the value of a point, or how useful it is, without any consideration of its infrangibility. Presumably the value of points decreases as the angles exceed 20°. The other function describes the mean lifespan of a point without any consideration of its value. Presumably the lifespans of points increase as the edge angles increase. The interactions between the conflicting value and longevity functions are at the heart of the model.

When the number of available points falls below some lower limit, more points are ordered. The template used for producing the new points is that point still in use found to

have the highest value. This template is taken out of service and used in the copying of new points. These new points can be expected to be imperfect copies, and so the new edge angles vary somewhat from that of the template, being produced randomly according to a specified distribution. As new points are produced they are put into service and their time of disappearance is calculated, varying randomly about the date selected by the longevity function according to some specified distribution. When a point disappears statistics are gathered on it.

Thus there are two types of entities in the model, points and orders. Each point has two attributes, angle and value. The angle is assigned at the time of creation of the point. The value is calculated from the angle. Each order has two attributes, the number ordered and template used for copying. There must be places to retain these entities, so two sets are available, a point set and an order queue. There are three kinds of activity in the model. The point entry activity is concerned with caring for a newly created point. The break point activity occurs when a point is lost or broken and decisions about whether an order should be placed are made. The copy activity is concerned with creating new points according to specification.

The programs presented are straightforward renderings of this model. The only parameter varying because of external considerations is the number that constitutes a full complement of points. The underlying notion is that, due to population or other changes, the required number of available points might change, and these changes could skew the overall distribution of points. The model can be complicated with other parameters.

For example, in the model presented, statistics are gathered for the whole time period. It is possible to do this over some specified subinterval of the total simulation time. Also, the value of points is judged statically at the time of creation. It is possible to make this judgement after some delay or as a function of the use history of the point. These are just two of the many ways the model can be embellished.

Two points are worth mentioning. First, there is nothing here that restricts the applicability of this model to projectile points. Any process of technological change can be studied with this model or some variation of it. Secondly, narrative descriptions of models such as this one are generally not complete, leaving many details unspecified. If they were complete they would be overlong and much of the detail would be lost in the prose. Natural language is not highly structured, and much of a narrative description is devoted to establishing structure. Programming languages, on the other hand, are very highly structured, especially the special-purpose languages. The placement of a program statement carries information, for example. Consequently, programs can constitute complex, condensed descriptions of these models.

Program 1
Line
1. PREAMBLE
2. TEMPORARY ENTITIES . . .
3.   EVERY POINT HAS AN ANGLE, AND A VALUE,
4.   AND MAY BELONG TO THE POINT.SET
5.   DEFINE ANGLE AND VALUE AS REAL VARIABLES
6.   DEFINE POINT.SET AS A SET RANKED BY HIGH VALUE

7.   EVERY ORDER HAS A NUMBER,
8.   OWNS A TEMPLATE,
9.   AND MAY BELONG TO THE ORDER.QUEUE
10.   DEFINE NUMBER AS AN INTEGER VARIABLE
11.   DEFINE TEMPLATE AS A FIFO SET
12.   DEFINE ORDER.QUEUE AS A FIFO SET

13. EVENT NOTICES . . . INCLUDE COPYING
14.   EVERY BREAK.POINT HAS A LOST.POINT
15.   DEFINE LOST.POINT AS AN INTEGER VARIABLE
16.   EVERY POINT.ENTRY HAS A NEW.POINT
17.   DEFINE NEW.POINT AS AN INTEGER VARIABLE

18. THE SYSTEM HAS A POINT.COUNT, AND A FULL.COMPLEMENT, AND A REORDER.LIMIT
19.   DEFINE POINT.COUNT AND FULL.COMPLEMENT AND REORDER.LIMIT AS INTEGER VARIABLES

20. THE SYSTEM OWNS A POINT.SET, AND AN ORDER.QUEUE

21. DEFINE EDGE.ANGLE AS A REAL VARIABLE
22. TALLY POINT.DISTRIBUTION (0 TO 90 BY 5) AS THE HISTOGRAM OF EDGE.ANGLE

23. END

24. MAIN
25. PERFORM INITIALISATION
26. **Instructions to set up dynamic changes in FULL.COMPLEMENT go here. When FULL.COMPLEMENT is found to be 0 the simulation terminates.**
27. START SIMULATION
28. **Instructions to write out the histogram go here.**
29. END

30. ROUTINE FOR INITIALISATION
31. READ FULL.COMPLEMENT, REORDER.LIMIT
32. CREATE AN ORDER
33. LET NUMBER (ORDER) = FULL.COMPLEMENT
34. CREATE A POINT
35. READ ANGLE (POINT)
36. FILE POINT IN TEMPLATE (ORDER)
37. FILE ORDER IN ORDER.QUEUE
38. SCHEDULE COPYING NOW
39. RETURN
40. END

41. EVENT POINT.ENTRY GIVEN NEW.POINT
42. DEFINE LIFETIME AND MEAN.LIFETIME AS REAL VARIABLES
43. LET MEAN.LIFETIME = Some function of ANGLE (NEW.POINT)

44. LET LIFETIME = EXPONENTIAL.F (MEAN.LIFETIME, 1)
45. SCHEDULE BREAK.POINT GIVEN NEW.POINT AFTER LIFETIME DAYS
46. ADD 1 TO POINT.COUNT
47. RETURN
48. END

49. EVENT BREAK.POINT GIVEN LOST.POINT
50. REMOVE LOST.POINT FROM POINT.SET
51. LET EDGE.ANGLE = ANGLE (LOST.POINT)
52. DESTROY LOST.POINT
53. SUBTRACT 1 FROM POINT.COUNT
54. IF POINT.COUNT IS LESS THAN REORDER.LIMIT
55.   CREATE AN ORDER
56.   LET NUMBER (ORDER) = FULL.COMPLEMENT – POINT.COUNT + 1
57.   REMOVE THE FIRST PROJECTILE FROM POINT.SET
58.   SUBTRACT 1 FROM POINT.COUNT
59.   FILE PROJECTILE IN TEMPLATE (ORDER)
60.   IF ORDER.QUEUE IS EMPTY
61.   SCHEDULE COPYING NOW
62.   REGARDLESS
63.   FILE THE ORDER IN THE ORDER.QUEUE
64. REGARDLESS
65. RETURN
66. END

67. EVENT COPYING
68. DEFINE WORKDAY AS AN INTEGER VARIABLE
69. REMOVE THE FIRST TASK FROM ORDER.QUEUE
70. FOR WORKDAY = 1 TO NUMBER (TASK),
71.   DO
72.   CREATE A POINT
73.   LET ANGLE (POINT) = NORMAL.F(ANGLE (F.TEMPLATE(TASK)), 3, 1)
74.   LET VALUE (POINT) = some function of ANGLE (POINT)
75.   FILE POINT IN POINT.SET
76.   CAUSE POINT.ENTRY GIVEN POINT IN WORKDAY + 15 DAYS
77.   LOOP
78. IF ORDER.QUEUE IS EMPTY
79.   RETURN
80. OTHERWISE
81.   SCHEDULE COPYING IN NUMBER (TASK) + 30 DAYS
82. RETURN
83. END

The SIMSCRIPT program

Program 1 lists the essential parts of a SIMSCRIPT program for our model. Note the use of a full stop (line 6) in place of a blank space in names more than one word in length.

The program consists of a PREAMBLE (lines 1 to 23) in which the parts of the system are described, a MAIN program (lines 24 to 29) which controls the starting, input and output of the program, an INITIALISATION ROUTINE (lines 30 to 40) which is called upon to start the execution, and several EVENT ROUTINES (lines 41 to 83) which describe actions the system takes when certain events occur.

SIMSCRIPT provides mechanisms to manage the entities and events. In lines 3, 4 and 6 a POINT is said to have a VALUE, and may belong to a POINT.SET which is a collection of

POINTs maintained in a certain order, with the POINT of largest VALUE coming first. This having been established, the statement on line 75 causes the system to insert automatically a specific POINT into POINT.SET at the position corresponding to its relative VALUE. The statement on line 57 has a very special meaning in the context of the PREAMBLE: the item with largest VALUE in POINT.SET is the one removed.

   The schedulling of events is also a system function. Events are considered to take place instantaneously. During the course of an event other events can be scheduled. At the end of an event, the timing mechanism finds the particular event next scheduled to occur, and transfers control to it. During the event POINT.ENTRY (line 41) an event corresponding to the loss of the new point is scheduled at line 45 to occur some days in the future. If nothing else has been scheduled to occur before this time, this BREAK.POINT will occur after the current POINT.ENTRY event ends. In general, however, several other events can occur in the interim.

Line 2. Temporary entities POINT and ORDER are system entities that are created, exist for a time, and are destroyed as the simulation proceeds. This statement applies to lines 3 to 12.

Line 3. Each occurrence of POINT has two attributes, an ANGLE (see line 73 for calculation) and a VALUE (line 44).

Line 4. POINTs in existence at any one time are collected together under the name POINT.SET.

Line 5. ANGLE and VALUE are real valued (fractional) quantities.

Line 6. The POINT.SET is maintained in a particular order, with highest VALUEd entry first. See line 75 for insertion into the set, and lines 50 and 57 for removal.

Lines 7–12. ORDER is the other temporary entity. It has one attribute, NUMBER, which is integer valued. ORDERs are collected together in ORDER.QUEUE, which is maintained in the usual way for orders, on a first-in-first-out (FIFO) basis. In addition, each ORDER may own a set of objects called TEMPLATE. ORDERs are stored in the queue at line 63 and removed at line 69.

Line 13. The descriptions of the information associated with particular event notices follow (up to line 17). COPYING (lines 67–83) is an event with no special parameters.

Lines 14, 15. Each BREAK.POINT (lines 49–66) has associated with it a LOST.POINT (one of POINT entities of line 3). Integer values are used internally as names of particular temporary entities.

Lines 16, 17. Each POINT.ENTRY (lines 41–48) event also has a POINT associated with it, called NEW.POINT.

Lines 18, 19. Variables that have meaning to the whole simulation program are listed. POINT.COUNT is the current number of POINTs, FULL.COMPLEMENT is the upper limit on the number of POINTs in existence at any one time, and when REORDER. LIMIT is reached new POINTs are ordered.

Line 20. POINT.SET and ORDER.QUEUE are system-owned collections, rather than being owned by a temporary entity.

Lines 21, 22. These two statements tell the system to construct a histogram automatically. POINT.DISTRIBUTION is the name of the histogram, EDGE.ANGLE is the variable being tallied. Whenever EDGE.ANGLE changes value (line 51) a one is added to the count for the range corresponding to the new value of EDGE. ANGLE. The increment is 5 degrees, ranging from 0 to 90 degrees. Statistics like MEAN and VARIANCE of EDGE.ANGLE could also be gathered here.

Line 23. END of the PREAMBLE.

Line 24. Here is where execution starts, at time zero.

Line 25. INITIALISATION (lines 30–40) is caused to occur. It is not a simulation event, but rather a routine to start things going.

Line 26. Statements to provide for the occurrence of an exogenous (externally caused) event go here. At particular times specified on data cards, the value of FULL.COMPLEMENT is changed. When the value of zero is read, the simulation is caused to cease.

Line 27. Here the simulation itself starts. Time is set to zero and the first scheduled event (set up at line 38) is caused to occur. The locus of activity remains here until simulation ceases.

Line 28. When simulation ceases the histogram and other values of interest are printed out.

Line 29. The end of execution of the program is signalled.

Lines 30, 31. Caused to occur at line 25. The upper and lower inventory limits are read in.

Line 32. The first order, for all the POINTs that start the system, is created.

Line 33. The NUMBER attribute of this order, how many POINTs are to be made, is to be FULL.COMPLEMENT.

Line 34. A POINT to serve as a TEMPLATE for the ORDER is created. This is the prototype point.

Lines 35, 36. The ANGLE of the prototype POINT is read in, and the POINT is filed in the TEMPLATE set of the ORDER.

Line 37. The ORDER just created is filed in the queue of orders. It is the only order currently in the queue, and will be removed whenever COPYING occurs.

Line 38. COPYING is scheduled as the first event of the simulation. It will produce NUMBER copies of the POINT stored in the TEMPLATE set of the next ORDER, which is the only order now in existence.

Lines 39, 40. RETURN is the point of logical ending of INITIALISATION. END informs us that the last card of INITIALISATION has been reached.

Line 41. The parameter of the event POINT.ENTRY, scheduled at line 76, is a POINT with the local name NEW.POINT.

Line 43. Some expression yielding a timespan as a function of the ANGLE attribute of the POINT called NEW.POINT is inserted here.

Line 44. The actual LIFETIMEs are exponentially distributed with average value MEAN.LIFETIME. A random number from the first random number stream is obtained, and used in the system supplied routine to obtain variates with the exponential distribution.

Line 45. The BREAK.POINT event (lines 49 to 66), which occurs at the end of the life of a POINT, is scheduled for LIFETIME days in the future. The parameter is NEW.POINT, the POINT newly entered into the system.

Line 46. It is recorded that a new POINT has been added to the system. See lines 53 and 58.

Line 49. The parameter of the event BREAK.POINT, scheduled at line 45, is a POINT with the local name LOST.POINT, which was referred to locally in lines 41 to 48 as NEW.POINT.

Line 50. The particular POINT called LOST.POINT, whose ejection from the system is the task of this event, is removed from the collection POINT.SET.

Line 51. The value of EDGE.ANGLE is set to that of the ANGLE of this particular POINT. The updating of the histogram (lines 21, 22) is automatically performed at this moment.

Line 52. The computer memory used to store the attributes of LOST. POINT is returned to the pool of available storage. Many thousands of POINTS might be created during a simulation, each requiring several words of memory. The other temporary entity, and all of the event notices also use storage from this pool. Memory locations used by an event notice are returned to the pool upon execution of RETURN. The automatic management of the available storage pool is a very important service of SIMSCRIPT.

Line 53. It is recorded that a POINT has been removed from the system. See line 46.

Lines 54 to 64. The IF statement provides for conditional execution. If the condition on line 54 is true (the number of POINTS currently available has fallen below the lower limit) lines 55 to 63 are executed, setting up a new ORDER. Whether or not the condition is true, statements following the REGARDLESS on line 64 are executed.

Lines 55, 56. A new ORDER is created, with NUMBER attribute set to the number of POINTS needed to bring the system up to full inventory.

Line 57. The first POINT in POINT.SET, that is, the POINT with highest value (see line 6), is removed and given the local name PROJECTILE.

Line 58. It is recorded that another POINT has been lost to use (see lines 46 and 53).

Line 59. This best POINT is used as the TEMPLATE of the newly created ORDER.

Lines 60 to 63. If no ORDERs are waiting to be processed, a COPYING (lines 67 to 83) can be scheduled to occur immediately. In any case the ORDER is inserted into the queue of orders. If there are other orders already in the queue, a COPYING will be scheduled for this order after the previous ORDER is finished (see line 81).

Line 67. There is no parameter for the event COPYING scheduled at line 38, 61 or 81. The information it needs is to be found among the attributes of the next ORDER in the queue.

Line 69. Obtain the first (longest outstanding, see line 12) ORDER and give it the local name TASK. This might be the initial order (line 37) or a later order (line 63).

Lines 70 to 77. The instructions between the DO statement (line 71) and the LOOP statement (line 77) are to be executed several times, first with WORKDAY equal to 1, then to 2, then to 3, and so on. The NUMBER attribute of the ORDER named TASK is the value that WORKDAY assumes the last time that the statements are executed.

Line 73. The ANGLE of the new POINT is calculated from the ANGLE of the POINT stored in the TEMPLATE set of the ORDER called TASK (see line 59). The new ANGLE is normally distributed about the old one with a standard deviation of 3 degrees. The first random number stream is used.

Lines 74, 75. The VALUE is calculated and the POINT is filed in its set ranked by the VALUE (see line 6).

Line 76. CAUSE is a synonym for SCHEDULE. A POINT.ENTRY is scheduled for this new POINT. It will occur in WORKDAY + 15 days. Thus the first point of the order appears 16 days later, the second on the 17th day, and so on.

Lines 78 to 81. If no more orders remain to be processed nothing is done, and new COPYING will occur because of line 61 only. If there is an order to process, COPYING will be rescheduled. It will occur 15 days after the last POINT from the current order is produced, at NUMBER (TASK) + 30 days.

The SIMULA program

Program 2 lists the essential parts of a SIMULA program for our model. System keywords are bold.

SIMULA is a block structured language, which means that all statements between a **begin** statement and the associated **end** statement are considered as a unit. Blocks can be nested. Thus the **begin** of line 1 matches the **end** of line 69, and all of the included statements belong to the **simula** program. Similarly the **begin** of line 15 matches the **end** of line 18.

Program 2
Line

```
1.   Simula begin;
2.      set orderqueue, pointset;
3.      element first;
4.      integer fullcomplement, reorderlist, pointcount, seed, i;
5.      integer array hist1 (1:19), hist2 (1:18);
6.      real firstangle, t;

7.      activity point (angle); real angle;
8.      begin real life, meanlife;
9.           meanlife: = some function of angle;
10.          life: = exponential (meanlife, seed);
11.          hold (life);
12.          pointcount: = pointcount −1;
13.          histo (hist1, hist2, angle);
14.          if pointcount les recorder limit then
15.               begin
16.                    activate new order (fullcomplement −
                            pointcount) at time;
17.                    pointcount: = pointcount −1;
18.               end;
19.      end;

20.     activity order (number); integer number;
21.     begin element X, template;
22.     real maximum;
23.          X: = head (pointset);
24.          maximum: = 0;
25.          for X: = suc (X) while exist (X) do
26.          begin
27.               inspect X when point do
28.               begin
29.                    if g (maximum) les g (angle) then
30.                    begin
31.                         maximum: = angle;
32.                         template: = X;
33.                    end;
34.               end;
35.          end;
36.          terminate (template);
37.          if empty (orderqueue) then activate copy at time;
38.          wait (orderqueue);
39.     end;

40.     activity copy;
41.     begin integer workday;
42.     real angle;
43.     start: if empty (orderqueue) then passivate;
44.          inspect first (orderqueue) when order do;
45.          begin
46.               activate first (orderqueue);
47.               for workday: = 1 step 1 until number do
48.               begin
49.                    angle: = normal (maximum, 3, seed);
50.                    include new (point (angle), pointset);
51.                    activate last (pointset) at time + workday
                            + 15;
52.               end;
53.               pointcount: = pointcount + number;
54.               hold (number + 30);
55.          end;
56.          go to start;
57.     end;

58.     for i: = 0 step 5 until 90 do
59.          hist2: = i;
60.     read (seed, reorderlimit, firstangle);
61.     first: = new point (firstangle);
62.     include (first, pointset);
63.     read (fullcomplement, t);
```

```
64.    activate new order (fullcomplement);
65.    next: hold (t)
66.    read (fullcomplement, t);
67.    if t > 0 then go to next;
68.    hprint (hist1, hist2);
69.    end simula;
```

The descriptions of the variables on lines 2 to 6 apply to the whole program. The description on line 8 applies to lines 9 to 18. The main program is stated only after all of the sub-activities are described. Therefore execution begins on line 58. Notice the similarity of variable names with the SIMSCRIPT program. Notice also that all of the various events associated there with POINTs are here gathered together as one activity, and similarly for ORDER.

In a SIMULA execution, several copies of each of the activities may be executing at any one time. A particular instance of an activity may execute for a time, cause itself to delay for a precalculated interval (see line 11), cause itself to become passive until some event in another activity activates it, or terminate itself.

Lines 2 to 6. *orderqueue* and *pointset* are the same as before, except that *pointset* is not maintained in a ranked fashion. Thus it must be searched for the best *template* (lines 23 to 35). *first* corresponds to the prototype POINT (program 1, lines 34 to 36). Variables *fullcomplement*, *reorderlist* and *pointcount* are the same as before. *seed* is the starting point for the random number stream. *hist1* and *hist2* are arrays used for building the histogram (line 13). Variable *t* is used to hold the time span until the next change in *fullcomplement*.

Line 7. The parameter of activity *point* is real variable *angle*. This *angle* is available only in routine *point*, up to line 19.

Lines 8 to 10. Exactly the same as lines 42 to 44 of program 1. *life* is an exponentially distributed random variate with *meanlife* as its average value.

Line 11. Suspend the execution of this particular *point* activity for the period of time specified by the value of *life* (see program 1, line 45).

Line 12. It is recorded that a *point* has left the system (see line 53) (see program 1, line 53).

Line 13. Update the histogram by counting one in the range corresponding to *angle* (see program 1, lines 22, 51).

Lines 14 to 18. If the condition is true then then execute lines 16 and 17. Otherwise go on. (See program 1, lines 54 to 64).

Line 16. Create a new instance of the activity *order*, and set it in operation. The parameter is the number of new *points* needed to bring the *pointcount* up to full value.

Line 17. Record the fact that another *point* is used, in this case for the *template* (line 36).

Line 20. The parameter for the processing of an *order* is the number of *points* ordered.

Lines 23 to 35. The *pointset* must be searched for the *point* with the maximum value. A standard technique for finding a maximum is employed.

Lines 23, 24. Start at the head of the list of *points* stored in the *pointset*. Assume that the *maximum* is greater than zero.

Lines 25, 26. Let X be the successor in the list of *pointset* items of the element just considered, while there is a successor. For X having this value execute the statements from lines 27 to 34.

Line 27. This is a standard SIMULA construction for accessing the variables which are defined in another activity. Within the range of this statement, lines 29 to 33, the variable values of the instance of the *point* activity being considered are available for calculations. In particular, the *angle* mentioned in lines 29 and 31 is

the *angle* of the particular *point* which we have singled out of the *pointset* for inspection.

Line 29. The function g is the value function which appears in line 74 of program 1. If the condition is true, then the current guess as to the value of *maximum* and the identity of *template* is wrong and must be updated.

Lines 31, 32. Update the values of *maximum* and *template*.

Line 36. At this statement *template* is the *point* with *maximum* value. It is removed from the system because it is used in the *copying*. See line 59 of program 1. Actually the only information used by the *copy* routine is the *angle* stored in *maximum* (see line 49).

Line 37. If there is currently no outstanding *order*, the *copy* activity has caused itself to become passive at line 43. Reactivate it in this case.

Line 38. Suspend execution of this instance of the *order* activity, and place it in the *orderqueue*. It will remain suspended while other *orders* are processed. When it becomes the first *order* in the queue, the parameter *maximum* will be inspected (line 49) and the activity will be reactivated (line 46), only to terminate (line 39) and be removed from the system.

Line 40. Only one instance of the *copy* activity ever exists. If there is no *order* to be filled *copy* becomes passive (line 43).

Line 43. If there is no *order* to be filled, *copy* places itself in a passive state, to be activated by execution of line 37. *start* is a statement label. When one *copy* activity is complete, control is transferred to this statement from line 56 so that the next *order* may be filled.

Line 44. This is the standard way of accessing variables of other activities. In particular the parameters local to the first *order* in the *orderqueue* are available in lines 46 to 54.

Line 46. Reactivate the next *order* to be processed. It placed itself in the *orderqueue* at line 38 some time in the past (see program 1, line 69).

Lines 47 to 53. Cycle variable *workday* in steps of 1 from 1 to *number*, and for each value of *workday* execute the statements on lines 49 to 51 (see program 1, lines 70 to 77).

Line 49. The *angle* of the new *point* is normally distributed around that of the *template* (*maximum*, the parameter of the *order* just reactivated) with standard deviation 3 (see program 1, line 73).

Lines 50, 51. A new *point*, with the newly calculated *angle*, is placed into the *pointset*. This instance of the *point* activity is scheduled to begin execution in *workday* + 15 days (see program 1, line 76).

Line 53. Update the running count of the number of *points* available.

Line 54. Suspend execution of the *copy* activity for a certain span of time (see program 1, line 81).

Line 56. After the suspension, reactivation occurs here. Return to line 43 to begin processing of the next *order*.

Lines 58, 59. The *hist2* array defines the intervals over which the counts are tallied. Here each interval is 5 degrees, and the range is for 0 to 90 degrees (see program 1, line 22).

Line 60. *seed* defines the starting point of the random number stream (cf. program 1, line 31).

Lines 61, 62. *first* is defined to be the first instance of the *point* activity, whose *angle* parameter is the just read *firstangle*. It is filed in the *pointset* (see program 1, lines 34 to 36).

Line 63. The remaining data are pairs of numbers, a *fullcomplement*, and a timespan *t* over which this *fullcomplement* is effective (see program 1, line 26).

Line 64. The first *order* is activated. The number ordered is *fullcomplement*. The *template* found in lines 23 to 35 will be the just filed first (and currently only) *point*. Activity *copy* will be activated now for the first time at line 37 (program 1, line 38). The *angle* used for duplication in line 49 will be *firstangle*.

Line 65. Execution of the main activity is suspended for *t* units of time. *next* is a statement label. Control is returned to line 65 from line 67.

Line 66. The new *fullcomplement* and its *timespan* are read.

Line 67. $t = 0$ is the signal to stop the simulation. If this is not the case, go to line 65.

Line 68. At the end of the simulation, print out the histogram (cf. program 1, line 28).

An early description of SIMULA can be found in Dahl and Nygaard (1966). Fishman (1973) gives examples of SIMSCRIPT and SIMULA programs for another simulation problem.

One can expect very many projectile points to be created during a simulation experiment. It is not as costly in computer resources to have a large number of SIMSCRIPT entities in existence as it is to have a large number of instances of a SIMULA activity in execution. Also, the interactions between the events of the model are not very complex. For these reasons the SIMSCRIPT program can be expected to perform somewhat more efficiently on this problem. However archaeologists can expect to deal with a wide range of problems that require both of these approaches to simulation.

References

Birtwistle, G.M., Dahl, O.J., Myhrhang, B. & Nygaard, K. (1973) *SIMULA, begin* Auerbach

Dahl, O.J., Myhrhaus, B. & Nygaard, K. (1968) *SIMULA 67 Common Base Language*. Report S2, Norwegian Computing Center

Dahl, O.J. & Nygaard, K. (1966) 'SIMULA – an ALGOL based simulation language', *Communications of the ACM* 9: 671–78

Doran, J.E. (1972) 'Computer models as tools for archaeological hypothesis formation' in D.L. Clarke (ed.) *Models in Archaeology*, Methuen

Emshoff, J.P. & Sisson, R.L. (1970) *Design and Use of Computer Simulation Models*, Macmillan

Fishman, G.S. (1973) *Concepts and Methods in Discrete Event Digital Simulation*, Interscience

Kiviat, P.J., Villanueva, R. & Markowitz, H.M. (1973) *SIMSCRIPT II.5 Programming Language*, Consolidated Analysis Centers

Kleine, H. (1971) 'A second survey of users' views of discrete simulation languages', *Simulation* 17: 89–93

Pred, A. (1967) *Foundations for a Geographic and Dynamic Location Theory, Part I. Lund Studies in Geography*, Series B, No. 27

Pred, A. (1969) *Behavior and Location: Foundations for a Geographic and Dynamic Location Theory, Part II. Lund Studies in Geography*, Series B, No. 28

Sammet, J.E. (1976) 'Roster of programming languages for 1974–75', *Communications of the ACM* 19: 655–69

Shannon, R.E. (1975) *Systems Simulation: The Art and Science*, Prentice-Hall

Shannon, R.E. & Wyatt, M.W. (1973) 'Discrete simulation languages users' survey revisited', *Simulation* 19: 26

Thomas, D.H. (1972) 'A computer simulation model of Great Basin subsistence and settlement patterns', in D.L. Clarke (ed.) *Models in Archaeology*, Methuen

Thomas, D.H. (1973) 'An empirical test of Steward's model for Great Basin settlement patterns', *American Antiquity* 38: 115–76

PART TWO

The simulation of settlement processes

In this introduction both the simulation of settlement systems and of a site's economic strategy are considered.

Settlement systems

Many of the problems connected with the study of settlement processes have already been discussed by Hamond (chapter 1) who notes the numerous difficulties associated with traditional approaches to the analysis of settlement patterns and looks to simulation as an alternative method of analysis. This introduction is intended to outline existing work on this topic and to suggest avenues for future applications.

Clarke (1972) examines the value of a random-walk model for the dispersal of early Neolithic (Bandkeramik) settlement on the European loess soils. This is considered a relevant model because, within the loess, a settlement on re-location 'is equally likely . . . to move to any of the nearest neighbouring acceptable location points in any direction' (ibid., p. 20). Following this random-walk procedure, sites are likely to return in time to former locations, and are constantly coming into fresh associations with other settlements. Although this degree of movement and contact between individuals is probably found in many societies, Clarke suggests that this type of model helps to explain the homogeneity and conservatism of Bandkeramik material culture.

At a more detailed level, Clarke (1972, pp. 24—6) simulated the development of Körös early Neolithic settlement near the Tisza river in a similar way. The random walk of settlements was allowed within the suitable dry loess terraces close to running water. To allow sufficient agricultural land for exploitation by each settlement, sites were not permitted within 2 km of each other. The distance moved by sites was also 2 km because of the advantages of remaining near the previously inhabited area. Simulated settlement for 500 years produced a palimpsest of sites which had continually returned to locations near or on earlier sites. Yet Clarke found that, despite the complexity and distortion of the palimpsest, random samples taken at 2%, 10% and 50% levels of survival still retained evidence of the 2 km distance between sites. This is an interesting initial consideration of a wider problem — what types of settlement pattern are most robust in the face of the blurring and distortion of post-depositional factors? Simulation could certainly be used to answer such questions.

Ammerman and Cavalli-Sforza (1973) have carried out an initial simulation of the same prehistoric phenomenon — the spread of the early Neolithic across Europe. Their model is more complex in that it involves two aspects — the random-walk movements of settlements and, in addition, the logistic growth of population. The end-result of the simulation of these combined factors is the gradual outward spread of a 'wave of advance'. In the simulation program, time and space are treated discontinuously and the process is carried out only linearly. Population starts at a density of 0.1 inhabitants per km^2 at the origin and has an initial growth rate of 3.9% per year reaching a saturation density of 5 inhabitants per km^2. Migration distances are assumed to be Normally distributed. The simulation gave rise to a wave front advancing at about 1 km per year. This type of simulation is certainly valuable in that, for example, its predictions might indicate areas where there had been greater resistance to the 'advance' from hunter-gatherer groups. Equally, however, it makes many assumptions about the nature of the spread of the Neolithic and it is conducted at an extremely general level at which testing of the assumptions is difficult. For example, the nature of the settlement migration is perhaps best studied at a more localised level.

At this more localised scale, Hodder (1977) again used logistic population growth and random-walk settlement moves to simulate the spread of early Neolithic settlement in the Untermaingebiet, W. Germany. Simulation of the development of the settlement pattern over four phases indicated areas in which the proposed model was inadequate and where changes in future simulations would need to be made. Often inspection of how the model does not work leads to the gaining of information about the process under study. When further examination of Neolithic settlement spread at the local level has been carried out, it will be of interest to return to the broader patterns noted above.

Other approaches to settlement simulation include the work of Thomas (1972, 1973). A model was developed in order to test Julian Steward's theory of Shoshonean subsistence patterns in the central Great Basin. The yearly round of activities in the Reese river valley in central Nevada, as suggested by Steward's hypothesis, is shown in fig. 1. The small plus's and minus's in circles indicate the yes, no answers to the questions in the diamond shaped boxes. Each activity is related to a type of environment, so the box in the top right of figure 1 indicates a rabbit drive involving both sexes in the lower sagebrush microenvironment. However, in the actual simulation only three activities were considered as far as change through time was concerned — pinon nut gathering, Indian ricegrass harvesting (ricegrass being the predominant seed gathered), and antelope driving. A considerable amount was known about the yearly variation in the availability of these three resources, allowing their detailed simulation. In the overall model (fig. 1), activities taking place in particular environments resulted in the deposition of particular tool types. Thus, running of the model produced predicted site locations, predicted densities of different artifacts in different environments, and predicted artifact patterns (random, regular or clustered). These predictions were found to correspond fairly well with the artifact patterns discovered in a detailed field survey of the Reese river valley. However, as Doran and Hodson (1975, p. 305) note, the part played by computer simulation in this procedure is very slight and the results could have been obtained by some straightforward mathematics. Nevertheless, this is a good example of an attempt to build a model containing a series of systemic relationships and which is able to output sets of data which can be directly compared with the archaeological evidence. It is in exactly this type of situation that fuller computer simulation is most valuable.

Another aspect of settlement which has been studied using simulation procedures is the relationship between the rank and size of sites (Hodder 1978). When the sizes of sites have been estimated, the sites can be ranked from largest to smallest and the relationship between rank and size plotted (fig. 2). Geographers have considered various processes which result in different rank–size relationships and the aim of the study was to determine the range of processes which could have produced particular archaeological data sets.

The data sets examined were: groups of univallate and multivallate Iron Age hillforts in southern England, Romano-British walled towns, Romano-British rural sites in the Fenlands, Early Dynastic I sites from the Diyälä Plains, Iraq (c. 2800 BC), Late Helladic sites from Greece, the lengths of earthen long barrows in southern England. These data sets represented a range of different types of site, different dates and areas, and different standards of data collection and fieldwork.

Several growth processes were used which, as the result of simulation, predicted rank–size relationships. Some of these processes were deterministic such as the predictions of central place theory and the random splitting model (Cliff, Haggett & Ord 1974). Others were stochastic such as the drawing of sizes for sites from a Normal distribution. In other stochastic procedures, the 'contagiousness' of larger populations attracting

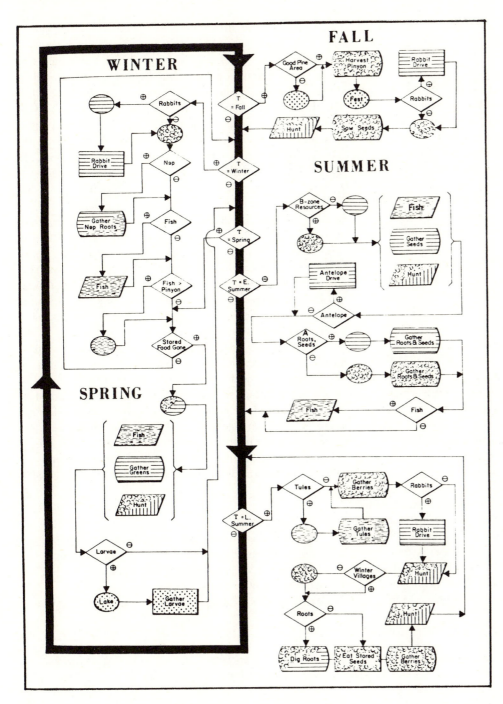

Fig. 1. Flow chart for the Shoshonean economic cycle. Source: Thomas 1973.

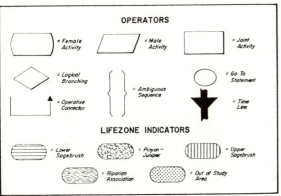

Key to symbols in fig. 1.

larger increments of population was considered. Units of size were added to settlements over time in such a way that larger sites attracted more units.

The simulations of the latter process began in phase I with the number of settlements actually occurring in a data set. The sizes of these sites were chosen at random from a uniform distribution between 1.0 and 20.0 (or from a Normal distribution with a mean of 10.0). Unit increments were then added to the settlements at random, but larger sites had a greater chance of attracting these increments. 600 units were added in this way, but the process was stopped at phases 2 (after 200 additions), 3 (400 additions) and 4 (600 additions). At each phase 20 separate simulations were carried out to produce average sizes for the nth rank settlements. At each phase, also, the size shares of each site were reassessed, and the shares were ranked, plotted, and compared with the actual data.

It was found that through time a more concave rank—size curve was formed as the bigger sites increased relatively faster. But a major failing of this approach is that spatial factors were not taken into account. The rate at which a settlement grows and attracts population partly depends on the size and number of neighbouring settlements. Thus a simulation similar to that just described was carried out including spatial constraints. Increments were allocated to the settlements in such a way that settlements in locations where there was less competition from neighbours grew faster, while larger centres retained a greater chance of attracting increments.

As a general result of the simulations, it was noted that flatter, less concave, rank—size curves often relate to the more unconstrained and purely random processes. Lower gradients indicate decreases in the 'organisation' or order in the settlement hierarchy, and increases in entropy. More structured and constrained processes such as long-term contagious growth and central place hierarchies produce more concave rank—size curves. But the way in which the archaeological data survive and are recovered also has an important effect on the rank—size graphs. Less-reliable data sets in which there has been

much 'blurring' and distortion are less likely to demonstrate organised, structured and highly concave rank—size curves unless the distortion is itself highly structured. For example, the Iron Age univallate hillforts (fig. 2a) cover a long period of time, are not all contemporary and probably include sites of very different function. Thus, even if a marked hierarchy ever existed within any class of these hillforts, it is blurred by the time it reaches the archaeologist. The multivallate hillforts (fig. 2b), on the other hand, cover a shorter period of time, are more likely to represent one class of site in the area studied, and are less susceptible to destruction and disappearance. Their concave rank—size curve suggests a particularly highly constrained situation. Certainly literary and other archaeological evidence suggest a strongly hierarchical society in the late Iron Age which the rank—size relationship might reflect. This simulation study, then, showed that each rank—size curve was the composite result of a complex balance between original forces, and survival and recovery processes. The work provided a basis for the detection and initial interpretation of 'organised' and constrained rank—size relationships.

So far, this introduction has considered processes resulting in the spatial and hierarchical pattern of sites. But simulation can also be used to examine the character and components of individual sites, and the processes which resulted in the frequency and arrangement of those components. Thus, attempts have been made to model the formation and deposition of evidence in present-day sites in East Africa (D. Gifford, personal communication) while O'Shea (chapter 4 below) considers the development of features within Pawnee sites.

Economic systems

Mention of within-site systems leads to the economic strategies carried out by settlements in the past. This topic would appear to hold great potential for simulation studies although there is little proof of this at the moment. J. Parkington (personal communication) is simulating the shell-

Fig. 2. The relationship between rank and size for (a) univallate and (b) multivallate Iron Age hillforts. The curves predicted as a result of allocating sizes from the Normal distribution are shown as dashed lines.

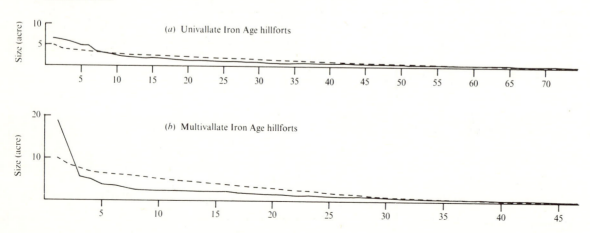

collecting strategies of coastal sites in South Africa in an attempt to reproduce various aspects of the shell assemblages in archaeological sites. For example, what levels of culling lead to decreases in the sizes of shells and changes in the population structure of the shell species?

This example illustrates one approach to the simulation of economic systems, based on individual sites and their environments. Such studies require a considerable knowledge of the possible economic activities involved. In many cases estimation of crop yield per acre, amount of grazing needed per sheep or cow, amount of winter fodder needed per animal and so on may be required. Where such data can be provided with some confidence, simulation offers the chance to link the various components of the economy into different types of system. Given a detailed soil and agricultural potential map around a site, economic strategies involving, for example, different fallow periods, different uses of the environment and different numbers of inhabitants, could be simulated in order to see which are most likely or which best reproduce the economic evidence recovered from the site.

A rather different approach to the simulation of economic systems would be to model the movement of sites into an area. Attention would be focused in such procedures on the particular environmental variables which had been selected in the location of sites (see Chadwick, chapter 5 below). One of the limitations of 'site-catchment analysis' is that a site and its territory are studied in a vacuum. If particular types of location have been specifically selected by the inhabitants of sites, this can only be demonstrated by considering the positioning of sites within the total environment. The spread of sites into an area could be simulated according to particular economic preferences. Comparison between the simulated and actual site distributions would provide information on the environmental factors most relevant in site location. This is a more objective approach than that followed in site-catchment analysis.

Another aspect of economic strategies is considered by Mosimann and Martin (1975). They begin with the fact that around 11 000 years ago a remarkable number of large mammals vanished from North America. These losses included three genera of elephants, six of giant edentates, fifteen of ungulates and various giant rodents and carnivores. Many theories have been put forward to explain these extinctions, but Mosimann and Martin examine the possibility that it was the arrival of man the hunter in North America which caused the 'overkill'. In their simulation of this process, 100 hunters of both sexes arrived from Alaska around 11 500 years ago and gradually spread southeastwards across the United States. Estimates are provided of the following parameters – initial prey biomass, prey carrying capacity, prey replacement or growth rate, initial human density, the ceiling of human density, the maximum human growth rate, and prey destruction rate. A 'front' of hunters gradually spreads across America, killing animals locally, but the 'front' is wide enough to prevent animals 'leaking' back into unoccupied areas behind the 'front'. By varying the parameter values they show that extinction of large fauna

by relatively small numbers of hunters is feasible. In addition, they demonstrate that the archaeological visibility of the hunters would be extremely low. It is possible that a relatively low density of discarded artifacts would have been produced. This is an attractive application of computer simulation in archaeology although there are necessarily many unknowns involved in the assignment of parameter values and the nature of the 'front' is perhaps rather unrealistic.

Settlement and economic systems clearly provide a rich area for simulation studies. This topic has attracted most simulation work in the past because fairly straightforward models can be employed and because the end-result, the settlement pattern, is readily and directly comparable with the archaeological data. In the following chapter Zimmerman provides a detailed introduction to the simulation of locational processes. O'Shea and Chadwick then give examples of the simulation of within-site processes and of the spread of settlement.

References

Ammerman, A.J. & Cavalli-Sforza, L.L. (1973) 'A population model for the diffusion of early farming in Europe' in C. Renfrew (ed.) *The Explanation of Culture Change*, Duckworth, London

Clarke, D.L. (1972) 'Models and paradigms in contemporary archaeology' in D.L. Clarke (ed.) *Models in Archaeology*, Methuen, London

Cliff, A., Haggett, P. & Ord, J.K. (1974) *Elementary Regional Structure: Some Quantitative Approaches to the Spatial Organisation of Static and Dynamic Regional Systems*, Cambridge University Press

Doran, J. & Hodson, F.R. (1975) *Mathematics and computers in Archaeology*, Edinburgh University Press

Hodder, I. (1977) 'Some new directions in spatial analysis in archaeology' in D.L. Clarke (ed.) *Spatial Archaeology*, Academic Press, London

Hodder, I. (1978) 'Simulating the growth of hierarchies' in K. Cooke & C. Renfrew (eds.) *A Mathematical Approach to Culture Change*, Academic Press, London

Mosimann, J.E. & Martin, P.S. (1975) 'Simulating overkill by Paleoindians', *American Scientist* 63: 304–13

Thomas, D.H. (1972) 'A computer simulation model of Great Basin Shoshonean subsistence and settlement patterns' in D.L. Clarke (ed.) *Models in Archaeology*, Methuen, London

Thomas, D.H. (1973) 'An empirical test for Steward's model of Great Basin settlement patterns', *American Antiquity* 38: 155–76

Chapter 3

Simulating prehistoric locational behaviour
Larry J. Zimmerman

Introduction

The perplexing question, why people locate themselves where they do, has become a focus for archaeology only since settlement pattern analysis developed as an important area of research in the early 1950s. Recent concern for the delineation and explanation of cultural processes has brought the question into sharper focus making prehistoric locational analysis a keystone of entire regional research efforts (Gumerman 1971). That such a focus is important is perhaps obvious: an individual or group has to be *somewhere* to exploit his (its) environment in a particular way and to relate to his (its) contemporaries in specified ways. Therefore, in many respects human location can be seen to serve as an integrative mechanism, an interface for several cultural subsystems.

Archaeological simulations of human location have been relatively rare, perhaps because locational decision-making is seen to be incredibly complex. Zubrow (1971*a*, 1971*b*, 1975) concerned himself with a model of environmental carrying capacity as a dynamic equilibrating system. As part of his model he simulated the impact of carrying capacity changes on size and location of human settlement in the Hay Hollow Valley of Arizona. Thomas (1971, 1972, 1973, 1974) used a function-specific model designed to simulate deposition of artifacts resulting from the ethnographic subsistence pattern of the Shoshone of the Great Basin as posited by Steward (1941). Even though his concern was primarily with artifacts, certain of his categories were directly related to settlement pattern. While both these situations dealt with locational behaviour as a somewhat peripheral issue, Zimmerman (1976a, 1977) focused on settlement as the central concern in a simulation of locational decision making of Central Plains tradition populations in the Glenwood locality of southwestern Iowa near the Missouri River.

All three simulations, no matter what the degree of consideration of locational behaviour, represent total society simulations, a class of simulation that treats a large number, though not necessarily all, subsystems of a culture. Total society simulations are extremely complex; the more subsystems to be modelled and integrated with other subsystems, the greater the order of magnitude of programming and verification problems. Yet, since anthropological archaeology is an holistically oriented discipline it would seem important that such simulations should eventually be done in order to test the feasibility of our reconstructions of lifeways and cultural processes (cf. Whallon 1972, p. 38).

To develop such a simulation is a very time consuming, demanding procedure that, once complete, seems far less frightening than it did at the start. Such a simulation for the Glenwood locality was attempted and had a modicum of success; an assessment of that effort might prove useful to those contemplating locational or other total society simulations. Consequently, this chapter is not an abridged version of the Glenwood simulation but rather a sort of flexible 'recipe' or list of 'helpful hints'. An effort is made to consider some of the key issues and problems of simulating locational behaviour as a total society simulation.

Some theoretical considerations

For small-scale societies, hunters and gatherers and horticulturalists, locational behaviour is primarily the result of individual or small-group decision making. The imperatives involved in such a locational decision are relatively few, and they operate within a framework of environmentally and culturally delimited parameters, functionally set by mutual interaction. To identify these imperatives, let alone the particulars of the parameters, is difficult, perhaps even impossible, even when one is personally involved in making the decision.

In other words, people have a conception of where persons in their 'situation' should or would prefer to live. They 'know' in a very general way what major factors (such as availability of key resources or distance to friends or relatives) contribute to their idea of proper location. The combination of these elements indicates locations that are acceptable according to culturally defined standards of quality of life. The parameters determining settlement location are 'fuzzy', complicated by interaction with each other, factors of lesser importance, and by a number of seemingly random factors. Within this 'fuzzy' framework people decide where to live. They control only some of the variables knowing in a general way the parameters of the imperatives and standards of life. Random factors they cannot control and seldom consider.

Still, they do make functional choices. Analysing these decisions even with direct access to the decision-maker is thus extremely difficult. Analysis of such decisions in prehistory must be considered even more tenuous.

A number of approaches to locational behaviour have been developed, primarily by economic geographers. Most models are concerned with spatial distribution and land-use patterns, and are essentially normative in that they deal with idealised patterns rather than actual spatial organisation of economic phenomena. The majority of techniques in archaeological application, most notably central place theory, are derived from this normative approach. Such approaches have not gone uncriticised by geographers.

The major criticism of the normative approach focused on its simplicity. Models in economic geography did not take account of the multiplicity of factors that influence spatial organisation (Harvey 1969, p. 369). Further, economic geographers 'failed or refused to regard any spatial distributions or array of economic features on the landscape as the aggregate reflection of individual decisions' (Pred 1967, p. 11). These arguments reflect behaviourist influence, which Pred suggests was only considered implicitly; economic geographers tended to accept the generalisations of the environmental determinists and their successors (Pred 1967, p. 11). Little direct attention was paid to the behavioural component of spatial distribution. In recent years economic geographers have realised that behavioural concepts must be introduced into their models. Some of the same criticisms can be levelled against the archaeologist who applies models from economic geography without bearing in mind their normative nature and general lack of behavioural components.

Locational theorists on the other hand were concerned primarily with behavioural components of spatial distribution in terms of 'economic man' models derived from economics, especially the optimising models of Von Neumann and Morgenstern (1953). The optimising models of human behaviour proposed an 'economic man', an omniscient, totally rational construct endowed with perfect predictive powers. He had one goal, that of maximising guided behaviour. 'Optimiser' strategies were those geared to reap maximum benefits from 'best'-choice decisions. Davenport's (1960) study of Jamaican fishermen and Gould's (1963) consideration of Jantilla, Ghana, farm planting strategies demonstrate the limited effectiveness of their models.

The efficacy of the optimising framework which assumed that units involved in decision-making acted 'in the guise of "absolutely rational", "unerring", economic man' (Pred 1967, p. 11) can be seen to be minimal. Major criticisms of economic man models in location theory focus on the logical consistency of assumptions of the motives ascribed to economic man and a rejection of the economic man and the high level of knowledge and abilities attributed to him. Man often operates in less than optimal ways but usually in ways that satisfy him in terms of needs (Washburn 1972). This satisfying behaviour is both culturally and situationally defined.

Pred's (1967, 1969) work suggests that perhaps even the satisfying models might not be entirely adequate. When faced with equal options, minimal amounts of information, and limited ability to use the information, man behaves 'randomly' or invents *ad hoc* rules by which to rationalise his choices. Pred therefore chose to view locational behaviour in terms of real world deviations from the norms provided in both the optimising and satisfying models. He consequently developed a behavioural matrix to account for variability in decision-making.

His behavioural matrix has two axes, one a scale of increasing ability to use information, the other a scale of increasing quantity and quality of information. Pred views decisions as adoptive–adaptive. At time 1 (T_1) when a decision-maker faces a decision with minimal ability to use information and little or no information his decision will be one that has equal probability with all others of being chosen. If the decision he adopts satisfies his needs, the next time (T_2) a decision needs to be made, he has available the information regarding the T_1 decisions and will *adopt* that same or at least a similar strategy again. If on the other hand his original T_1 choice fails to satisfy his needs he will select another different option from the matrix. Given the information about the inferior T_1 strategy, he will choose either a slightly or vastly different option from the matrix at T_2. He increases the probability that a more satisfying strategy will be selected; he thereby *adapts*. At T_n he will select an optimal, though rarely achieved, strategy. What Pred's matrix allows, that the optimising and satisfying models do not, is the input of random factors, changing abilities to make decisions, and ways to account for real world deviations from 'normal' behaviour.

Consideration of human location in these terms is much like that stated earlier. These more realistic, less normative models bridge the gap between approaches to human location that Hole and Heizer (1973) suggest as characteristic of archaeology and geography. Realistic behaviours can be considered, random factors can be included, and specific problems or data sets can be examined within an adaptive framework. In spite of the utility of these approaches to location, translations of general models developed in other disciplines to particular archaeological problems present further difficulties.

Applications of all the locational models discussed above have been relatively easier in geography than they would be in archaeology. Geographic problems have, in the main, considered living, usually Western, cultures. They therefore usually have abundant data and can meet the criteria that Hägerstrand (1952) suggests as being necessary for adequate implementation of most geographic models — that data must be complete and capable of quantitative analysis. Completeness of data must not be restricted to one moment in time, and moments should succeed each other at short intervals to give a good idea of order and continuity in the processes under consideration. In archaeology the data are generally incomplete and rarely adequate for one moment in time let alone for short intervals that allow for any real conceptualisation of the processes with

which we deal. Archaeological concerns with locational behaviour processes overlap those of the geographer. Archaeology, however, falls short when comparing adequacies of data sets necessary for analysis of the complex variables and their relationships involved in locational behaviour.

Archaeological locational problems can perhaps be best considered in two ways. Precise relationships between pertinent locational variables can often be determined by the application of heuristic statistical techniques to a data set. These techniques are similar to those suggested in Haggett (1965) for geography and applied in archaeology by Green (1973) and Washburn (1974). If the data sets are adequate and temporal control is otherwise available, the key variables in locational behaviour and their interactions can be demonstrated. Selection of variables to be considered in the data set is either intuitive or it simply uses those variables most often considered important to location (Trigger 1968). Processes or relationships in statistical form are often difficult to visualise if one is not familiar with statistical usage. The degree of contribution of each of the variables is often not entirely clear. The result even with adequate data can be confusing; with poor data the picture can be even more out of focus. When data sets are not adequate for meaningful statistical evaluation another approach to locational problems can be used — model building. Relationships and processes are no more difficult to conceptualise than those that are expressed statistically.

Model building can begin with relatively little data at hand. Variables relevant to the locational problem can be generated intuitively or drawn from existing models. The variable relationships can then be deduced. Ultimately, the model can be tested by comparison of a real data set, however weak, with the data generated by the hypotheses. The model of particular utility for long-term relationships and processes is a simulation model in which the precision of the data is not a key. It is the processes and hypothesised relationships which are paramount to the success of the model.

Actually the statistical approach and the model-building approach are complimentary and circular. The inductive methods of the heuristic statistical procedures can generate precise, realistic hypothetical structures to build hypotheticodeductive models. Intuition need not play a key role. If, however, data are not available nor easily accessible, they must be generated. This can be accomplished with simulation modelling.

The utility of simulation

The process of simulation encompasses the design and study of a model of a system; motivations for its use come from a number of sources. As an abstract model becomes less abstract and general and more realistic and specific, it also becomes more intractable mathematically. 'We cannot easily determine the behaviour of systems whose variables are discontinuous, stochastic, and intimately related to many other such variables in a multiplicative fashion' (Wyman 1970, p. 1). We do witness such complexity in the real world and can often best comprehend complexity only if we deal with it in as realistic a fashion as possible. Consequently 'simulation's most prominent attractions are intelligible results and freedom from the constraints of mathematical ignorance' (Dutton & Starbuck 1971, p. 4). The implications of relationships that are non-linear or irregular in some other fashion can be explored without restriction to some mathematically convenient assumptions. Simulation does, however, impose some degree of logical rigour on an investigator by causing him to analyse the temporal structure of modelled processes or systems. For computer simulations this quality is inherent, in that if assumptions are not logically structured, no output will be produced. If an investigator builds an operating program he is forced to consider temporal sequence or at least to specify which operation comes before which other operation; in this way he moves towards a comprehension of causality. Simulation is a particularly useful technique when the real system or situation under consideration is not available for direct manipulation as with prehistoric cultural systems. The extension of a model of an operating system through time is useful as a predictive device, but without the real system, inference drawn from the model remains hypothetical as the inference is only as adequate as any underlying assumptions concerning real system environment or operations.

Those instances where simulation can be usefully employed, but when the real system is not available, pinpoint the greatest disadvantages of simulation. Even though the simulator has too little information to specify the relational and temporal assumptions to be incorporated into his model, he is required to specify them in very precise ways. He is consequently often induced to substitute conjecture or speculation for investigation and fact. Further, the computer languages used in simulation often vary in their facility such that even with precise, adequate information, the conceptual structures of the simulator cannot be realised in the program (Zimmerman 1976b). Finally, the search for realistic forms of output sometimes tends to overshadow the needs for realistic associations between the input and the output. All in all, the simulator is faced with major problems whenever he attempts to create a realistic simulation model.

The quest for realism in an extreme form can lead to what has been labelled 'Bonini's paradox' (Bonini 1963, p. 136) or the complexity dilemma. Simulation models are so constructed that assumptions and functional relations may be as complex or realistic as possible, so that some observed causal process can be better understood. The outputs of the model may resemble reality in such a way that the model will be deemed by the investigator to be an accurate representation of the real process. But, with the model's complex set of assumptions and their relations, the simulation is no easier to understand than the real process. If the researcher, 'hopes to understand complex behaviour, he must construct complex models, but the more complex the model, the harder it is to understand' (Dutton & Briggs 1971, p. 103). Since the purpose of science is to make things simpler, constructing a model as complex or more complex than reality is self-defeating.

Simulation, then, as the controlled manipulation of symbols representing a real system, is a means by which an investigator can study any particular system without actually manipulating the system itself. Its goal remains an understanding of some causal process. Simulation allows the application of a rather rigorous logical framework to an extremely complex situation that is either difficult or impossible to analyse mathematically. Consequently, the use of simulation to analyse the behaviour of total societies as reflected in locational decisions, a system often deemed too complex to analyse quantitatively, might seem a reasonable step.

Locational behaviour as a total society simulation
Dutton and Briggs (1971, p. 103) define a simulation of behaviour in terms of conditions that must be satisfied. These conditions are such that a simulation must: (1) examine a behaviour process; (2) give a theory or model which describes and explains the process without ambiguity; (3) show how the process is affected by its environment; (4) be formulated in such a way that inferences about the process may be verified by observation. Behaviour process is defined as an activity that undergoes transformation through time, depending partly on the initial state of the environment and the subsequent response to that environment by the activity. The activity may both operate on its environment or be determined by its environment. Their view of behaviour is essentially systemic. Their conditions could be a definition for most dynamic models. Simulations of behaviour processes have been executed effectively for relatively low-level human phenomena, particularly in psychology and business management (Starbuck & Dutton 1971, pp. 31–102), but few have dealt effectively with the broader behavioural phenomena of human aggregates.

The reason for this relative paucity of broader behavioural simulations is that while it may be possible to study a total society it is impossible to study a total society totally (Pool 1967, p. 45). There is no such thing as a complete description of even the smallest event, let alone a complete description of a total society. As an investigator, one must select from the infinite range of alternative good descriptions. Consequently, there may be an infinite number of problems to be solved and an infinite number of solutions to each of those problems. Seeking an absolutely correct single solution to a problem has led to frustration and confusion; if even at the lowest levels the frustration and confusion exists, how much greater must it be for individuals working at higher, more complex behavioural levels?

The strictures of missing data or 'infinite' data have been suggested as a rationale for not studying total societies (a suggestion that would hurt archaeology badly), and abandoning simulation which requires such precise information for the structuring of models. However, it is not true that a simulation is no more useful than its data (Pool 1967, p. 57). The interest of using a simulation lies as much or more in the study of process as in the measures of particular real world parameter values. If the mechanisms by which a process operates are understood or at least hypothesised by an investigator they can still be structured for simulation. Parameter estimations or arbitrary figures can be used for the data necessary to the system's environment or operations. The results derived will probably not be a correct solution for the particular real world problem but the hypothesised structure of a process will be examinable. Perhaps by comparison of the real system results with the results derived from the estimated 'ball park' parameters in combination with the understanding of the process a means for more precisely estimating the real problem data can be generated. Simulation in this instance becomes an ever more specific and accurate cyclical procedure. At any rate, the best that can be hoped for, given the limitations of the study of total societies, is a simulation bound to be a representation of but one or a few aspects of a society, never all aspects.

Thus, when simulation is used to examine prehistoric locational decisions all the factors noted above come into play. Such decisions involve numerous elements from many cultural subsystems and their interfaces as well as input from the system's environment. Such simulations therefore necessarily become total society simulations. In considering locational behaviour in prehistory the data are not often good, so must be estimated. In most cases then, simulations of locational behaviour will not be correct solutions to a problem related to a particular real world archaeological manifestation but will be an examination of an hypothesised structure of a locational process. As noted by Mosimann and Martin (1975, p. 313) 'simulations can prove nothing about prehistory', but they can show that a particular locational model is feasible given certain assumptions and conditions.

Locational theory into locational simulation

The translation of a number of theoretical considerations into an operational simulation model of locational behaviour is not an easy task. Armed with limited data for a particular problem and perhaps only a limited scheme as to how locational decisions might have been made the task may seem especially formidable.

At this point all the theoretical considerations seem far removed from one's actual archaeological problem. Perhaps it should be so, for locational theory is only an abstraction from reality. Theory can at this point be temporarily put aside. It has probably already oriented one's thought about the problem and will in essence be tested by the simulation.

The first and most beneficial thing to remember is that simulation is a rather exacting procedure requiring considerable attention to detail. Consequently it is imperative that the operation be guided by strict methodologically sound procedure. Mihram's (1972) article 'The modelling process' provides an excellent outline of such a procedure. Simulation model builders are urged to examine it carefully. His scheme is summarised here.

Mihram (1972, p. 625) sees six stages to the procedure. It is imperative before any model is constructed that the designer first consider what the specific goals of his model are to be, that is to say, what are the appropriate measures of the

performance of the system. This *model's goals* stage is basic to the later selection of the variety of model to be used. Once the selection is made, the salient components of the system being modelled, their interactions and relationships, and the system's dynamic behaviour mechanics are isolated in the *system analysis* stage. *System synthesis* consists of organising the system's behaviour in accordance with the system analysis stage, in other words, developing a computer program. The model's responses are then compared in the *verification* stage with those which would be anticipated if the model's structure was indeed prepared as intended. The responses resulting from the verified model are compared with the observations of and measurements from the real system. This is essentially an effort at *validation*. The final stage of *inference* is concerned with the definition of experiments with and comparisons or response from the verified and validated models. The process is essentially cyclical; at any stage one can drop back to an earlier stage if problems are encountered. If the results produced by the model are deemed to be inadequate, the only assumptions remaining are that the system being modelled is behaving in such a complex and irrational way owing to incomprehensible forces or that the model that we have constructed is simply inadequate (Morrill 1965, p. 14). If the latter is seen as the difficulty, the only solution is return to an earlier stage in the modelling process.

Simulating locational behaviour

A simple statement of *modelling goals* before research proceeds can be an extremely useful tool. The modelling goals not only act as guides to investigation procedures but also determine whether or not the simulation has been successful when it is complete. Goals should therefore be very broadly stated. As an example the modelling goals for the Glenwood I simulation are stated below.

The goals of investigation of Glenwood settlement patterns in general are:
(1) To account for the variability previously noted in Central Plains tradition settlement patterns of the Glenwood locality;
(2) To understand to some degree the processes by which locational decisions might have been made by inhabitants of the locality;
(3) To operationalize and test the implications of a number of assumptions about or reconstructions of Central Plains tradition culture for settlement patterns. Specifically, an explanation of settlement variability in systemic, dynamic terms is seen as desirable. It should however be phrased as realistically as possible so that the investigator can more readily understand its operation, including the impact of randomness on system behaviour. Some means of testing the explanation is also desirable, preferably the generation of simulated settlement patterns that can easily be compared with known settlement distribution. (Zimmerman 1976a, p. 65)
These goals have components that are both general,

relating to the broader problems of locational processes, and specific, stating that a certain kind of model is desirable. The model must in this case be realistic and testable by comparison of real and simulated settlement distributions. With model goals stated at two different levels of specificity, flexibility can be maintained but particular goals are visible and can be directly monitored for progress throughout the model-building process.

While the modelling goals are important and somewhat difficult to state, the most demanding stage of the modelling process is the *system analysis* stage. A locational system comprises a number of constituent elements and the intrinsic mechanisms which relate those elements to each other. Thus, the system analysis stage involves determining which elements of culture are important to locational decision-making and the more or less precise relationships of those elements. This consists of 'exiling to the environment those elements which, though they may from time to time affect system entities significantly, are never affected by any of the elements (entities) intrinsic to the system' (Mihram 1972, p. 626). In other words one must conceptualise two important units, the locational system and the environment. System analysis becomes a sorting process.

Isolating the components of the locational systems can be difficult if one is working with very few data. As noted earlier, intuition may play an important role in selection of these factors. Important factors that determine settlement can also be found in such works as Trigger's (1968) article 'Determinants of settlement patterns'. In the case of the Glenwood I simulation an algorithm was provided by Anderson and Zimmerman (1976) which outlined many of the key considerations for Glenwood locality settlement. In Thomas' BASIN I simulation his Shoshone settlement/subsistence model had been provided by Steward (1941). One's familiarity with the literature of the culture under examination will probably provide clues as to whether one can use an extant model or must develop a new one. If a large quantity of high quality data exists for the culture it may well be useful to apply a number of statistical techniques to provide clues of what might have been the salient considerations leading to locational decisions. With at least some of these components determined one can begin to build a loosely structured model.

With Glenwood I, model building began with an attempt to conceive of settlement as a dynamic decision-making process that could be repeated an infinite number of times. Consequently the decision-making symbolism of computer flow-charts was used to structure the decision-making process for location. A simple open-ended flow chart was prepared for location of a single lodge, a process that could be repeated many times for any number of lodges. That flow chart, slightly modified, is presented in fig. 1.

The basics of the flow chart are relatively simple. After initiating the system, the active core of the model, the population, is controlled via rules for birth, death and mating. If the population changes, new territory to support that population

is allocated near the lodge. If a new family is started, a new lodge location and territory are necessary. The locational decision is made from available locations via a set of rules. If the rules for a location are met, a new lodge is located. Both the population core and location rules are influenced by environmental input by way of environmental carrying capacity (ECC). The ECC leaves open the possibility of environmental change in an area.

A general flow chart like the one presented here could be used in any number of archaeological problems relating to the development of settlement. For Glenwood I it pinpointed three major areas that needed detailed analysis; natural environment, demography, and locational rules. The probability is high that at least these three areas will be important to most simulations of locational behaviour; ways to develop these areas of the model therefore deserve some examination.

The first major step in analysis is to 'create' the environment in which the people under consideration made their decisions. Since the environment is by definition exterior to the system, merely providing input to the system, it may be well to consider the environment as separate from the decision-making process temporarily. Information in the form of environmental carrying capacity as noted in the flow chart can simply feed information to the system. While the key elements of the environment important to decision-making may differ from culture to culture most will probably consider topography and available natural resources.

As was the case with the Glenwood I simulation, precise data that would provide an exact reconstruction of environments of the past are rare. One may be forced to accept Butzer's (1971, p. 49) suggestion that, 'the ultimate key to

Fig. 1. Simplified flow chart for simulation of locational systems.

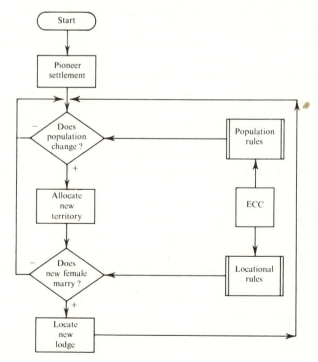

paleo-ecology is provided by the modern distribution of similar features'. A reconstructed environment will therefore be a combination of information derived from floral and faunal remains from archaeological sites in the locality and the distribution of modern species assuming that modern and past distributions are similar. Unless one can demonstrate otherwise, a stable topography may also be assumed.

To handle the environment in a detailed way could be an extraordinary simulation in itself; consequently generalisation is necessary. Thomas (1972) did this by considering the availability to the people of certain species or by grouping species into particular life-zones. Zimmerman (1977) did the same by dividing the locality into five resource-zone types, each resource-zone being comprised of flora and fauna potentially used by local populations. These resource-zones and their locations in space can actually be placed into computer memory. This can be accomplished by placing a grid system over a map of the locality with resource-zones mapped in. For Glenwood I, United States Geological Survey topographic maps were used. This grid divided the forty square mile locality into square mile units with each of these units divided into 100 units. Each of these 4000 data points therefore covered 6.4 acres (2.6 ha). The major resource-zone type was then recorded for each unit. Topographic information was derived in the same way. The average elevation for each unit was recorded and rounded to the nearest preselected contour interval. The topographic averaging process can be tested by using the data to reconstruct a contour map of the locality or even a three-dimensional projection to see if the abstraction resembles reality. The number of data points or the size of the grid system depends largely on the stamina of the individual doing the coding. Whatever the number of grid units the data can be put into data matrices directly accessible to the locational system. If one wishes, changes can be made in resources or topography simply by causing a program systematically to change them to other resource types or elevations at some later point in time, thus simulating climatic change, erosional processes, or whatever might be desired.

Demographic data for particular cultures, like environmental data, may not be available. Some mortality data may be available through detailed analysis of skeletal populations from burial areas, but even then important life data such as age of marriage or year of first parturition may be missing. Consequently, much of the data must be derived by ethnographic analogy with societies at similar levels of culture and living in similar environments. Important information to be considered is mortality, age of marriage, first parturition, sex ratio, and fecundity. These data will probably be of more utility if structured into probability tables.

Unless one has some sort of precise geneological information for the culture, which is highly unlikely, one cannot make a totally 'realistic' demographic core for one's model. This segment of the model thus becomes a function of probability and the impact of randomness on the system becomes important.

Other issues that enter into the demographic core of the model that may be directly accessible from the archaeological record via ceramics or similar artifacts are the kinship systems of the population. Matters to be considered are preferred marriage patterns (e.g. locality exogamy vs. endogamy) and descent systems which may have an important impact on residence patterns.

A set of rules whereby people actually make their locational decisions is that key segment of the model that links the demographic components to the natural environment. As noted, rules can vary widely depending on individual or cultural standards of what 'makes' a proper location. There are usually relatively few rules and they tend to be given priorities by individuals or groups. Therefore when rule 1 is applied to the set of available locations, the set is reduced to those that met the requirements of the rule. Rule 2 is then applied to that set, further reducing the number. This procedure can go on as long as one has rules and remaining choices. When one runs out of choices the decision is made. When one runs out of rules, *ad hoc* rules are invented or the choice becomes random. Conceptualising locational rules in this way will ease programming during the synthesis stage. It also gives the opportunity to test the impact of randomness on the system again both in terms of what determines the set of possible locations at any given moment and in terms of choices made when no more rules exist.

While conceptualising the rules in this fashion is not particularly difficult, selecting and giving priorities to the rules can present problems. Areas that should be considered are preferred residence patterns (matrilocality, etc.), available resources in the area, especially proximity to water, elevation, and minimum or maximum distance to friends and relatives. Some of these rules may be dependent on others. For example distance to relatives may depend on availability of resources. Locating a lodge too near another may well deplete area resources, and would thereby preclude use of that location.

The locational rules for Glenwood I might serve as examples. These rules focused primarily on territorial allocation and post-marital residence. The primary rules were economically oriented. The location of a lodge needed to be in an area where there was adequate resource potential to support a nuclear family unit. This rule was directly linked with the subsistence system of the people which was a mixed hunting-gathering/horticulture pattern. Each family unit therefore had to have available enough units of particular resource-zone types to support a nuclear family. The ideal location within this set of possible places was seen to be on ridgelines near the oak—hickory resource zone, so that the people could gather nut crops easily, but not in it, since trees would have had to be cleared in order to plant crops. The ideal location was then within a resource-zone, an ecotone of forest and grassland. Since it is likely that at least two of these units would be available, and since one of these units was deemed necessary to support a single person, a further choice existed. Given more than one unit, that unit with the highest elevation was selected.

If units were of equal elevation, the decision was random.

These rules functioned once a potential territory was selected, but given a forty square mile area, many territories of adequate size and composition would be available to support a nuclear family. Consequently a second major group of rules was used to narrow the choice. A new household was established when an eligible female married. For this female a rule of proximal matrilocality went into effect: the available territory meeting subsistence requirements was selected that was the nearest to the bride's mother. When the youngest daughter of a family married she simply took over her parents' territory on their deaths.

In the Glenwood I simulation these locational rules were specifically stated and given priorities. During such a simulation it is possible to change the locational rules at some time if that is an important part of the model — as it was in the Glenwood I simulation when severe climatic change was assumed to have reduced the available natural resources drastically. The point is that these locational rules can be very flexible or rigid depending on the desire of the model builder. Changing them is a relatively easy matter.

System analysis provides the base on which a model is built, a framework to which continual reference is made as system synthesis occurs. Weaknesses of various model segments may exist in the system analysis stage that do not become apparent until programming of the model actually is under way. Certain segments will have a much larger data or assumptive base (e.g. environment and population) on which to build components and linkages. The locational rules pose the fewest problems for synthesis and the environment the most. Many of the difficulties with the system structure only become apparent during the verification stage of model building. System analysis therefore becomes a continually reiterative process. Ultimate boundaries must, of course, be set lest one becomes trapped in the complexity dilemma.

Many of the conceptual structures that are to be programmed in the *system synthesis* stage will be generally organised in the system analysis stage. The major task of synthesis, then, is transformation of these general structures into a computer program. Probably the single most important step in synthesis is the selection of a programming language.

Selection of a language can pose serious problems for the archaeologist. Most archaeologists have had little computer training beyond introductory courses in FORTRAN or a similar language. Many have not even had that degree of experience and perhaps have used nothing more than a few 'number-crunching' library statistical routines (Zimmerman 1976b). With this small experience the prospect of developing an original program of such complexity can be frightening. In this case the archaeologist should make every effort to consult a specialist in computer programming. The problem should be expressed to that individual in as clear a set of terms as is possible. One will probably find that communication can be difficult since neither person is likely to be familiar with the field of the other. With the aid of the specialist a language suitable for the simulation can be selected.

Many languages, like FORTRAN, were not designed with simulation as a goal; programming a simulation in them may be very difficult and in fact, often wasteful. Therefore the language that is selected should be suitable: the model builder must be able to comprehend it and to communicate problems about it to the specialist. Further, the language should be accessible to the programmer, that is to say it should be available on the computer system on which he will be working. Cost must also be a consideration.

In the case of the Glenwood I simulation, the language SIMSCRIPT was selected after a number of very frustrating attempts to program in FORTRAN Y and extended discussions with a computer specialist, Daniel Moore (see chapter 2 above, where SIMSCRIPT is described). SIMSCRIPT proved to be far more suitable in that it retained the familiar FORTRAN-like words, phrases, and symbols, but it was also event oriented, generalised, and an almost 'natural' language making it useful for organising, analysing, and modelling the structure and behaviour of a complex locational system.

Programming in many respects seemed much like the analysis of the system. However, in one aspect it was far more demanding. The analysis had to be made operational, that is, made far more specific so that it could be programmed. This was done in close collaboration with the specialist who would often say, 'This is far too general and I can't do anything with it.' Thus one is forced to conceive of the environment, demography, and locational rules in increasingly specific and logical ways. What happens in programming is that one proceeds most easily by using the top-down method, that is, programs are built starting with routines that are generalised and then subroutines are developed that are ever more precise in their functions. In Glenwood I, for instance, 8 subprograms handled the seemingly simple task of determining the location of a lodge and continually monitoring the environment to see if the lodge's location remained within a territory adequate to support the lodge's inhabitants — actually only a small part of the entire simulation. This may seem excessive but this degree of specificity may be needed to develop a realistic simulation. Every extra statement seems to make verification of the model's behaviour more difficult, but output devices incorporated while programming can simplify the chore immensely.

One further matter must be given a great deal of thought — the nature of the output of the program desired by the model builder. While it may be acceptable to derive just locations from the program using some kind of x-y coordinate system, one should try to program as many output functions as possible into the program. One may well want to know the year or season in which a location was established, population statistics, and allocation of resources to support the people in the location. Instead of x-y coordinates alone, one may also be able to generate a line-printed map showing the locations so that one can inspect distribution patterns visually. In short, programming as many output functions as possible or considered useful may provide later benefits.

The utility of many output devices becomes most apparent in the *verification stage*. Verification is the most demanding and potentially frustrating part of the simulation process, done for the purpose of determining the logical consistency of the program. Put more simply, it is done to see if the model is behaving in the way in which the programmer intended. This stage can be likened to the term computer programmers often use, 'debugging'.

The first problem of verification is simply getting the program to run on the computer. To complete a run the program must be logically constructed according to the rules of the computer language used. Many programming errors tend to 'creep' into such a complex kind of simulation. Most language manuals however, have a section to assist in working out these sorts of problems and the computer specialist again is invaluable in finding and correcting these errors.

However, just because the computer program runs, one should not assume that the system is behaving as one anticipated; such may well not be the case. The importance of being able to monitor the system variables becomes almost immediately evident when one carefully examines the first runs of the program. It is not enough to have just a final map or list of locations printed at the end of the simulation runs. A locational model's complexity demands much more. To this end it is extremely useful to include as many monitoring devices as possible into the program as noted in discussion of the synthesis stage.

In Glenwood I, even though the simulation ran without programming errors, examination of the output from monitoring devices indicated that problems had cropped up. For example, construction of population curves to verify the performance of the model's stochastic demographic core indicated excessive births, certain women bearing children each year up to five years after their death. While this is perhaps an interesting medical phenomenon, it is simply not known in reality! A simple change solved the problem. Many other sorts of errors are much more difficult to detect and, once detected, to solve.

Verification must be done very carefully and few assumptions of proper system behaviour should be made. The entire verification procedure for Glenwood I took approximately a year to complete. Even then, more verification could perhaps have been done. When one seems to have the system functioning properly, a minor change in a subprogram can have a profound impact on another segment of the model. Changes in seed numbers of a random number generator can cause havoc in the system. A model that seems to be behaving well in the 100th iteration can be fouled in the 1000th iteration by some unique circumstance. Persistence in verification will solve most problems.

Other than solving logical problems to make the program run correctly, there are some positive benefits to be gained from verification. During this stage one sees most clearly how the system operates and the impact of one subsystem on another. Also, errors that appear are not always bad, and can in fact provide avenues toward the solution of some conceptual or even programming difficulties which the model builder may

have had. In other words, verification has both its frustrations and rewards.

Just as the verification stage in a model's development serves as a check on the system synthesis stage, the *validation* stage is undertaken to check the system analysis stage. Validation is accomplished by comparing the responses from the verified simulation with the corresponding responses of the real locational system. If valid results cannot be generated, one returns to analysis and makes alterations in the model. With simulation under ideal circumstances experimentation is conducted with both the simulated and real systems. Obviously this cannot be done with prehistoric culture systems. Consequently any inferences that are drawn from the simulation must be tentative. Formal validation procedures very often involve the use of high-powered statistics. However since the real locational system is not available for experimentation and since the assumptive base for the simulation is probably large, informal validation procedures will need to be developed.

The major task, then, is to compare the distribution of the real locations with those that have been simulated. While one might naively hope that one's simulation will generate a settlement distribution that corresponds one-to-one with the known settlement distribution in the study area, one must realise that such a fit is highly improbable.

Two general approaches can be used in informal validation. The first, which should not be underrated as an analytical tool, is visual inspection of maps showing both the real and simulated distribution of locations. By comparing the two one can often easily see areas in which there are settlements in reality and none in simulation or vice versa, or one can perhaps begin to spot trends of settlement movements into certain locations. These may not be as obvious using the other approach, statistical analysis. Several statistical techniques are available in order to test the goodness of fit in settlement distribution as discussed in Haggett (1965). One-to-one comparisons of locations are possible but may not be meaningful. More useful perhaps are statistics that simply test the dispersion or nucleation of settlement across an area.

Two techniques are useful for this kind of comparison, nearest-neighbour analysis as applied by Washburn (1974) to Pueblo I–III sites in New Mexico or the coefficient of dispersion as used by Thomas (1973) in his Reese river valley study. Both measure the deviation of a distribution of a population in space from a random distribution toward either a clustered or anticlustered pattern. The former is somewhat more complex to apply than the latter with approximately the same information resulting.

The statistics developed will show a tendency for a distribution of locations to be clustered or dispersed. When derived for both the real and simulated settlement patterns a comparison is possible that shows how far apart the two are. Experimentation with and alteration of the model may be oriented toward achieving similar measurements for the real and simulated patterns.

A combination of both visual and statistical validation was used for Glenwood I. While a perfect fit of coefficients of dispersion and visual congruity was never achieved, a level that was deemed satisfactory visually and statistically was met. For validation, the use of many different techniques should be considered and is recommended.

With the first efforts at validation analysed, one begins to notice areas for possible experimentation with either the parameters or the structure of the model. All the frustrations of system analysis and verification should be put aside at this point, because now the real enjoyment of the simulation begins. One should make every effort to play with the program, asking questions of the sort, 'What if I change the . . . ?'. This kind of play will lead to many important insights into the behaviour of the system in terms of the impact of particular variables on locational decisions. As each run with altered components is rejected one essentially tests the feasibility of certain assumptions about the locational system being played with and goes back to limited reanalysis of the system. This basically results in *inferences* made about the system.

In the case of Glenwood I, many parameters were changed. The primary avenues for experimentation were manipulations of time, climatic fluctuation, and location of pioneer settlement in the Glenwood locality. The result of these experiments led to inferences that the duration of occupation in the locality was far shorter than suspected (this was independently corroborated by radiocarbon dates unknown at the time the simulation was being done), that climatic change had little influence on settlement of the people, that the known distribution of lodges could simply have been the result of preferred postmarital residence patterns rather than alterations in locational rules due to decreased availability of resources, and that locality population levels were far smaller than suspected. While proof for these inferences cannot come from the simulation, corroboration may come with further research focused on these ideas. Again, simulation proves nothing about the prehistory but merely shows that certain ideas are or are not feasible.

An assessment of locational simulation

The intent of this paper has been to provide a sort of primer on the simulation of locational behaviour. To do this, general theoretical conceptions of how locational decisions are made were considered, in order to provide a framework from which to discuss total society simulations with location as a focal point. Mihram's (1972) scheme of the modelling process with modelling goals, system analysis, system synthesis, verification, validation, and inference as major stages was presented as a profitable approach to the construction of a locational simulation. Within each of these stages a number of suggestions and examples derived from Zimmerman's (1976*a*, 1977) Glenwood I simulation were offered as a 'recipe' for locational simulation. While every attempt was made to suggest potential benefits to be derived from simulation as well as potential problems and weaknesses, a final general assessment of simulation of locational behaviour might be useful. It should be noted that while locational simulation is the central issue, many of these comments could apply to any variety of computer simulation.

The major weakness of locational simulation is that it attempts to model a cognitive process of an individual or group and how their perceptions of a number of natural and cultural environmental factors relate to satisfaction of their needs in terms of choice of position on the landscape. The information necessary to build a truely adequate and realistic simulation is perhaps unknowable and even if available would create such complexity that it could not be simulated at reasonable cost. In a sense, however, this weakness can be viewed as a strength: patterns of settlement similar to reality *can* be generated with relatively little complexity. Reality can thus be simplified and made comprehensible. Simplicity and generality allow one effectively to follow the interaction of variables that influence location.

At the same time, the use of simulation entails detailed, precise analysis of locational processes that must be logically acceptable to the computer. This necessary attention to detail creates an intense involvement in the simulation process that is unique. The programmer becomes a variable in the process that is as important as any other variable. One becomes almost personally involved with the culture being simulated and in a sense becomes a cultural 'button-pusher', providing situations to which simulated beings must react. This involvement promotes serendipity, and one often encounters some totally unexpected situation that offers insights into the locational model's particular behaviour or about one's own thinking about the modelling processes. Out of serendipity come new avenues of experimentation.

Simulation should not be considered a panacea for archaeological problems of locational behaviour; it has many liabilities. The computer is in a sense very limiting. One can conceive many possibilities for a model that are beyond the capabilities of the language one selects, or at least beyond one's ability to program in that language. This can be most frustrating. One must also recognise that proper formal validation for archaeological simulations is impossible and that all inferences drawn from the research are suspect.

Finally, and not of least importance, is the fact that computer simulation is expensive. If one's model is complex and one's programming abilities limited costs can be high. Total costs for the Glenwood 1 simulation were about $3000 with each successful run costing around $25.

In all, the benefits to be gained from locational simulations outweigh the liabilities. If one remembers that simulations prove nothing about prehistory they can be a most useful tool. They are simply methodological devices which allow the researcher a great deal of freedom to hypothesise and provide a limited test of those hypotheses. They do not provide 'the' answer even if 'the' answer can be found.

Simulation for the archaeologist can allow a shift away from the artifacts themselves toward their systemic context and their behavioural correlates if that is seen as desirable for a particular problem. Simulation makes total society study in archaeology feasible; its implementation would seem to be a reasonable methodological extension for locational analysis in archaeology.

References

Anderson, A.D. & Zimmerman, L.J. (1976) 'Settlement/subsistence variability in the Glenwood locality, southwestern Iowa', *Plains Anthropologist* 21: 141—54

Bonini, C.P. (1963) *Simulation of Information and Decision Systems in the Firm*, Prentice-Hall

Butzer, K.W. (1971) *Environment and Archaeology: An Ecological Approach to Prehistory*, Aldine-Atherton

Davenport, W. (1960) *Jamaican Fishing: A Game Theory Analysis* (Yale University Publications in Anthropology, No. 59), Yale University Press

Dutton, J.M. & Briggs, W. (1971) 'Simulation model construction' in J. Dutton & W. Starbuck (eds.) *Computer Simulation of Human Behavior*, Wiley

Dutton, J.M. & Starbuck, W. (1971) 'The plan of the book' in J. Dutton & W. Starbuck (eds.) *Computer Simulation of Human Behavior*, Wiley

Gould, P.R. (1963) 'Man against his environment: a game theoretical framework', *Annals of the Association of American Geographers* 53: 290—7

Green, E.L. (1973) 'Locational analysis of prehistoric Maya sites in northern British Honduras', *American Antiquity* 38: 279—93

Gumerman, G.J. (1971) *The Distribution of Prehistoric Population Aggregates* (Prescott College Anthropological Reports, No. 1), Prescott College Press

Hägerstrand, T. (1952) *The Propogation of Innovation Waves. Lund Studies in Geography*, Series B, No. 4

Haggett, P. (1965) *Locational Analysis in Human Geography*, Arnold

Harvey, D. (1969) *Explanation in Geography*, Arnold

Hole, F. & Heizer, R. (1973) *An Introduction to Prehistoric Archaeology*, Holt, Rinehart & Winston

Mihram, G.A. (1972) 'The modelling process', *IEEE Transactions on Systems, Man, and Cybernetics* SMC-2: 621—9

Morrill, R.L. (1965) *Migration and the Spread and Growth of Urban Settlement. Lund Studies in Geography*, Series B, No. 26

Mosimann, J.E. & Martin, P.S. (1975) 'Simulating overkill by Palaeo-indians', *American Scientist* 63: 304—13

Pool, I.S. (1967) 'Computer simulations of total societies' in E. Klausner (ed.) *The Study of Total Societies*, Doubleday

Pred, A. (1967) *Behavior and Location: Foundations for a Geographic and Dynamic Location Theory, Part I. Lund Studies in Geography*, Series B, No. 27

Pred, A. (1969) *Behaviour and Location: Foundations for a Geographic and Dynamic Location Theory, Part II. Lund Studies in Geography*, Series B, No. 28

Starbuck, W.H. & Dutton, J.M. (1971) 'The history of simulation models' in J. Dutton & W. Starbuck (eds.) *Computer Simulation of Human Behavior*, Wiley

Steward, J. (1941) 'Culture element distribution: XIII, Nevada Shoshone', *University of California Anthropological Records* 4: 209—359

Thomas, D.H. (1971) *Prehistoric Subsistence-Settlement Patterns of the Reese River Valley, Central Nevada*, University Microfilm

Thomas, D.H. (1972) 'A computer simulation of Great Basin subsistence and settlement patterns' in D.L. Clarke (ed.) *Models in Archaeology*, Methuen

Thomas, D.H. (1973) 'An empirical test of Steward's model for Great Basin settlement patterns', *American Antiquity* 38: 155—76

Thomas, D.H. (1974) 'An archaeological perspective on Shoshonean bands', *American Anthropologist* 76: 11—23

Trigger, B. (1968) 'The determinants of settlement patterns' in K.C. Chang (ed.) *Settlement Archaeology*, National Press Books

Von Neumann, J. & Morgenstern, O. (1953) *Theory of Games and Economic Behavior*, Princeton University Press

Washburn, D.K. (1972) *An Analysis of the Spatial Aspects of Site Locations of Pueblo I—III Settlement Patterns Along the Middle Rio Puerco, New Mexico*, University Microfilm

Washburn, D.K. (1974) 'Nearest neighbor analysis of Pueblo I—III settlement patterns along the Rio Puerco, east New Mexico', *American Antiquity* 39: 315—35

Whallon, R. (1972) 'The computer in archaeology: a critical survey', *Computers and the Humanities* 7: 29—45

Wyman, F.P. (1970) *Simulation Modeling: A Guide to Using SIMSCRIPT*, Wiley

Zimmerman, L.J. (1976*a*) *Prehistoric Locational Behavior: Computer Simulation of Central Plains Tradition Settlement in the Glenwood Locality, Mills County, Iowa*, University Microfilm

Zimmerman, L.J. (1976*b*) 'Selection of languages for archaeological simulations: SIMSCRIPT', *Newsletter of Computer Archaeology* 11: 30—8

Zimmerman, L.J. (1977) *Prehistoric Locational Behavior: A Computer Simulation* (Reports of the State Archaeologist of Iowa, No. 10), University of Iowa Press

Zubrow, E.B.W. (1971*a*) *A Southwestern Test of an Anthropological Model of Population Dynamics*, University Microfilm

Zubrow, E.B.W. (1971*b*) 'Carrying capacity and dynamic equilibrium in the prehistoric Southwest', *American Antiquity* 36: 127—38

Zubrow, E.B.W. (1975) *Prehistoric Carrying Capacity: A Model*, Cummings

Chapter 4

A simulation of Pawnee site development
John M. O'Shea

Introduction

In the eighteenth and nineteenth centuries on the North American Plains, two long-established life-ways came into a brief and intense contact which resulted in the eventual destruction of an entire culture complex. The Plains villages, which once to Coronado represented El Dorado, and which now remain only as circular depressions in these dwindling areas of unploughed prairie, offer a unique opportunity for the simultaneous study of culture history and archaeology. To the archaeologist, the historic Plains villages are seen as the final act in a tradition which had successfully adapted to the prairie environment for nearly a millenium. To the ethnohistorian, they are the source for exhaustive ethnographic and linguistic documentation and analysis, supplemented by accounts of travellers, trappers, soldiers, and missionaries concerning the customs and life styles of the village inhabitants.

This study represents an attempt to merge the information from these various sources in modelling the local settlement strategy of a historic Plains village and the archaeological remains which it produced. The basic goals of this study are (1) to evaluate the ethnographic and historic descriptions available on the settlement strategy of the Plains villages, and (2) to illustrate the effects of such a strategy on the formation of archaeological remains.

For the purpose of this study, we are concerned with those elements of the occupation which will be incorporated directly into the archaeological record, and the rate at which they are incorporated through time. Fruitful work could be undertaken on the simulation of the making, use and disposal of tools, or on the accumulation of various occupational debris, but since this example is conceived as a pilot and illustrative study, it will concentrate on those coarser features of the occupation, such as the number of structural remains and storage facilities, and on the changing size of the population.

Computer simulation will be employed as the means of setting the model in operation. The simulation will be used to approximate the local settlement strategy as the result of an ordered series of stochastic 'events'. The outcome of these events should not only reflect the current status of site occupation, but will also be used to generate, with certain assumptions, a selected set of the archaeological remains that would be produced by the occupation.

The process of simulation consists of the ordered passage through a series of steps (Mihram 1972, p. 211). These steps, from the statement of the model's goals, through system analysis, system synthesis, verification, validation, and inference have been described in chapter 3. This paper will review first the relevant ethnographical background and source material for the critical parameters, and will then discuss the formalisation of these elements into a simulation model; followed by a discussion of model validity.

The Plains Village
In this study we will examine the site strategy relating to the earthlodge and cache pit complex associated with the Plains village tradition. This tradition, which appeared on the Central Plains before AD 1000 and which persisted into the nineteenth century, was a successful Plains adaptation which relied equally on hunting and riverine horticulture (Willey 1966, p. 320). The mixed economic posture was well suited to the Plains environment with its extremes in temperature and marked fluctuations in precipitation (Wedel 1961, p. 24). Settlements of the historic period (from 1780 onward) were located on the terraces of the tree-fringed rivers and streams which dissected the grassy rolling prairie uplands. These waterways not only provided rich land for garden plots of maize, beans, squash and sunflowers, but also were a source of scarce water and timber. Bison were overwhelmingly the principle prey in the hunting economy, but elk, deer and smaller animals were also taken.

Two distinctive features of the Plains village groups were the large timber and sod earthlodges and the deep bell-shaped storage pits. Historically the lodges were large circular structures with a diameter of 8–15 metres (25–50 feet) and built slightly below ground level (see fig. 1). The lodges were typically supported by four to eight large centre posts, with smaller posts and poles around the circumference of the lodge to maintain the crossmembers which supported the massive walls of thatch and sod (Wilson 1934, p. 358). Structures of this general type were common throughout the Central and

Northern Plains from approximately AD 1500 until the destruction of the Indian cultures in the nineteenth century and appear to have been an innovation of the Caddoan speakers of the Central Plains. Earlier (c. AD 700–1500), lodges were of a rectangular shape and were somewhat smaller, though they appear to have been constructed and organised in much the same manner. The large storage pits were customarily dug to a depth of 2½–3 metres (8–10 feet), assuming a 'bell' shape, with a narrow neck and mouth, expanding out and terminating in either a flat or rounded base. It was in these deep caches that the year's precious agricultural harvest was stored, and other possessions were hidden during those periods when the bulk of the band was away from the permanent village on the annual bison hunts (frequently all but four or five months of the year (Dunbar 1880, p. 275)).

With this background into the Plains village tradition as a whole, the study will concentrate on the Pawnee of what is now central Nebraska as a particular and representative example. The Pawnee were chosen for simulation because of the good documentation of the tribe from historical and ethnographic sources, because they remained somewhat shielded from the early effects of the intensive European trade on the Missouri mainstem which so radically transformed all the Plains groups, and because they, as a group, appear to have great antiquity as Plains inhabitants (Grange 1968, p. 121).

The Pawnee are thought to be represented prehistorically by the archaeological Lower Loup Phase, and earlier, from the Upper Republican groups (Ludwickson 1975). They were Caddoan speakers related to the Arikara to the north and the

Fig. 1. Plan and section of typical Pawnee earthlodge (after Weltfish 1965).

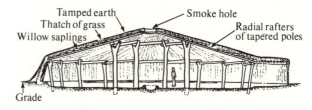

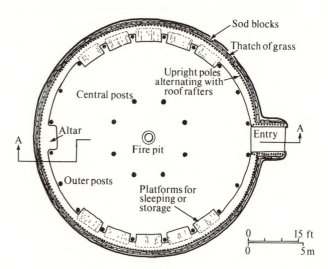

Wichita to the south. Their villages were found on a 200 km
(120 mile) stretch of the Platte and Loup river valleys from
just above the north fork of the Loup river on the west to the
confluence of the Elkhorn and the Platte rivers on the east
(Grange 1968, p. 8). The Pawnee were traditionally divided
into four independent bands known as the Grand Pawnee,
Republican, Tapage, and the Skidi (Dunbar 1880, p. 260). Each
band seems originally to have been made up of several semi-
autonomous villages, but in the eighteenth century, the
Pawnee villages had begun to coalesce and ultimately each of
the bands had formed into a single village. In the nineteenth
century as the pressure of marauding horse-borne nomads
and epidemic disease increased to intolerable limits, the bands
combined into still larger villages and ultimately were removed
to Indian territory in Oklahoma (Wedel 1938, p. 8). The
Pawnee ceremonial, social, and economic systems were
governed by a distinct annual cycle, which saw the bands
travelling *en masse* on great bison hunts in the summer and
winter, crop harvesting and storing in the autumn, and cel-
ebrating a great ceremonial season in the spring (Weltfish
1965, p. 86).

The model

With this brief introduction, we can begin to abstract
from the data available on the Pawnee those elements which
will be of importance in the modelling of the Pawnee settlement strategy. The first set of elements which the model
requires are those relating to the rate at which houses and
storage pits were constructed on the site during the period of its
occupation. To determine this, we need to know the average
use-life of these features, their relation to each other, and the
initial number of each at the founding of the settlement.
Another element which will directly influence the archaeological interpretation is the relation of the human population
to the number of lodges occupied, and the way in which population growth would be manifest on the site. An additional
important consideration is the average length of time a particular site was occupied before it was abandoned as a whole,
and the preferred community size, if one existed. Other factors, such as the potential of natural disaster as an element of
lodge attrition, and the likelihood of independent movement
of one or of a group of households instead of total community
relocation, must also be explored.

The most fundamental parameter necessary for the simulation of the earthlodge will be the length of time a single
structure was likely to be used before it required replacement.
Weltfish's (1965, p. 88) informants suggested that a lodge
could be used for a maximum of fifteen years (an estimate
which agrees with the ten to twelve years given by Wilson's
(1934, p. 358) Hidatsa informants). It is clear from Weltfish's
account that the critical decision was whether simply to effect
repairs of the existing lodge or to rebuild it completely,
remembering that it was necessary to anticipate at least two
years in advance in order to procure and season the raw
materials needed for such a task (Weltfish 1965, p. 362). The

usual causes of the short life expectancy of these massive
structures was the rotting of timbers, sod deterioration and
their infestation with rats and parasites.

The nature and use of the deep external caches in the
Plains villages appear to be somewhat more variable than the
other components. Among the Hidatsa, the external caches
were large and deep; each family making exclusive use of
several (Wilson 1934, p. 391). Among the Pawnee, however,
one large external cache per lodge appears to have been the
norm; though the produce of each family was kept separate in
the shared cache. Weltfish (1965, p. 268) does mention
though, that wealthy men or chiefs among the Pawnee
occasionally did use more than one cache.

Population growth within the current context will be
evaluated in terms of the increase in the number of lodges
occupied at any one time on the village site. It is important to
determine then, how the actual human population related to
the number of lodges on the site. These large earth lodges were
spacious (Carelton (1943, p. 14) noted that 100 to 175 individuals could congregate in a single lodge), and were usually
occupied by 20 to 60 individuals (Catlin 1965, p. 62; Oehler
& Smith 1914, p. 27; Morgan 1965, p. 135). Among the
Pawnee this averaged 30 to 40 individuals from two or more
extended families per lodge who may or may not have been
related (Weltfish 1965, p. 14). This association between families within the lodge formed the basis of the productive unit
within the society; each lodge acting as a relatively independent and self-sufficient entity. The tight economic integration
of the households added to the complexity of marriage
arrangements and prevented simple increase in the number of
lodges as a result of the establishment of new households. This
tendency, in addition to a series of restrictive marriage prac-
tices and a form of sororal polygyny, served to inhibit the
expression of growth as a function of an increase in the number of households.

In the actual formalisation and implementation of the
model, certain decisions were made concerning the nature of
various events which could not be readily documented ethnographically. The first parameter considered is the likelihood of
locating a new lodge or a reconstructed lodge on the current
site, or moving outside the area. In historic times, for the most
part, relocation does not seem to be the choice, since the
vulnerability to raids of small isolated settlements made them
almost suicidal (cf. Fletcher & La Flesche 1911, p. 95). The
loose village endogamy practised by the Pawnee would also
have worked against relocation. However, there must have
been cases where the effort involved to procure the materials
necessary for the construction of the lodge would have made
the relocation alternative attractive (though it would probably
be in the context of a series of households relocating together).

For the purpose of this preliminary model, the probability of the non-local construction of a lodge, which was
needed either as a replacement because of attrition, or as a
new lodge because of population growth, will be ¼ as opposed
to ¾ in favour of local construction. In the case of natural

disaster, the probability of non-local construction was set at ½ to model potential reliance on relatives in perhaps another village as an equally viable source of shelter and aid.

Another parameter which was not directly available was the maximum use-life of the deep storage pits. Lacking ethnographic guidance, two alternative life expectancies were tested: one which assumed the pits to have a relatively long use-life, approximately twenty-five year maximum (i.e. longer than the lodge use-life); and a shorter expectancy of about ten years maximum (less than the lodge use-life). Fig. 2 illustrates the effect of these two parameters on the simulation of archaeologically visible sites. This figure will be discussed later in terms of model validation.

A third parameter which required estimation was the potential for population increase on the site. The demographic modelling of the population presents an extremely complex problem owing to the unstable conditions experienced by the Pawnee, and is clearly beyond the scope of this study. Therefore, each lodge was assigned an equal probability of splitting as a result of population growth. The probability of such an event would need to be low in view of the factors already mentioned relevant to the establishment of new households. A simple probability of increase was established, and tested in a Bernoulli trial for each house in each modelled iteration. A cumulative probability could not be assigned to this situation, since lodge membership was frequently re-shuffled. The rate finally used in the present case was a 5 percent probability that a particular lodge would produce a new household in the five year interval. (In the Pawnee example this is equivalent to a growth probability of 0.5 percent per family per year.) Some experimentation was undertaken using a rate of 10 percent per iteration, but this led to a too rapid increase in the local population. The 5 percent figure tends to maintain the village population at a relatively constant level by just balancing the local system's out-migration. A major difficulty in estimating this parameter lies in the fact that there is no source of good

ethnographic or historical documentation to use as a basis for comparison.

The on-site population was determined in each cycle by a random integer value from a Normal distribution with a mean of 32 individuals, and a standard deviation of 6. Again, no cumulative record was kept of individual lodges because of the non-biologically based changes which frequently altered lodge membership.

The model allows the site to be abandoned as the result of the slow relocation of lodges outside the test frame. For the Pawnee, however, it is well documented (cf. Grange 1968, p. 18) that the villages often did move *en masse* from one site to another. Dunbar (1880, p. 257) noted that the normal length of site occupation among the Pawnee villages was eight to ten years. To simulate this effect, a process was written into the model which determined at the beginning of each cycle whether the village as a whole would relocate. This was done by allowing the site to be occupied a certain number of cycles, determined by a normal distribution with ten years as its mean. This resulted in site occupation ranging from five to fifty years in duration. A histogram reflecting an arbitrarily selected series of occupation times can be seen in fig. 3b. A potential source

Fig. 3. Length of continuous site occupation: (a) historic Pawnee, number of sites = 16; (b) simulation estimates, number of sites = 18.

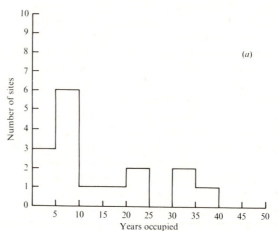

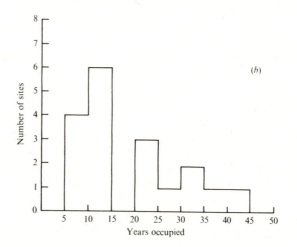

Fig. 2. Simulation of archaeologically visible storage pits and lodges generated by varying the use-life of the pits compared with the archaeological results.

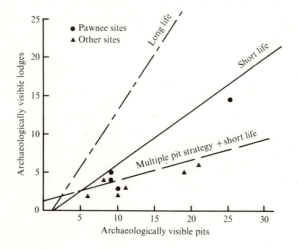

of bias in this procedure, which will be mentioned again, is the fact that since the model was incremented in five-year cycles, a site could not be occupied for less than one cycle, or five years, which will cause some divergence from several known historical examples.

The model building has concentrated, so far, on deriving the ethnographic elements of the system. These parameters must now be further modelled in order to reflect their cumulative appearance as archaeological remains. As was noted earlier, the frame of reference of this study is assumed to be the small unit of space on which the settlement lies, and as such correlates with an archaeological site. Any household which is relocated, or other activity which takes place outside this frame of reference, is eliminated from further interaction.

Two other assumptions are necessary for our generation of the archaeological remains. First, it is assumed that there exists no clear-cut spatial arrangement of features within the site, other than the physical necessity that two features do not occupy the same location in space at the same time. In this sense, the model will contain less information than an excavator might hope to discover on an actual site such as the overlapping of structures or the segregation of different occupational episodes as discrete spatial units. Additionally, the model assumes perfect archaeological preservation, with no loss of features due to post-depositional effect, and that the site is completely excavated. With these assumptions the archaeological remains can be modelled simply as the cumulative record of the site's occupational history. It should be mentioned that the effects of post-depositional sampling or systematic bias resulting from the excavation strategy could, with little difficulty, be incorporated into this model, and could be especially relevant in those cases where settlement is being studied on a regional level. However for purposes here, it was deemed most appropriate to illustrate the patterning without these effects — to simulate the ideal archaeological recovery and preservation.

The formalisation of the ethnographically modelled decisions into 'events' can be simply illustrated by a flow

diagram. Fig. 4 represents the events involved in the decision to repair or rebuild the lodge. It starts at connector A; the first decision (1) reflects the repair or rebuild question. If the answer is no, the house will not be rebuilt. The variables do not change and control passes to the next event (B). However, if the decision is yes, this leads to a second decision (2); will the new lodge be constructed locally? If yes again, the number of occupied houses on the site remains unchanged, but the number of archaeologically visible houses increases by one ($Y = Y + 1$). If the result of the second decision is no, then the number of houses occupied on the site decreases by one ($X = X - 1$), while the record of households moving away is incremented by one ($W = W + 1$) and there is no change noted in the archaeological record. The result of a simple simulation run based only on this set of decisions is illustrated in fig. 5.

In a general way, the model approximates the Pawnee strategy by looping through a series of event routines and recording the state of the variables through time. The clockwork of the simulation is based on a simple, discrete change model, where time passes in equal units (cf. Mize & Cox 1968, p. 105) of five years each and where each increment is equivalent to one iteration through the model. During each interval a series of tests are undergone to determine the state of the

Fig. 5. Examples of simulation results: (a) results produced by simple lodge attrition only; (b) results including the possibility of local population increase.

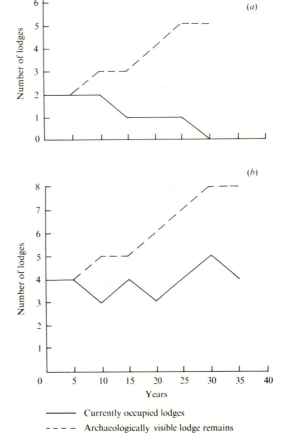

Fig. 4. Flow diagram of decisions involved in lodge reconstruction. See text for explanation.

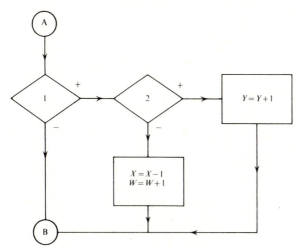

site features for that cycle, after which a report is issued which outlines the present status of these features. The maximum number of cycles permitted in the present model was fifty — the equivalent of 250 years of simulation time. If during the run, the site was abandoned, an integer number distributed uniformly from one to one hundred determines the number of iterations which would pass before the site would be reoccupied. If this number, when added to the number of iterations already simulated was greater than fifty, it was assumed that the site was not reoccupied and the run ended at that point. If, on the other hand, the number was still below the 50 maximum, the site was reoccupied at that point and allowed to run again until the 50 cycles had been reached.

Excluding the initialisation process, the program can be envisaged as passing through five basic stages in each iteration of the model. These steps are summarised in fig. 6. The model first determines whether the site as a whole will be abandoned. If so, a routine tests whether the site will be reoccupied; if not, a final report is issued and the run ends. If the site is not abandoned, the next event determines which if any, of the existing lodges are destroyed through natural disaster. Those destroyed are either rebuilt locally or move outside the test frame. If no houses remain on the site after this step, the routine determines whether the site will be reoccupied. Assuming that a portion of the lodges survive, these are then tested to determine which will be rebuilt during the five-year interval. For those which must be rebuilt, it must be decided whether construction will be undertaken within the site area or outside it. It will also be necessary to determine whether a new cache must be constructed if the household remains on the site. A similar test must be made for the pits currently in use, with those no longer usable being abandoned and replaced. The

final event of the series evaluates the potential for population increase for each lodge which survives on the site; if the increase does take the form of a new lodge, the location of its construction must be determined. At the end of the cycle, a report of the current state of the site is made. If the time limit has not been reached the clock is incremented by one and the cycle is repeated; if it has, a final status report is recorded and the simulation terminates. Fig. 7 shows a sample run through the model charting four variables. This summarises schematically the ordering of the events in the model and the logic behind the organisation.

The status reports of the program include the number of lodges and caches currently in use on the site, the number of lodges and pit caches visible archaeologically, the size of the population, the number of iterations and the number of simulation years represented, the maximum size of the settlement at any time during the run, the number of years that the site was unoccupied and the number of households that moved outside the test frame during the run. These variables then give both a running account of the status of the site at any given time, and provide a cumulative log of the changes which take place on the site through simulation time.

Discussion

The first step in the validation process was to compare the results of the simulation with the ethnographic sources from which the parameters were derived. Clearly, if there is not good correspondence between them, we must return to the model verification step to determine the cause. Having done this, we then move to compare the results with real observations which were independent of the model's formulation. This process was admittedly coarse in the present case and relied to a certain extent on data that were themselves not always beyond question, such as the estimates of village size and population made by traders and military commanders, and the dependence on many excavations, which while

Fig. 6. Simplified flow diagram of the decision process.

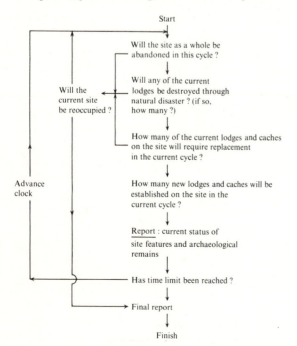

Fig. 7. Sample simulation results. Initial number of lodges was set at 4.

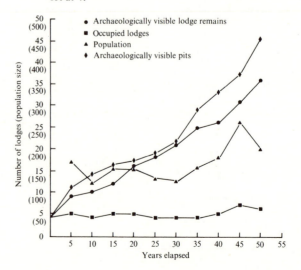

thorough for their day, may not have yielded an accurate representation of the evidence occurring on the site. Also, since by definition the model assumes perfect preservation and recovery, we must expect some variation between our model and actual observation.

As a first test, a series of historically derived estimates of standing population and village size (see Hyde 1951, p. 364) were plotted and compared with the trend produced by a series of simulation runs (fig. 8). The simulation results are summarised as a least-squares regression line (after Hays 1973, p. 630) employing population size as the dependent variable. Similarly, regressions were also calculated for the Pawnee sources and also for a series of Middle Missouri estimates included for comparison. The agreement between the simulation and the historical sources for the Pawnee is very good. The figure also demonstrates an apparent divergence in lodge population between the Pawnee and the historical Middle Missouri groups (here the Mandan, Hidatsa, and Arikara).

Fig. 2 summarises the relationship between the simulated archaeologically observable lodges and storage pits, using different use-life estimates for the storage pits. These are then compared with a series of known archaeological remains. Owing to the scarcity of extensively excavated Pawnee sites, estimates could only be obtained from four sites, 25PK1, 25WT1, 25BU1, 14RP1. For comparative purposes a set of other village sites from varying periods where estimates could be made, were also plotted, including 39ST14, 39ST30, 25TP1, 25PT13, 25NC1, 39ST16, 25HT3. Regression lines were plotted for both the long and short life expectancy models. Additionally, an alternative process was incorporated which allowed a multiple storage pit strategy coupled with a short use-life. Its results are summarised in fig. 2. The outcome of this test is somewhat ambiguous. The non-Pawnee villages show a reasonably good fit with the multiple pit strategy. The Pawnee sites remain situated between the multiple and single pit adaptations, though they perhaps support the shorter use-life model.

Fig. 8. Population size and number of lodges estimated by simulation (solid line), and from Pawnee (dashed line) and Middle Missouri sources. Regression lines have been used to summarise the relationships.

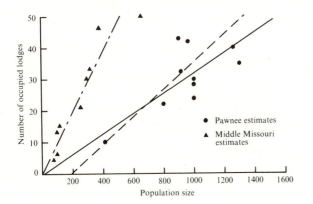

A third test of the model's ability to imitate the Pawnee site behaviour was attempted by comparing the duration of occupation from a series of historically documented Pawnee sites (see Grange 1968, p. 18) with the occupation durations of a series of arbitrarily selected simulation runs (fig. 3). The overall correspondence is fair. Because the simulation did not allow a site to be occupied for less than a five-year interval, the distribution's peak is shifted as illustrated in the figure.

These tests unfortunately can evaluate only some of the aspects of the model proposed here. The most critical parameter which must remain unvalidated for lack of evidence is the rate at which lodge attrition occurs. The ultimate evaluation of this parameter and the other aspects of the model must await the complete and detailed excavation of one or more of the historically documented Pawnee settlements. Despite these limitations the reasonable agreement between the observed conditions and the simulation results is encouraging at this elementary level.

Conclusions

This study represents a first, crude attempt at modelling the critical physical events or decisions which determine the Pawnee settlement strategy. Despite its preliminary nature it does highlight several important points. First, given the data currently available, it appears to confirm the accuracy of the ethnographic assertions concerning the organisation of and decisions affecting the Pawnee villages. Secondly, it illustrates clearly the dangers inherent in the 'static' interpretation of settlement remains caused by the basic indeterminancy of such factors as length of occupation, population size, and site re-occupation in most archaeological contexts.

The model, though useful in its present form as a heuristic device, requires further elaboration before it could be used effectively as a means of further study of prehistoric settlement remains. Most important is that it requires a means of portraying the spatial organisation of and relationships among the various features on the site through time. It would also be necessary to expand the scope of the model to a regional scale, for despite the illustrative value of a single-site model, the testing of hypotheses relevant to the overall settlement strategy would require that the various lodges and villages be continually traceable through their particular movements and interactions. In such an expanded framework, specific hypotheses concerning population size, duration of settlement and the dynamics of site-use could be formulated and tested. Such future study would be especially valuable in areas where fine-grained chronological control cannot be assumed.

The model presented in this study has only scratched the surface of the potential sources of information that could be used, not only ethnographic and historical, but also the archaeological evidence which could be employed to validate the model and to elaborate it further. It is hoped that this preliminary study may have served to draw attention to the kind of data which exist for study on the Plains and to emphasise the potential sources of error inherent in the uncritical interpretation of the archaeological remains from settlement sites.

Acknowledgement

I would like to thank John Ludwickson for invaluable aid and advice throughout the course of this study.

References

Carelton, J.H. (1943) in Lewis Pelzer (ed.) *The Prairie Logbooks, Dragoon Campaigns to the Pawnee Villages in 1844.* The Cayton Club

Catlin, G. (1965) *North American Indians, Volume 1*, Ross and Haines

Dunbar, J.B. (1880) 'The Pawnee Indians, their history and ethnology', *Magazine of American History* 14(4): 241–81

Fletcher, A.C. & La Flesche, F. (1911) *The Omaha Tribe* (Twenty-Seventh Annual Report of the Bureau of American Ethnology to the Secretary of the Smithsonian Institution 1905–1906), US Government Printing Office.

Grange, R.T. jr (1968) *Pawnee and Lower Loup Pottery* (Nebraska State Historical Society Publications in Anthropology, No. 3), Nebraska State Historical Society

Hays, W.L. (1973) *Statistics for the Social Sciences*, 2nd edn, Holt, Rinehart & Winston

Hyde, G.E. (1951) *The Pawnee Indians*, University of Oklahoma Press

Ludwickson, J. (1975) 'The Loup river phase and the origins of Pawnee culture', MA. thesis, University of Nebraska

Mihram, G.A. (1972) *Simulation: Statistical Foundations and Methodology*, Academic Press

Mize, J.H. & Cox, J. (1968) *Essentials of Simulation*, Prentice-Hall

Morgan, Lewis H. (1965) *Houses and House-life of the American Aborigines*, University of Chicago Press

Oehler, Brn.G. & Smith, D.Z. (1914) 'Description of a journey and visit to the Pawnee Indians', *Moravian Church Miscellany 1851–1852*, New York

Wedel, W.R. (1938) 'The direct historical approach in Pawnee archaeology', *Smithsonian Miscellaneous Collections* 97(7)

Wedel, W.R. (1961) 'Plains archaeology, 1935–1960', *American Antiquity* 27(1): 24–32

Weltfish, G. (1965) *The Lost Universe*, Basic Books

Willey, G.R. (1966) *An Introduction to American Archaeology, Volume 1*, Prentice-Hall.

Wilson, Gilbert L. (1934) 'The Hidatsa earthlodge', *Anthropological Papers of The Museum of Natural History* 133: 340–420

Chapter 5

**A computer simulation of
Mycenaean settlement**
A. J. Chadwick

Introduction

The simulation of settlement is a field in which there has been relatively little work (Haggett 1965), and this chapter is an attempt to apply the technique to part of Greece in the Bronze Age. It illustrates how it is possible to use even the limited and tentative data base that is available to archaeology to produce some interesting results, albeit subject to a considerable number of if's and but's. A model is by definition only a simplified representation of reality, and as such it is only one of numerous ways of looking at any particular situation. The virtue is that such an exercise forces the investigator to formulate his ideas into a concrete and testable form, and hence allow them to be refuted, found inferior, or superior to existing approaches. Simulation is only one technique for doing this, and certainly cannot be used in all situations, data often being the major constraint. The advantage of it lies in the ability to conduct experiments, and try a wide range of alternatives, something not usually possible outside the physical sciences.

From experience three stages can be identified in the production of a model, though they are certainly not discrete, nor used in the work below explicitly. The model should have a clear objective, otherwise the ends can become subservient to the means. The available theory, even if rejected, and data need to be carefully analysed to provide a framework for both evaluating the results, and keeping in touch with the real world. From these, a set of hypotheses can be generated, which can then be tested, and in the process give rise to more ideas. Given sufficient data, simulation may well be an appropriate means of doing this, but any such model must be simple. The latter point is very important because as a model becomes more complex, it becomes harder to calibrate, let alone interpret, the parameters, or evaluate their significance. Simulation should not be approached by attempting to adjust some data to fit a new found technique, for which it is probably not suitable.

The data for the two models discussed below come from the work of the University of Minnesota Messenia expedition – UMME (McDonald & Rapp 1972). This project was set up in the early 1960s by Professor W.M. McDonald, with the aim of reconstructing the Bronze Age environment in a region covering the largest possible extent of the Kingdom of Pylos, as given in Homer. It was from the palace at Ano Englianos that Nestor set off to fight at Troy, and this was the first place Telemachus arrived at in his search for his father Odysseus. The area UMME used will be referred to as Messenia (fig. 1), an area bounded by the sea on the west and south, the Taygetos mountains to the east, and a line just north of the Alpheios river. The term Pylos will be confined to the much smaller area between the sea, the mountains, and the Neda and Nedon rivers, preferred by some as the bounds of the Kingdom (J. Chadwick 1976). Messenia was studied by a team of archaeologists, ancient historians, agriculturalists, botanists, geologists, philologists, surveyors and others, each from their own discipline's point of view. For our purposes the items most of interest are those on the physical geography, and the search for Mycenaean sites.

Fig. 1. Messenia. Source: UMME.

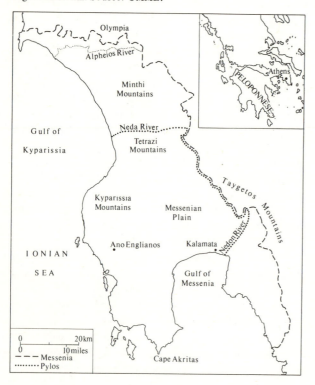

Messenia is a region some 3800 km^2 in area, with a maximum length of 100 km and width of 50 km. It consists mainly of mountainous relief made up of limestones uplifted during the Tertiary. To the east the Taygetos mountains rise to heights of over 2000 m, forming a very solid barrier to the influence of any power centred on the Plain of Sparta. The foothills are pierced in a number of places by precipitous gorges, of which the Nedon river is an example. To the north the Alpheios is one of the major rivers of the Peleponnese, rising in Arcadia. South of it lie the Minthi and Tetrazi mountains, bordered by a narrow, coastal plain, and divided by the gorge of the Neda river. Further south parallel to the coast run the Kyparissia mountains, which eventually degenerate into a series of isolated hills surrounded by a dissected erosion surface down towards Cape Akritas. Between the two mountain chains, and divided in half by the low Skala ridge, is the Messenian plain. This is the area which gives the region its agricultural wealth, with 40% arable compared to the national average of 28% (UMME).

The aim of the first model built (A. Chadwick 1977) was to convert the settlement pattern given by UMME for Middle Helladic (circa 1600 BC), to that for Late Helladic IIIb (circa 1250 BC). It was hoped that the process of analysis and testing involved would allow something to be said about the mechanisms involved in settling the area during the period. As more than one process can produce the same result, any findings are only suggestive, not definitive. However they could be used to support independent sources of information, for example documents. Very few of the 94 sites in Middle and 169 sites in Late Helladic have been investigated, identification and dating relying for the most part on surface finds of sherds. Potential sites were identified by UMME from air photographs, using a set of preconceived ideas as to Mycenaean site location. Thus, the problems of dating, the difficulties of finding sites in areas of intensive agricultural use, and possible bias, mean that the resulting maps may be subject to considerable amounts of error. The model however treats the two maps (fig. 2) as accurate, or at least representative samples, because otherwise no progress is possible. This assumption must be borne in mind when interpreting the results, and of course their value may be limited if the maps are later shown to be radically wrong.

Map analysis

The first step in analysing the two patterns was to construct Thiessen polygons around each site, that is regions such that every point within them is closer to that place than any other. They are constructed by bisecting lines joining each place to its surrounding neighbours, and taking the smallest enclosed space. A number of problems were encountered on the land boundaries of Messenia, where due to a lack of information some polygons had to be left open. This procedure defines for every place the number and location of first-order neighbours — those places with contiguous polygons. Middle Helladic sites have an average of 4.77 first-order neighbours, and Late Helladic 5.04, compared with the expected value of

5.788 theoretically derived by Dacey (Haggett & Chorley 1969). The mean first-order neighbour distance decreased from 6.00 km to 4.46 km, while the mean nearest-neighbour distance fell from 3.27 km to 2.21 km. Fig. 3 shows the raw data frequency distributions. Bintliff (1977) has suggested that there is a regularity in the order of 5 km between larger Mycenaean settlements, for which the above figures give some support allowing for the fact that they ignore size.

A similar exercise was carried out for Pylos using only those sites which UMME estimate had populations of 100 or more, an arbitrary figure. These estimates are based on the area of the site, so far as it could be determined, times a constant multiplier, so that sites with smaller populations and for which an estimate was not possible are excluded. The 81 sites involved produce a mean first-order neighbour distance of 5.44 km. However, for places with 500 or more people the figure is 11.91 km. This emphasises the scale dependency of the result. If the population estimates are ranked and plotted the resulting curve can be approximated by the expectation produced if the population were divided up at random (A.

Fig. 2. Middle and Late Helladic settlement patterns in Messenia (derived from UMME data).

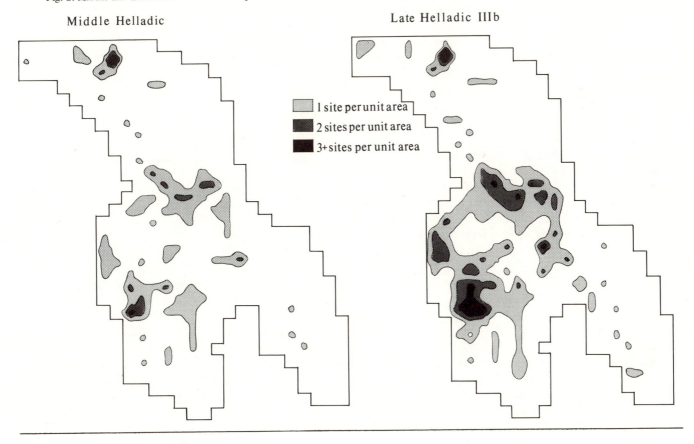

Middle Helladic   Late Helladic IIIb

☐ 1 site per unit area

■ 2 sites per unit area

■ 3+ sites per unit area

Fig. 3. First-order neighbour distances.

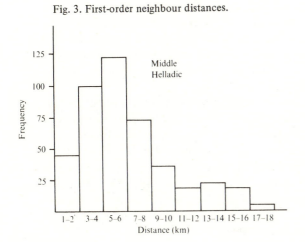

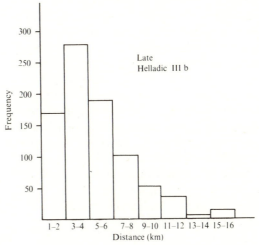

Chadwick 1979). This again brings out the continuous nature of settlement as a phenomenon, both across space and down the hierarchy, in contrast to the discrete steps of, for example, central-place theory. Randomness also provides a useful explanatory tool as will be seen below.

Nearest-neighbour analysis (King 1969) was carried out on 1st, 2nd, furthest, and average first-order neighbour distances. This produces a bounded statistic which compares the average of the straight line distances from all settlements to their *n*th neighbour against a theoretical value, derived assuming a Poisson distribution. The results suggest that the two patterns are random, but that they do exhibit some sign of clustering. This combined with a straightforward visual examination of the distributions suggested that they consisted of a series of clusters, probably centred on good agricultural land, surrounded by less densely settled areas. These could possibly have emerged by spread outwards from a series of initial centres located at random, though biased toward the more fertile areas. The gap between the two periods consists mainly of an infill of the existing pattern, with only a little expansion into previously unsettled areas.

Quadrat analysis (Rogers 1974) was carried out by covering the maps with a 2 × 2 km celled lattice of 1109 quadrats, and counting the frequency of cells with 0, 1, . . . , *n* settlements. The resulting frequency distributions (table 1) can be compared with those generated by various theoretical models, the procedure being repeated for 4 × 4 km and 6 × 6 km cells grids to check for scale dependency (Harvey 1968). The first model to be fitted was the Poisson:

$$P(x) = \frac{e^{-\lambda}\lambda^x}{x!} \qquad (x = 0, 1, \ldots, n) \qquad (1)$$

where $\lambda = \sum_{i=1}^{n} x_i f_i / N$

The model assumes that every cell has the same probability of independently receiving 0, 1, . . . , *n* settlements, derived from λ which is estimated as the mean number of sites per cell in the observed distribution. This implies that there is no directional bias in the operation of the settlement process, in other words there is stationarity in space, to borrow a term from time series analysis. The goodness of fit was evaluated using chi-squared and Kolmogorov-Smirnov tests (Siegel 1956), the latter being the more powerful test. The former however gives an indication of the fit in all classes, but suffers from degrees of freedom problems (*N*−2 for the Poisson, *N*−3 for the negative binomial), and the need to combine expected values below 5. A 99% significance level was used throughout, to minimise the risk of a Type I error (rejecting the null hypothesis when it is in fact true). The Poisson model is often found to be a good fit at small cell sizes, but breaks down at the higher, and this was the case with the settlement data. The scale dependency of the result suggested that a better alternative could be found, so the negative binomial was fitted (Williamson & Bretherton 1964);

Table 1. *Frequency distributions of 2×2, 4×4, and 6×6 km lattices.*

Settlements per cell:		0	1	2	3	4	5	6	7	8	9
2 × 2 km	LH:	958	135	14	2	–	–	–	–	–	–
N = 1109	MH:	1019	87	2	1	–	–	–	–	–	–
4 × 4 km	LH:	195	74	31	6	1	1	1	–	–	–
N = 309	MH:	233	61	13	1	1	–	–	–	–	–
6 × 6 km	LH:	70	40	22	11	2	2	3	1	–	1
N = 152	MH:	95	33	14	8	1	1	–	–	–	–

Table 2

	Lattice I	Lattice II
Generalised *k*:	*k*	*ks*
p:	*p*	*p*
Compound *k*:	*k*	*k*
p:	$\dfrac{a}{a+1}$	$\dfrac{a}{a+s}$ where $a = \dfrac{p}{1-p}$

$$P(x) = \binom{x+k-1}{k-1} p^k (1-p)^x \qquad (x = 0, 1, \ldots, n) \qquad (2)$$

where $p = \bar{x} / s^2$
$\qquad k = \bar{x}^2 / (s^2 - \bar{x})$

This model fits for all cell sizes, and both time periods. The problem is that it suffers from over identification; that is there are a number of different generating processes which produce the same end result, of which two are relevant to settlement studies (Cliff & Ord 1973). The pattern could have been generated by the generalised model, in which a series of clusters of settlement are distributed at random (Poisson), but the number in each group follows a logarithmic distribution, implying some form of contagious spread from a set of initial centres. The alternative is the compound model which is like the Poisson model described above, except that λ is not constant for every cell but varies across the map following a gamma distribution. There are a number of ways of sorting out the most appropriate model, and fortunately the simplest gives an unambiguous result. The method involves looking at the expected changes in the *p* and *k* parameters as against the actual, as *s* quadrats are combined to form larger cells. The expectation is shown in table 2.

In every case, that is for the 4 × 4 km and 6 × 6 km lattice at both time periods, the smallest absolute difference was between the actual value and the expected value for the compound model, derived as above. This result was also obtained by doing the same analysis for Pylos using sites with populations over 100. Cliff and Ord suggest that this result can be interpreted as showing that the settlement patterns are essentially random, but biased by the varying utility of the underlying environment.

Model 1

The brief physical description of Messenia has shown that it is far from being an isotropic plain, so this result is not altogether surprising. On the assumption that the land's varying potential was a key factor in determining settlement location, an environment surface was constructed, generalised in fig. 4. This uses the 2 X 2 km cell grid as a basis, and represents an attempt to synthesise a number of factors thought relevant to Mycenaean settlement (the darker the shading, the more 'attractive' a cell is). This is an area where a little more research into the desirable features would yield some improvements. The raw data were derived from maps given in UMME, though in retrospect a soil map would probably have been more use than the geomorphology one used. It was assumed that one of the key variables would have been easy access to a reliable source of water, either from a spring or permanent stream, as the Mycenaeans do not seem to have built wells (UMME). Defence does not seem to have been an overriding concern, in the latter period at least, as witnessed by the lack of walls around the palace at Ano Englianos. UMME record that in 1935 in the village of Karpofora, near Kalamata, there were

two main sources of water, one 400 m down a steep slope, and the other 1000 m away and 60 m down a much gentler gradient. A round trip with a donkey to collect some 115 litres of water took 45 minutes to the nearer source, and 1 hour to the further. On this basis it would seem reasonable to suggest that approximately 1 km would be a maximum carrying distance, though it might be necessary to go considerably further at the height of summer. A water resource map was produced from the UMME map, based on data from the Greek Agricultural Ministry, by marking off areas within 1.2 km and 2 km of any permanent stream or spring. The inner zone was given an index value of 3, the middle 2, and the outer 1. Quite apart from the arbitrary distance imposed, this begs the question whether the hydrological conditions have changed significantly over the past 3000 years. On the assumptions of a stable climate, a much greater forest cover, and a lack of man's interference with the watertable, conditions were probably wetter. There is no way of taking this into account other than by constructing the map on a generous basis.

Fig. 4. Messenia raw environment surface.

The other main variable considered is the land itself, both its suitability for settlement and for agriculture. This raises a conflict because especially where flat land is scarce it will be settled next to, not on, though at this scale it is probably not very significant. The UMME map of Messenian geomorphology, derived from air photographs and ground survey, has 13 different classes, which were collapsed into the three below on a rather *ad hoc* basis.

Class 1	Class 2	Class 3
Gorges	Alluvial plain	Alluvial slopes
Mountain	Coastal plain	Hill land
Mountain shoulder	Dissected Kampos	Kampos
Rock ridges	Ridges	Pliocene terrace
Scarps		
Swamps		

Class 1 contains only 6% of Late Helladic sites, and represents fairly clearly the most undesirable areas. Class 3, with 77% of sites represents the best land, and the problem was what to put in Class 2 with 17%. It was especially difficult to know in what class to put 'alluvial plain'. This land could have been drained and irrigated, and hence highly productive, or it could have been marsh, or it may not have existed at all, having been formed by later alluviation (Bintliff 1975). Its placing in Class 2 is a compromise.

Both maps were covered by the 2 X 2 km cell grid used in the quadrat analysis, and an index value entered for each cell. The basic rule was to enter the class that had 50% of the quadrat, though in a few cases this was broken where it would have resulted in the omission of a significantly sized zone that straddled the grid lines. In all doubtful cases the rule was to be generous in favour of the highest value. The combination of the two resulting maps posed something of a problem, straight addition or multiplication not producing satisfactory results, as well as assuming that a water index value of 2 was equal in value to a geomorphology index of 2, an unfounded assumption. An analysis was made of the original maps as to the distribution of sites in the Late Helladic in relation to the 9 possible index combinations.

Table 3. *Number of sites in relation to index values*

Water index	Geomorphology index		
	1	2	3
1:	8	1	22
2:	5	6	30
3:	7	18	72

This was turned into the grid (table 4) which very approximately preserves the proportions of that above, and this was used to produce the surface. Thus a cell with a water index of 2, and a geomorphology index of 3 receives a surface value of 4. However as it stood the map ignored the effects of

the sea as being a source of food and a means of communication. Accordingly an arbitrary value of 2 was added to all coastal cells to produce the final environment surface. The grid is also interesting in that it shows that for the Mycenaeans the quality of the land was more important than the availability of a good water supply.

Table 4. *Surface value in relation to index values*

Water index	Geomorphology index		
	1	2	3
1:	1	1	3
2:	1	1	4
3:	1	3	9

This inevitably introduces an element of circularity into the argument, in that the process of forming the environment surface could merely pick out the areas where the settlements are, thereby making it a trivial problem to simulate the pattern. In practice this is not the case, partly because of the crudity of the combination process, but more importantly because the end result produces plenty of attractive locations that were never settled. For example there are quite a few of these in the area between the Alpheios and Neda rivers. The surface acts as a constraint on the simulation, not a determinant — a fine distinction that has to be made. The essence of this sort of model is discovering constraints which are necessary for a successful simulation, but are not in themselves sufficient. Early trials without the surface were disastrous, while as will be seen below it is not sufficient by itself.

Using this surface it was possible to construct the first model, which rests on the assumption that the environment is the sole determinant of settlement location apart from the factor of chance. All simulation work was carried out on the University of Cambridge IBM 370/165, with programs written by myself in FORTRAN. The only library subroutine used was that for drawing a contour map on the plotter, the example being the settlement maps. The environment surface was originally mapped by a program of my own, but has subsequently been redone using SYMAP, on the facilities of NUMAC at the University of Newcastle-upon-Tyne. The environment was first converted to probabilities by dividing each value by the grand total, and then 75 random numbers were obtained from a standard pseudo-random number program. The number 75 represents the difference between the Middle Helladic total of 94 sites, and the Late Helladic of 169. To save search time these were sorted into ascending order, and then located along with the existing Middle Helladic distribution. This can be done very simply as shown by the tabulated example below. In stage I the original values in the cells are converted to probabilities, and then in stage II they are cumulated and ranged from 1—10 (or 0—9; 0—10 is not the same as the bottom cell acquires an extra number). A random number is then collected from a uniform distribution, for example 5, and the new site located, in this case in cell 3.

Cell:	1	2	3	4	5
Value:	1	2	3	3	1
Stage I:	0.1	0.2	0.3	0.3	0.1
Stage II:	1	3	6	9	10

The rules for this model can be stated:

(1) the choice of the location of a settlement is random, but
(2) the probability of a particular cell attracting a site is directly proportional to its environment surface value;
(3) the location of any settlement is independent of any other.

Thirty simulations were generated using the 2 × 2 km cell lattice, but it was felt unreasonable to expect the model to be accurate to 2 km when no details of local environment conditions were included. So the results were aggregated into the 4 × 4 km cell grid for testing the goodness of fit, which also had the advantage of making visual inspection easier because of dealing with a 29 × 25 rather than a 50 × 57 block of figures. Testing the fit of a spatial model is difficult, and it was done in three ways. First the aspatial fit was evaluated by counting the cell frequencies of sites, and comparing them with the Late Helladic using a chi-squared test. This provides a rough guide, but it makes a fundamental assumption about the data, which affects any statistical test on spatially arranged data. The chi-squared test assumes, in common with other statistical tests, that the individual data values are independent of one another, or put another way they are not spatially auto-correlated. In many cases the problem may not be significant, and there are ways around it (Cliff, Martin & Ord 1975), but it should be appreciated because of the interdependence of archaeological data.

Spatial autocorrelation can be put to good use in testing the spatial fit of the simulations (Cliff & Ord 1973). A residual map is formed by taking the expected distribution away from the observed, producing positives where the model has over-estimated, and negatives where it has underestimated. The test is best conceived of by imagining the positives coloured Black and the negatives Grey. The number of joins between Black and Grey cells can then be counted, and compared with the result that would be expected if they were randomly located. Clumpings of positives or negatives would be detected as being autocorrelated, and imply a systematic bias in the model. The actual statistic used preserves the magnitude as well as the direction of the sign:

$$I = \frac{n \sum\limits_{i=1}^{n} \sum\limits_{j=1}^{n} w_{ij} x_i x_j}{\sum\limits_{i=1}^{n} \sum\limits_{j=1}^{n} w_{ij} \sum\limits_{i=1}^{n} x_i^2} \qquad (i \neq j) \qquad (3)$$

where n = the number of non-zero residuals
x_i = the residual in the ith cell
w_{ij} = the elements of a weights matrix, in this case:
w_{ij} = 1 if i and j meet at a side or vertex
w_{ij} = 0 otherwise.

The non-zero residuals are taken as the map structure rather than that of all cells, as Cliff and Ord feel this is more realistic when there are areas much less likely to be involved than others, due for example to remoteness. A binary set of weights was used, but any set could have been specified, the problem being the need for some theoretical reason for the choice. The statistic can be standardised in comparison with the random expectation, and a procedure followed to evaluate a set of simulations performance; see Cliff and Ord. The overall test asks the question: could the actual (Late Helladic) pattern be a member of the population of simulations generated by a model? The final method was a straightforward visual comparison, on the grounds that if it looks right, it is right. This may not be very precise, but it is the only way of finding out where the model is going wrong, and as a result being able to work out why.

The initial model passed the aspatial test easily, but totally failed the spatial one. Examination of the simulations showed that while a good spatial spread was being achieved, the distribution was not nearly peaked enough where required. This result is not altogether surprising as the model assumed that the settlement location is independent, which patently it is not.

Model 2

In a settlement system primarily dependent on an agricultural base, villages need at a minimum to be spaced out to allow each a sufficient area of land to grow enough produce to support their populations. A zone of exploitation can be defined, here to be called a territory, which one place is more likely, though it does not necessarily do so, to exploit than any other. The concept need not be tied down to a contiguous geographic space, but following on from Hudson (1969) it can be conceived as an abstract n-dimensional space, defined by social, economic, and political factors. Translating this back into geographic terms could produce a highly fragmented set of zones, for example picking out the places with which a port trades. In the Mycenaean case, given the subsistence agricultural base, it seemed reasonable to assume that the territory could effectively be regarded as a contiguous spatial unit. It is of course impossible to define the actual areas, but the Thiessen polygons can be used as surrogates. Thus the environment surface was modified so each cell recorded a value for the resources in that cell, and those around. This was done by producing a distance decay term

$$Q_j = 150.59 - 154.47 \,(\text{Log}\, D_j) \qquad r = -0.93 \qquad (4)$$

where Q_j = Frequency of neighbours at distance j
D_j = Distance from the central point to the Thiessen polygon boundary

This was used in a form of potential model, derived from Wilson's (1970) production constrained gravity model. In retrospect the resulting surface was not radically different from the old, so the operation is probably not very significant.

$$E_i^m = \sum_{j=1}^{n} F_{ji} + E_i \qquad (5)$$

$$F_{ij} = A_i E_i E_j f(d_{ij}) \qquad (6)$$

$$A_i = 1/\sum_{j=1}^{n} E_j f(d_{ij}) \qquad (7)$$

where E_i^m = the modified environment surface value for the ith cell

E_i = the original environment surface value

F_{ij} = the 'flow' from the ith to the jth cell

$f(d_{ij})$ = the distance decay term, from (4) above

The original idea of carrying out a simulation of settlement came from reading Hägerstrand's excellent book (1967), along with its perceptive postscript by the translator Pred. His work was concerned with the diffusion of innovations in an agricultural community, and demonstrated the detailed empirical base that is needed for such work. His model operated on the notion that while the media would make known the existence of an innovation, for example TB controls, actual adoption would not occur until a non-adopter heard about it first hand from a current user. To replicate this he derived what he called an information field, a set of probabilities based on the distance decay of frequency of telephone calls. These probabilities were placed over each existing adopter, and a random number used to locate the new user of the invention. The model was made more realistic by allowing for the variable density of potential adopters, the resistance to change, and other factors. There seems to be no theoretical reason why a similar type of approach might not work with settlement.

The settlement process is analogous, except that new places have to be spaced out, owing to the need for territory, from all existing places, not just one. The construction of the model assumes that the dominant feature is one of infill, rather than an extension of the settlement frontier. In using the concept of territory it must be stressed that this need not be a single unit in space. Nevertheless this has been assumed here as it seems reasonable and is also simple. A settlement field was generated by fitting a curve to the Middle Helladic first-order neighbours data (fig. 3) of the form

$$Q_j = -0.68 + 8.21 \, (\mathrm{Log} \, D_j) - 5.84 \, (\mathrm{Log} \, D_j)^2$$
$$r = 0.84 \qquad (8)$$

where D_j = Distance from the central point to j

This produces, when rotated through 360°, the values entered in the cells of a 17 × 17 lattice, and when converted to probabilities, the chance of finding a first-order neighbour that distance from the blank central quadrat. The resulting shape, shown in cross-section in fig. 5, is best described as that of a log normal doughnut. The exact shape of the curve is scale dependent, for a much larger cell size than 2 × 2 km would have resulted in a negative exponential curve.

After several intermediate models, described in detail elsewhere (A. Chadwick 1979), the following was evolved. The settlement field was placed over each occupied cell, multiplied by the transformed environment surface to bias it, and then scaled to sum to an index value between 1.0 and 6.0. The purpose of this index value was to allow for the effects of population, on the assumption that places with a large number of inhabitants would tend to require more land to support them, and therefore be relatively less attractive to settle near. This argument would not of course apply, for example, to an administrative centre drawing tribute from a wide region. Previous versions of the model had tended to concentrate new settlement too much in existing areas. The UMME population

Fig. 5. Cross-section of the settlement field.

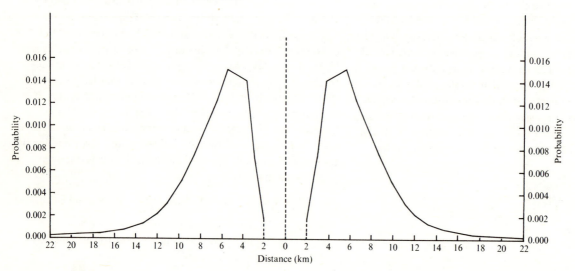

figures are not extensive enough to use, so the transformed environment surface was used as a surrogate, on the dubious assumption that the higher it was, the higher the population would be. Thus the index value, which also takes into account the number of sites in a cell, was set high for cells with presumed low populations, and vice versa. This procedure was repeated for every occupied cell, the resulting values cumulated for each quadrat, and converted into probabilities for the whole map. Apart from being extremely crude, the index has the disadvantage of using the environment surface twice, in opposite roles, seemingly negating its effect. In practice, and this is the only defence, it works by cutting down the concentration problem produced by adding the settlement fields on top of each other. In retrospect it would have been better to leave them as probabilities, and multiply them together. The problem arises because of the model's Hägerstrandian origins, which mean that the location of new settlements is derived from looking out, largely independently, from existing places. A much better approach would be to turn the whole thing round, and ask the question, what is the chance of getting a new site in this cell, given its 'attractiveness', and the current settlement distribution?

10% of the existing number of sites were then allocated using random numbers. Actual entry to a cell was dependent on the number of current occupants, being immediate for an empty quadrat. With one site the chance of entry becomes 0.66, with two 0.33, and with three 0.0 because no Late Helladic cell, in the 2 × 2 km lattice, has more than 3 sites. The 10% figure is a compromise between the cost in computer time, and the ideal of recalculating the map probabilities after each site has been located. The model was cycled in this fashion until the Late Helladic total of 169 sites was reached, and then the test procedures were carried out. On the computer the settlement field can be calculated in one stage using equations (6) and (7), with E_i put equal to the population index, E_j to the transformed environment surface values and $f(d_{ij})$ derived from equation (8). Messenia fitted into a (57,50) array, which was embedded in the centre of a (67,60) array so that the settlement field could be placed over each possible cell without the subscript values going negative. This saves up to 4 time-consuming IF statements, in return for using more space, which was sensible on the computer used. As in the first model the random numbers were sorted into ascending order, though this introduces a slight bias in giving the northern half of the map first pick. There is no point, with this type of model, in spending a lot of time in an attempt to produce a highly efficient program which will only run relatively few times.

The rules of the final model can be stated:
(1)   the location of settlement is random, but
(2)   the probability of access to any particular cell depends on
    (*a*)   its transformed environment surface value,
    (*b*)   its location relative to all existing sites, taking into account their populations,

(*c*)   the number of current occupants (sites).

Another problem that was met in the evolution of the final model was that of reflective frontiers (Yuill 1965). These result from the settlement field total being concentrated into a smaller area, and hence having proportionately more influence on the final probability map. Along the coasts and the eastern mountain margin this did not cause any problems, but along the northern frontier it did, causing a regular overestimation of sites along the Alpheios. The *ad hoc* solution was to repeat the top two lines of the environment surface as two new lines to the north, and use them in creating the settlement fields, but not in calculating the final possibility map. This makes this frontier partly absorbent, but allows for the effect of unknown settlements to the north. The ideal solution would be to include data for a larger area, but only carry out the test procedures within a central core.

This model can just be accepted at a 99% significance level. That is the Late Helladic distribution could just be a member of a population of 49 simulations. Fig. 6 gives an example of a simulation, which is in the spirit, if not the letter, of the desired result. The model suggests that the key factors controlling the growth of the settlement pattern between the two periods were the environment, the spacing effect of the territory, population size, and a stochastic element. The latter represents the outcome of a large number of individual decisions, which may have perfectly rational reasons at the time, but whose net effect is random to the observer at this

Fig. 6. A simulated Late Helladic settlement pattern.

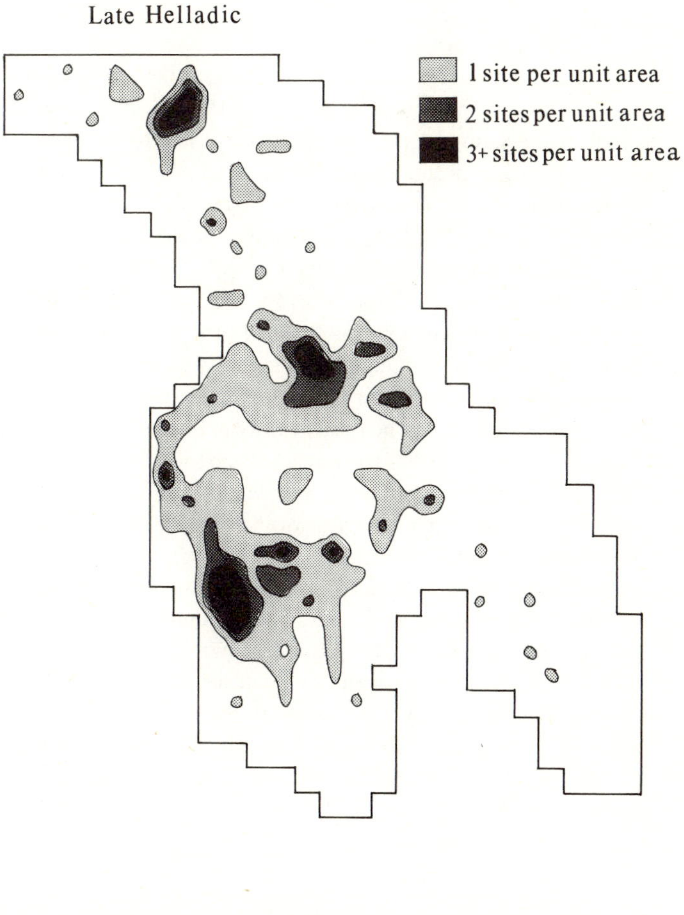

Late Helladic

scale. This ties up with Curry's (1964) notion of the random spatial economy, which, simply put, says that location in space is random, but subject to constraints. This is essentially the same argument that underlies Wilson's reformulation of the gravity model used above; entropy maximisation subject to constraints. Hudson's ideas provide a framework within which to view the operation of these constraints, and also the idea of competition between place for what is, at a given technological level, an essentially fixed supply of resources.

The model can be criticised on many grounds, the most obvious being that it is only descriptive, not explanatory, and it totally ignores time. There is nothing in the model to say whether the new settlement appeared overnight, or over a long period of years. The results of the quadrat analysis imply that the change was an infill process in the voids in the existing pattern, and not a result of splitting off from older settlements, which would produce clustering in line with the generalised version of the negative binomial. Bintliff (1977) has suggested that this period was marked by some fragmentation of existing places, owing to the emergence of satellites within their territories. Some evidence is provided for this in the frequency distribution of nearest Middle Helladic neighbours to new sites, which has a flat peak in the 1—4 km range, compared with the Late Helladic average of 2.21 km. Whatever the exact process involved, the varying potential of the environment, and the pressure on its resources seem to have been major constraints in controlling settlement location. However, the problem still remains of why the settlement pattern grew, and in particular the influence, causes, and nature of population growth.

Population growth

An attempt was made to tackle this problem by building a simple model of population growth, with built-in random variations. Because of the assumptions that had to be made, and some rather circular arguments used to produce the input populations, the actual results are of little use. It does however demonstrate in principle how it might be possible to build a model, and the data requirements involved. The basic problem is to produce population estimates for a series of regions for two time periods, and a plausible set of birth and death rates. Some of the parameters could be derived from empirical studies of cultures in similar technological states, and a study of colonisation by such peoples could yield useful parallels. The use of regions rather than quadrats introduces a scale shift that would pose problems in trying to produce a combined settlement generation and location model, if such an exercise were thought worthwhile.

The model was basically a simple cohort survival population model (Wilson 1974). In this the population is divided into age groups, or cohorts, in this case blocks of 10 years; 0—9, 10—19, . . . etc. A birth rate operates on the childbearing cohorts, taking due account of the lack of disaggregation by sex, while each is aged by means of a survival rate (1— death rate). The model operates in discrete jumps of 10 years from t to $t + T$.

$$P_1 (t + T) = \sum_{r=\alpha}^{\beta} b_r(t, t+T)P_r(t) \tag{9}$$

$$P_r (t + T) = s_{r-1,r}(t,t+T)P_{r-1}(t) \qquad r > 1 \tag{10}$$

where $P_r(t)$ = the population in cohort r at time t.
$b_r(t,t+T)$ = the birth rate from time t to $t+T$ in cohort r
$s_{r-1,r}(t,t+T)$ = the survival rate from cohort $r-1$ to r, t to $t+T$
α, β = limits of the child bearing cohorts

The birth and death rates were subject to random fluctuations by drawing random numbers from a Normal distribution with a small variance, after allowing for the effect of a crude index of resource pressure. An internal migration element was allowed for within the system of regions, using equations (6) and (7), though not from outside. The model states, very simply, that the population in region i at $(t+T)$ equals that at (t) — deaths + births + immigration — emigration. This is crude, but at least simple, the numbers of parameters being kept to a minimum, though some have to be arbitrarily decided. The actual model produced suggested that the population growth between Middle and Late Helladic took place in the order of 120 years, which ties up with the archaeological evidence. Given the uncertainties involved, such a model is best used for exploring a range of possibilities as to what might have happened, and what could not, rather than trying to say that x did occur.

I hope the above has provided some pointers to the way in which simulation might be useful in looking at settlement processes, and in particular the advantages from a theoretical point of view of a stochastic rather than a deterministic framework. It is easy to see how very much more complicated models could be produced, though they would probably be of little practical use. There is no point in building something which cannot hope to be tested because of the lack of an adequate data base. At the same time, given a lot of patient research and fieldwork, sufficient information can be obtained to test at least simple hypotheses about the settlement process in a particular area. A model can never prove anything, but it may be possible to give concrete reasons for preferring one theory over another. In the end one may only replicate one's ignorance, but at least one may discover how ignorant one really is.

References

Bintliff, J.L. (1975) 'Mediterranean alluviation', *Proceedings of the Prehistoric Society* 41: 78—84
Bintliff, J.L. (1977) *Natural Environment and Human Settlement in Prehistoric Greece* (British Archaeological Reports) Oxford
Chadwick, A.J. (1977) 'Computer simulation of settlement development in Bronze Age Messenia' in J.L. Bintliff (ed.) *Mycenaean Geography — Proceedings of the Cambridge Colloquium*, Cambridge
Chadwick, A.J. (1979) 'Settlement Simulation' in K. Cooke & C. Renfrew (eds.) *A Mathematical Approach to Culture Change*, Academic Press, London
Chadwick, J. (1976) *The Mycenaean World*
Cliff, A.D., Martin, R.L. & Ord, J.K. (1975) 'A test for spatial autocorrelation in choropleth maps based on a modified X² statistic', *Transactions, Institute of British Geographers* 65: 109—29

Cliff, A.D. & Ord, J.K. (1973) *Spatial Autocorrelation*, Pion, London

Curry, L. (1964) 'The random spatial economy: an exploration in settlement theory', *Annals of the Association of American Geographers* 54: 138–46

Hägerstrand, T. (1953) *Innovationsförloppet ur korologisk synpunkt.* Translated with a postscript by A. Pred (1967), as *Innovation diffusion as a spatial process*, University of Chicago Press

Haggett, P. (1965) *Locational Analysis in Human Geography*, E. Arnold, London

Haggett, P. & Chorley, R.J. (1969) *Network Analysis in Geography*, E. Arnold, London

Harvey, D.W. (1968) 'Pattern, process, and the scale problem', *Transactions, Institute of British Geographers* 45: 71–8

Hudson, J.C. (1969) 'A location theory for settlement', *Annals of the Association of American Geographers* 59: 365–81

King, L.J. (1969) *Statistical Analysis in Geography*, Prentice-Hall, Englewood Cliffs, New Jersey

McDonald, W.A. & Rapp, G.R. Jnr. (eds.) (1972) *The Minnesota Messenia Expedition*, University of Minnesota Press

Rogers, A. (1974) *Statistical Analysis of Spatial Dispersion: the quadrat method*, Pion, London

Siegel, S. (1956) *Nonparametric Statistics for the Behavioural Sciences*, McGraw-Hill, New York

Williamson, E. & Bretherton, M.H. (1964) *Tables of the Negative Binomial Distribution*, Wiley, New York

Wilson, A.G. (1970) *Entropy in Urban and Regional Modelling*, Pion, London

Wilson, A.G. (1974) *Urban and Regional Models in Geography and Planning*, Wiley, London

Yuill, R.S. (1965) *A Simulation Study of Barrier Effects in Spatial Diffusion Problems* (Michigan inter-university community of mathematical geographers discussion Paper, No. 5), University of Michigan

PART THREE

Simulation in population studies

The simulation of population changes in archaeology is intimately connected with settlement studies as the two previous chapters have shown. It is often in settlement patterns that the archaeologist hopes to be able to identify demographic change. This is further seen in a study by Zubrow (1975) to be outlined here.

The flow chart used by Zubrow is reproduced in fig. 1. The process starts with a small population in a single settlement. Population grows and environmental conditions change and new settlements are located. The population of each settlement is limited by a maximum which decreases as resources diminish. With depleted resources, settlements aggregate and finally become extinct. The four components in the model are: a population growth function, a population resource check (*NSP*) which checks population size against available resources, a settlement locator which determines where a new settlement will locate, and a longevity function which determines how long a settlement will exist before becoming extinct for reasons apart from insufficient resources.

The model could be used to simulate the spread of population and settlements onto different environmental zones in a particular case – the spread of settlement between AD 200 and 1500 in Hay Hollow valley, Arizona. Fig. 2 shows the total population and numbers of sites predicted at different time periods for this area by four simulations. Fig. 3 shows the actual number of rooms and sites recovered archaeologically from the same area.

It was decided that 'all the simulations fit the archaeological record in respect to general configuration' (ibid., p. 108) although no tests of the fit are carried out. The parameter values for the birth rate, for example, which provided the best visual fits to the data could be identified and further understanding of the working of the system was gained. As Zubrow (1975, p. 103) admits, this is not a complete analysis. Only 8 simulations were run so that few combinations of parameter values could be examined. However, it remains an interesting example of an attempt to build a complex simulation model.

A study of demographic change by Wobst (1974) was intended, not to reproduce a particular set of archaeological data, but to understand the relationship between different variables affecting the size of Palaeolithic bands in general. Wobst was particularly interested in the 'mean equilibrium size' of these bands, this being defined as the 'number of people which can consistently provide group members with suitable mates upon reaching maturity' (ibid., p. 157).

In his simulation a uniform environment is supposed containing a network of regular hexagons each inhabited by a

Fig. 1. A model for population growth and settlement (pop., population; res., resource; set., settlement; mig., migration). Source: Zubrow 1975.

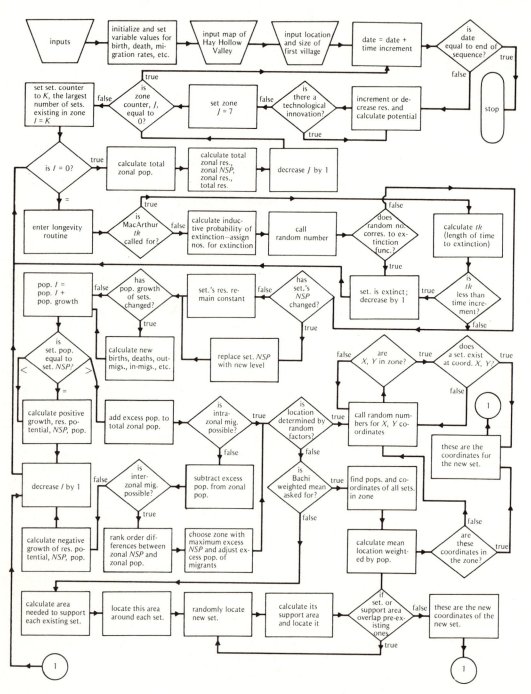

band. Each individual in the total population is given a name, age, sex, place of residence and marital status. All individuals are aged by one year and their status is changed as required. For example, some individuals enter the marriage pool and marry the compatible partner who lives nearest. Some females give birth to children which have a stated probability of being live, male or female, and some individuals die according to additional probability rules. Next, bands which are too small join larger bands and bands which are too large split into two sections. This stochastic simulation was written in FORTRAN and was run for 400 year cycles, in some cases with the addition of cultural restrictions such as incest taboos and post-marital residence rules. It was found that, under different combinations of parameter values, the minimum equilibrium size of bands varied within a relatively narrow range and that the actual size depended on mortality, fertility, sex ratio, and cultural rules on the mating system. Wobst also suggested that the results could be used to predict the spatial extent of Pleistocene societies.

A large number of assumptions had to be introduced into

Fig. 2. Simulations of the total population and total number of sites according to the model in fig. 1 (*B*, birth rate; *D*, death rate; *V*, migration velocity; *L*, longevity alternative). Source: Zubrow 1975.

Fig. 3. Total number of rooms and sites recovered from the actual area covered by the simulated map. Source: Zubrow 1975.

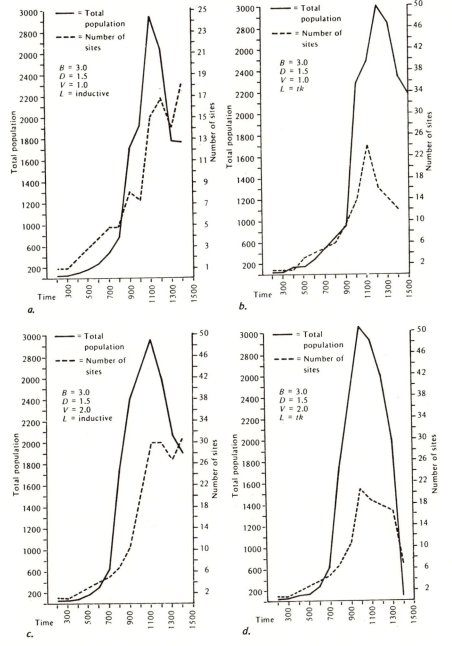

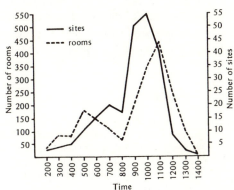

this study which is more concerned with understanding the working of a system than with trying to mimic a particular set of archaeological data. A more practically relevant study, referred to in the following chapter, is that by Levison, Ward and Webb (1972). They tried to understand the settlement of the islands of Polynesia by simulating the drift of boats according to the winds and currents of the area. Other factors introduced were the chances of survival at sea and the risk of gales. Whenever a boat, having started from one island, drifted within sight of another island it was assumed to land there. Their simulations showed that much of the occupation of the islands could have been the result of accidental drift but that the major voyages would have involved some intentional navigation. Problems connected with the occupation of Polynesian islands are further discussed in chapter 6. This study by Black exemplifies many of the aspects of population studies mentioned in this introduction, and it is a good example of the use of computer simulation to aid the comprehension of complex systems.

References

Levison, M., Ward, R.G. & Webb, J.W. (1972) 'The settlement of Polynesia: a report on a computer simulation', *Archaeology and Physical Anthropology in Oceania* 7: 234—45

Wobst, H.M. (1974) 'Boundary conditions for palaeolithic social systems: a simulation approach', *American Antiquity* 39: 147—78

Zubrow, E.B.W. (1975) *Prehistoric Carrying Capacity: a Model*, Cummings, Menlo Park

Chapter 6

**Polynesian outliers: a study in the
survival of small populations**
Stephen Black

Introduction

Polynesia, Micronesia and Melanesia represent three traditional geographical regions or culture areas within the island world of the Pacific. Although these regional distinctions provide some information on the distribution of people, languages and cultures, the areas are far from internally homogeneous. Melanesia offers the extreme case where the attribute which best describes the overall character of the region is its diversity (Howells 1973; Terrell & Fagen 1975). In addition to important internal variation, the boundaries between areas grow far less distinct under close scrutiny (Howells 1973, p. 168), and archaeological evidence now suggests that in the past cultural continuity existed across what are now seen as boundaries (Green 1973; Golson 1971).

Early theories on the settlement of Polynesia accepted the racial and cultural boundaries of the three areas as distinct and immutable, and it was thus necessary to allow culturally and racially pure Polynesians to migrate into Polynesia untainted by their passage through the inhabited islands to the west. Evidence for such a movement was seen in the communities of Polynesian Outliers (see fig. 1) who inhabit small islands within Melanesia (Churchill 1911; Capell 1962). The classification of communities as Polynesian Outliers has been based almost entirely on their linguistic affinities with Polynesian languages (Pawley 1967) although lists of culture traits have also been used in one of the most thorough attempts at classification (Bayard 1976).

Archaeological and linguistic evidence now suggests that Polynesian culture developed within Polynesia based on ancestral forms in eastern Melanesia (Green 1967, 1973, 1974; Golson 1971). Similarly, Polynesian Outliers are no longer seen as remnants of an earlier eastern migration, but rather as later movements of people from western Polynesia (Bayard 1976; Pawley 1967). This latter view raises interesting questions about the prehistory of the islands now occupied by Polynesian Outliers. Were these islands previously inhabited by other groups? If so, what happened to these earlier populations when the Polynesian colonists arrived, and is the event documented in the archaeological record? Is the present Polynesian population derived exclusively from the original settlement, or do most populations represent the result of multiple settlement?

The computer simulation of Polynesian voyaging by Levison, Ward and Webb (1973; Ward, Webb & Levison 1973) has provided useful insights into the probability of accidental drift voyages making landfall on the small islands occupied by the Polynesian Outliers. Using drift voyages beginning from nine islands in Polynesia, they produce contact probabilities for Outliers from different source areas (Levison, *et al.* 1973, p. 57; Ward, *et al.* 1973). They find a high correspondence between the set of likely sources produced by their voyaging results and the set of links proposed on the basis of linguistic and cultural comparisons (Ward, *et al.* 1973). Yet they caution that their probabilities cannot be equated with rates of immigration from different sources, for the results do not take into account differences in the frequency with which vessels might leave various islands (Levison, *et al.* 1973, p. 24).

Archaeological investigations have now been undertaken on several Outlier islands, but their results and interpretation have been quite varied. Davidson (1970, 1971, 1974) investigated Nukuoro, the northernmost of the Outliers, and found that she was unable to identify any evidence of cultural replacement during an occupation sequence spanning the past 600 years. Throughout the sequence Nukuoro material culture is similar to the atoll-adapted material culture of nearby Micronesia, and she suggests that 'Either the ancestors of the

Fig. 1. Polynesian Outliers in Melanesia.

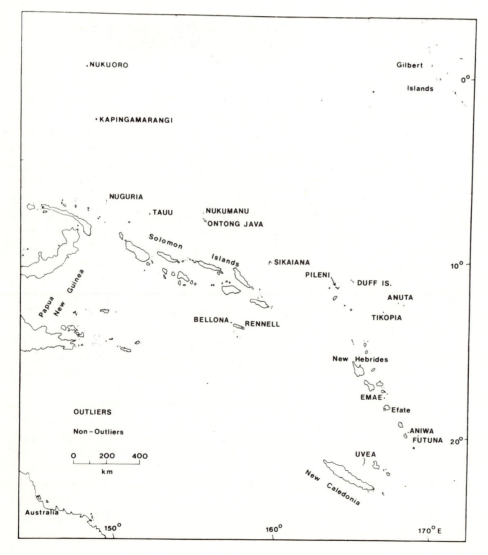

present Polynesian inhabitants of Nukuoro arrived there after adaptation to Micronesian atoll life on some other island, or they mingled with and replaced a previous Micronesian population without leaving any sign of this in the known archaeological record' (1974, p. 273). Similarly, Outliers located nearer Melanesia have produced a range of artifacts which reflect the material culture of that area. In the Duff Islands, excavations on Taumako and Kolua have produced an occupation sequence for the past 500 years (Black & Green 1977; Davidson 1974). This sequence has not revealed abrupt signs of cultural replacement, in common with results from Futuna (Shutler & Shutler 1968), and Fila and Mele (Garanger 1972, p. 88; Shutler & Shutler 1968) off the coast of Efate in the New Hebrides.

Continuity of the prehistoric sequence is also suggested in the case of Rennell and Bellona (Poulsen 1973; Black & Green 1977; Chikamori 1975). This interpretation is interesting for two reasons: (1) there is evidence for imported pottery on Bellona, and (2) both atolls share a traditional history of a pre-Polynesian population. The interpretation of the 6 pottery sherds recovered from one site is very problematic because of their low numbers and lack of diagnostic features. Although pottery is not now manufactured in Polynesia, there is ample evidence to suggest that it once was (Green 1973; Groube 1971). The pottery in Bellona is associated with a radiocarbon date in the first century BC (Polach 1973; Poulsen 1973) which precedes the traditional arrival of the present population at approximately AD 1300. Poulsen (1973) has suggested that with the exception of the loss of pottery, Bellona shows continuity over a 2000 year sequence. He also suggests that the traditional earlier population may be the direct ancestors of the present population. Alternatively, Davidson observes that the building of earth and stone mounds on Bellona after AD 1000 may suggest a later introduction from Polynesia, as mound building in Samoa and Tonga arise at about the same time. If this later introduction is accepted, she suggests that the traditional earlier population need not have been Polynesian (Davidson 1974).

The pottery recovered from Bellona is not unique to that Outlier. Plain pottery has been reported on Ontong Java although no archaeological investigations have been undertaken (Davidson 1974; R.C. Green, personal communication). Excavations by Kirch and Rosendahl (1973a, 1973b, 1976) on Anuta have also produced pottery (707 sherds) and a wide range of material culture. They suggest that Anuta was initially occupied by a pottery-using people. This group was present by at least 950 BC and survived perhaps until AD 500. Kirch and Rosendahl suggest the island was then unoccupied until after AD 1500 when it was resettled by the present Polynesian speakers (Kirch & Rosendahl 1973b, 1976). Concluding their interpretation, Kirch and Rosendahl observe that 'as the archaeological sequence of another Outlier has been revealed, we are made increasingly aware that both multiple origins and cultural replacements may be the rule rather than the exception in Outlier Polynesia' (1976, p. 244).

Cultural replacement is a poorly understood process, and it is not at all clear how it might be represented in the archaeological record. Although human biologists can offer a simple model for the genetic consequences of migration between two populations, no similar model exists for cultural traits. Vayda (1959) has reviewed some aspects of cultural replacement with reference to small islands. He argues that a small group of colonists arriving on the shores of a large and well populated island will have little if any genetic or cultural impact, but if a group of colonists arrive on an island which is either uninhabited or has a very low population the colonists may strongly influence the genetic or cultural inventory of the population. Implicit in Vayda's discussion is a correspondence between cultural replacement and population replacement. Complete cultural and population replacement is only likely if an established community is at high risk of extinction and we know *a priori* that the island has a long (although possibly discontinuous) occupation sequence. Multiple settlement is likely if an established community is at low risk of extinction. Although the former case might present a unique event of sufficient magnitude to be observed in the archaeological record, the latter would in practice be indistinguishable from a locally evolving sequence. Davidson observes that in the case of the Polynesian Outliers 'it is doubtful to what extent archaeology will be able to identify correctly the arrival of Polynesian language speakers, or to disentangle the evidence of effective settlement by groups of people from chance contacts and sporadic introduction of new traits' (1974, pp. 273–4). Acknowledging the lack of archaeological data, it may nevertheless be possible to establish at a theoretical level some expections about cultural replacement for the Outlier communities. In assessing the likelihood of cultural replacement we must first establish the probability that a local population of a given size (whether a founding group or an existing community) will become extinct. The problem of successful colonisation by founding populations is one which has been explored in greater detail by population biologists and biogeographers, and it is to their work that we now turn.

Model

MacArthur and Wilson (1967) have suggested that the number of species on an island is the result of a dynamic equilibrium between colonisation by new species and extinction of those already present. Thus the composition of the biota of an island may have a high turnover rate while the number of species present approaches an equilibrium value (Diamond 1969; Schoener 1974; Simberloff & Wilson 1969, 1970). The fate of a given species on an island is determined by that species' immigration and extinction rates: a species whose average time to extinction is less than the average time between arrivals of new colonists will not, in general, persist. The average time to extinction for such a population is dependent upon many factors, including: (1) K, the carrying capacity of the environment for that species, (2) λ, the per capita birth rate, (3) μ, the per capita death rate, and (4) N, the size of the founding population. For small founding populations and for islands with small K, the average time to extinction is low. Species which are good colonisers are those which maximise λ/μ and pass rapidly through the early stages of low population size and high vulnerability to demographic accident (MacArthur & Wilson 1967; MacArthur 1972, p. 89). Those species for which an island has a small carrying capacity must always remain in more immediate danger of extinction.

The rate of immigration of species to an island is dependent upon the distance between that island and the source area for prospective colonists. For a given species important factors affecting dispersal are the mean overseas dispersal distance and the form of the survivorship probability distribution (MacArthur & Wilson 1967, chapter 6). Dispersal of species is also aided by stepping-stone islands which may act as staging areas for dispersal, provided they are capable of supporting populations of the species. This notion of stepping-stone islands is developed in Bayard's (1976) view of the settlement of some Outliers by other Outliers, and has been interpreted in cultural terms by Kaplan (1976). Finally, the number of colonists of a given species arriving on the shores of an island is ultimately a function of the number leaving the source area.

Richter-Dyn and Goel (1972) have extended the original model for extinction proposed by MacArthur and Wilson giving it a more realistic, but necessarily complex and lengthy mathematical treatment. Using a single sex model they show that for a given λ and μ there is a critical size n_c such that if a population reaches this size it is bound to colonise and persist for an immensely long time. They also derive several expressions for the probability $P_s(N,m)$ of the population reaching size N from initial size m before going extinct. For the MacArthur and Wilson (MW) model (1967 p. 414) with carrying capacity K

$$P_s(N,m) = \begin{cases} \dfrac{1-(\mu/\lambda)^m}{1-(\mu/\lambda)^N} & N \leqslant K \\[2mm] 0 & N > K \end{cases} \qquad (1)$$

As Richter-Dyn and Goel suggest, the MW model is somewhat crude in its application of density dependent controls as it allows the population to increase exponentially until it reaches K. The models proposed by Richter-Dyn and Goel offer more realistic and gradual density dependent control for populations near K. However, in the early stages of colonisation when numbers are small, all of the models give quite similar results. The MW model is used here for the calculations that follow.

It is now possible to estimate values for the minimum population size (n_c) which will assure survival at some pre-assigned probability. These values of n_c are independent of the carrying capacity of the island. Richter-Dyn and Goel (1972, p. 415) derive the expression $n_c > 3/\log(\lambda/\mu)$ for the critical population size if we accept a 0.001 chance of failure among 'successful' populations. Values of n_c for various ratios of λ/μ are given in table 1 rounded to integer values.

Given the assumptions of the model, the estimates for

Table 1. *Values for critical population size (n_c)*

λ/μ	n_c	λ/μ	n_c
1.1	73	1.6	15
1.2	38	1.7	13
1.3	26	1.8	12
1.4	21	1.9	11
1.5	17	2.0	10

n_c suggest that under ordinary circumstances only a small population (and one easily supported by the smallest of the Polynesian Outlier atolls) would be required to assure success.

The probability of reaching size n_c (hence assured success) for smaller founding populations may be estimated using equation (1) where $N = n_c$ and m is the size of the founding population. Some values of $P_s(N,m)$ are given below in table 2. These values for $P_s(N,m)$ again suggest that given the assumptions of the model a 'small' canoe-load of voyagers may be sufficient for successful colonisation.

Table 2. *Probability of success for small founding populations.*

Size of founding population	Values for λ/μ		
	1.5	1.3	1.1
1	0.33	0.23	0.09
3	0.70	0.54	0.25
5	0.87	0.73	0.37
7	0.94	0.84	0.48
9	0.97	0.91	0.58
11	0.98	0.95	0.65

In the interpretation of these results it is important to consider further the assumptions of the model as it might apply to human populations. The first qualification that must be introduced is the extension of this single-sex model to a bisexual species. In any bisexually reproducing species both a male and female of reproductive age are required to produce offspring. The mention of reproductive age also carries with it further necessary complications. As Richter-Dyn and Goel (1972, p. 423) note, the incorporation of the age distribution of the population would require a multivariate generalisation of their results where the population is broken up into a number of age classes, each characterised by different λ and μ. Although it may be possible to extend the model to an age-specific two-sex case the mathematics involved would prove quite formidable. In addition the interaction between the two sexes is of crucial importance in the modelling of human population dynamics. Human groups practice marriage and have preferences and prohibitions regarding marriages (and matings) between individuals who stand in certain biological or socio-logical relationships. Further constraints include the age at which individuals may marry, the number of spouses they may have, and the preferred age differences between spouses. Although some preliminary work has been undertaken attempting direct estimates for the effects of these factors (Dyke 1971; McFarland 1970) we do not yet have explicit mathematical relationships and it is not possible to extend the model for two-sex interactions in a straightforward manner.

Computer simulation offers one approach to the analysis of mathematical models when direct solutions are not available or extremely tedious. Simulation is often the only practical alternative when the model under study contains a large number of interrelated variables and complex interactions. Yet the adoption of a simulation approach is no panacea; many problems remain. These may profitably be discussed within the framework of models developed by Levins (1966, 1968). Levins observes that a model may generally be characterised by its success in retaining three desirable qualities: generality, reality and precision. He further suggests that a single model cannot excel in all three. For example, a gain in reality in a single case (perhaps through the inclusion of factors unique to that situation) leads to a sacrifice in generality for all cases. These three qualities are involved, in varying proportions, in the choice of simulation model and experimental design.

The generality of the results from simulation models must be a matter of some concern for they often represent only a local rather than global mathematical analysis. Unless the parameters and variables involved in the model are adequately sampled from their respective universes it is not easy to interpret or generalise from the results obtained. There is always a need for explicit experimental design and the treatment of results in a probabilistic framework. If the model does contain a large number of interrelated variables a multivariate statistical analysis is essential. The inevitable constraints of available time for both humans and computers assures that a thorough and exhaustive research design is never possible if the system is truly complex. The alternatives appear to be a loss of reality resulting from the exclusion of important variables, and a loss of precision (through greatly increased variances) resulting from extremely small sample sizes. The choice of a particular design and its resultant mixture of reality, precision and generality must be based on the problem under investigation and the hypotheses being tested. This choice may significantly alter the result of an analysis.

There are several published accounts of simulation studies on the demographic consequences of marriage rules and the minimum size for endogamous populations. The results to date have not provided a consistent picture of the effects of varying marriage rules on population growth. In fact, the effects of incest prohibitions on population growth have ranged from a negative effect, through no effect, to an increase in growth in three different studies (Weiss 1975a).

Hammel and Hutchinson (1974) examined the effects of 4 levels of incest avoidance on a population of 65 persons.

They used conditions of high mortality balanced by high fertility to produce populations which were near zero growth under conditions of no incest avoidance. Average growth rate over a 100 year period was the only variable examined, and the results are not subjected to any statistical tests. Increasingly restrictive incest prohibitions do appear to decrease the average rates of growth for the small sample studied.

MacCluer (1974) and MacCluer and Dyke (1976) have also reported studies of the effects of incest prohibitions. Using a low fertility and mortality regime and founding populations of 100 and 200, MacCluer observed the effect of incest prohibitions extending to second cousins. Several variables are examined independently, but no statistical tests are applied to the results. MacCluer suggests that 'even in populations as small as 100 incest prohibitions do not appear to result in a greatly diminished rate of population growth, and most individuals are able to find mates' (1974, p. 218). In a more recent study MacCluer and Dyke (1976) have extended this analysis to include three marriage types at two levels of mortality and fertility. They use four founding populations (300, 200, 100, 50) and the marriage types include no marriage, strict monogamy, and strict monogamy with an incest prohibition extending to first cousins. Results are again presented without statistical analysis although the tables shown appear to support the authors' observation that 'under a range of constant demographic conditions, endogamous populations may have a high probability of survival even if they consist of as few as one hundred to two hundred individuals' (1976, p. 11). MacCluer and Dyke also suggest that 'avoidance of first cousin marriage has more serious demographic consequences in populations with low than in those with high fertility and mortality' (1976, p. 10). Populations experiencing low mortality and fertility also appear to achieve greater rates of growth (1976, p. 6). This observation parallels the conclusions concerning the advantages of low mortality and fertility (versus high mortality and fertility with an equivalent growth rate) arrived at in models of colonisation (MacArthur & Wilson 1976; Richter-Dyn & Goel 1972).

Morgan (1974) has also examined the survival of small closed populations under conditions of high and low mortality, and monogamous marriage. In a set of experiments using no incest prohibitions and founding populations of 100 and 200, Morgan found that populations experiencing low mortality and fertility survived longer than those experiencing high mortality and fertility. Younger founding populations were more favourable for growth, and large founding populations ($N = 200$) survived almost twice as long as small ones ($N = 100$). In a further experiment he observed the effect of incest prohibition, clan exogamy, and remarriage prohibition on a population of 200 experiencing low mortality and fertility. Average growth rate for 3 one hundred year blocks was examined in a split factorial analysis of variance (ANOVA) design. When clan exogamy was required the only significant main effect was the growth rate across the 100 year blocks. This effect was also significant when clan affiliations were ignored, but contrary to expectation under these conditions the incest prohibition significantly increased population growth! The general effect of clan exogamy was to reduce population growth.

McArthur, Saunders and Tweedie (1976) have examined the success of very small founding populations using a model based on mortality and fertility patterns which have been established from direct experience with the demography of Pacific populations (McArthur 1968; McArthur *et al.* 1976, p. 310). Their simulated populations were all monogamous, and were subject to either no incest rules, or prohibition against marriage between siblings and between parents and offspring. The initial populations of 3, 5, and 7 couples were generated stochastically for each run from a given age distribution. Although the method of randomly generating each founding population increases the generality of their results, McArthur *et al.* have introduced error variance into their results and sacrificed precision. They subsequently discover that 'the evolutionary course of all of the populations is so variable that there is no predictability in either the period of time needed to attain some specified size, or the time that those which failed to survive persisted before eventually heading for extinction' (1976, p. 322). No statistical analysis is presented for the results, although some tests of significance were apparently carried out (1976, p. 313). Examining the fate of populations over a 500-year period McArthur *et al.* suggest that larger and younger founding populations are more successful. They also observe that 'the imposition of incest taboos has no significant effect in general on the probability of extinction, but there is a suggestion that the smaller the founding group the greater the effect such restrictions would have in diminishing the likelihood of success' (1976, p. 314).

Granting the general observation that younger founding populations subjected to low fertility and mortality are at an advantage (MacArthur & Wilson 1967; Richter-Dyn & Goel 1972; Morgan 1974; MacCluer & Dyke 1976; MacCluer 1974; McArthur, *et al.* 1976) there remains no clear picture of the significance of marriage rules on the behaviour of small populations. MacCluer and Dyke believe that 'some measures are much better than others as indicators of a population's potential for survival' (1976, p. 12) and suggest several suitable measures. Given the conflicting results which have appeared so far with different models using varying measures of success, it seems essential to consider the results of a single study in a multivariate framework.

The experiments reported in this study were performed on a computer simulation model called ISLAND. The experimental design is described following a brief description of the model. An overview of ISLAND is illustrated in fig. 2, which follows an individual through his or her lifetime. Each person born into the population is assigned an age at death. If this age at death is less than the earliest age at marriage, his or her record is removed. Age at marriage is set at a fixed value for males (15 years in this study) and assigned for females by adding a lognormally distributed random variable to a set mini-

mum age (Skolnick & Cannings 1974, p. 177). Females who survive to marry, and all males who pass age 15 enter the marriage pool.

The marriage system operates by marrying a given female and her most suitable suitor (as determined by the societies' marriage rules). The program makes the unrealistic assumption that the parties involved in the marriage always choose to follow as closely as possible their societies' rules for marriage, and only if there are no eligible males will a marriage not take place. This marriage system is different from those used in other programs (MacCluer 1973; Morgan 1974; Skolnick & Cannings 1974) which weight each potential male according to their desirability and assign a marriage stochastically by generating a random number. These other models include a fixed probability of not marrying which is apparently independent of the desirability and numbers of potential mates. The assumption that all who may marry will do so seems justifiable in the case of Polynesia, where marriage is virtually universal (McArthur 1968).

The choice of most suitable suitor is based on a generalised multivariate procedure. Each male eligible for marriage in a given year is given a numerical score relative to each eligible female. The procedure is to score each male on several orthogonal axes (3 are used in the present study) and derive the Euclidian distance to each male from the origin. Males who are prohibited for some reason from marrying a given female are given a negative score on that axis and excluded from further consideration. The axes used in this study represent kinship category, clan, and age difference between prospective partners. This multivariate approach may easily be generalised to consider *n* attributes for marriage suitability including genotype, financial gain from marriage, etc. The importance of one axis relative to another is realised by scaling the score awarded on the different axes.

As two individuals are picked for marriage they enter a separate family-building routine. Most demographic simulation models treat the production of offspring by yearly rates, in a manner analogous to risk of mortality. Although the calendar year is a pragmatic time-frame for sampling mortality, it obscures much of the interesting details of human reproduction. Yearly treatment does not allow for any control over the independent variables which produce yearly birth rates: fecundity, pregnancy wastage (abortions and stillbirths), and postpartum sterile periods. Specialised models which include these variables have been developed (Henry 1972; Sheps & Manken 1973) and have added much to the understanding of the biological and cultural bases of fertility. These models work in months (an approximation to the ovulatory cycle) and provide information on birth intervals which is entirely lost in models which use yearly fertility rates. Skolnick and Cannings (1974) have used a family-building routine which operates in months and is combined with a yearly mortality routine. A similar hybrid form has been used for ISLAND. In operation, a couple enter the family-building routine upon marriage and complete a reproductive history. The family-building routine is terminated on the death or sterility of one spouse, and the couple is returned to the main program in the appropriate year.

Output from the program includes numbers of births, deaths, unmarried females, unmarried males, and population size for each year. At decade intervals this information is supplemented by a frequency count of individuals by sex and age class. Following the frequency counts the program calculates three different statistics: child dependency ratio, juvenile/adult ratio, and divergence from stable population. The child dependency ratio (Pressat 1972, p. 356) is defined as P_{0-4}/F_{20-44} where P stands for persons of both sex in the ages covered by the subscripts, and F stands for females. This index provides a general measure of population growth

potential and may be useful for small populations as it is less sensitive to random fluctuations in vital events than are yearly birth-rate statistics.

The juvenile/adult ratio (Pressat 1972, p. 358) measures the proportion of the adults in a given population who will be replaced by the current juvenile cohort. This statistic is calculated as the ratio P_{15-39}/P_{40-64}. As with the child dependency ratio, this statistic provides a general measure of population success. If the value of the juvenile/adult ratio falls below replacement level (1.0) for several years, then the population is in danger of extinction.

The third statistic calculated is the divergence of the observed age distribution from an expected age distribution in

Fig. 2. Path of an individual through the program ISLAND.

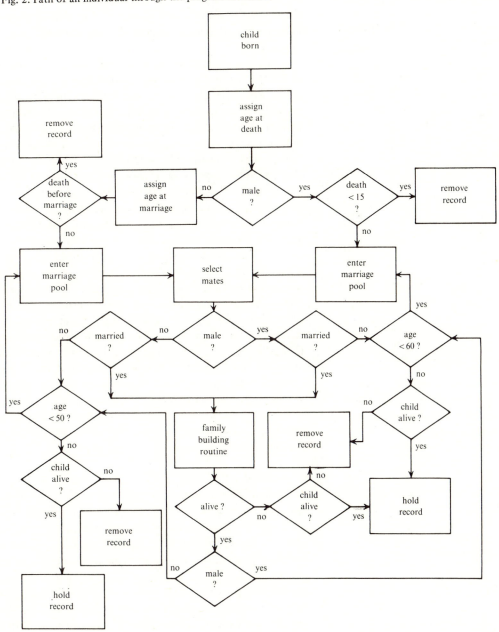

Table 3. *Experimental design*

Incest prohibition	Clan rules ignored (C0)		Two exogamous clans (C2)	
	Founding population		*Founding population*	
	N = 40 (N4)	N = 80 (N8)	N = 40 (N4)	N = 80 (N8)
I0				
I1				
I2				

(I0) Random Mating
(I1) Prohibits the following: siblings, parent-child, grandparent-grandchild.
(I2) Prohibits all marriages between first cousins and closer relatives.

Table 4. *Age and sex composition of founding populations*

Age Class	N = 40 ♂	N = 40 ♀	N = 80 ♂	N = 80 ♀
00–01	2	1	2	1
02–04	2	3	3	5
05–09	1	3	6	5
10–14	0	3	4	4
15–19	3	5	6	10
20–24	3	2	6	4
25–29	2	2	4	4
30–34	2	1	4	2
35–39	0	0	0	0
40–44	1	0	1	2
45–49	1	0	1	0
50–54	1	0	1	1
55–59	1	0	1	1
60–64	0	0	0	1
65–69	0	0	0	0
70–	1	0	1	0

Table 5. *Values for reproductive variables*

Fecundity (monthly probability of conception) = 0.20
Probabilities for pregnancy wastage

Age class	Stillbirth	Abortion
15–25	0.10	0.20
26–40	0.10	0.20
41–50	0.20	0.40

Post-conception sterile period
(gestation + infertility in months)

Stillbirth	9 + 3
Abortion	3 + 1
Live Birth	9 + 6

a stable population. This measure is suggested by MacCluer and Dyke (1976, p. 11) as an informative one in the study of population extinction:

$$\text{DIVERG} = \left(\sum_{i=1}^{18} (O_i - E_i)^2 \right)^{1/2}$$

Finally, the program reports the mean and variance for three variables over the entire simulation run: parity for females who have completed their reproductive history, age at marriage for females, and age at marriage for males.

It is relatively easy to compile a long list of variables which might affect the success of a small founding population: size of group, marriage system, mortality schedule, fertility schedule, sex ratio, age composition, biological relationships along the members of the group, etc. Many of these variables are made up of a number of interrelated variables, for example the fertility schedule is a product of factors such as age at marriage, age at menarche, fecundity (monthly probability of conception), post-partum sterile period, proportion of foetal wastage, and age at menopause, among many others (Davis & Blake 1956). It is far more difficult to choose an experimental design which achieves a reasonable level of generality and precision in its results without sacrificing realism. The design chosen here represents one such compromise. Only three variables are manipulated in the factorial ANOVA design shown in table 3. Ten replicates were made for each cell in the design, thus the entire experiment represents 120 individual runs of the program ISLAND, each run lasting for 200 simulated years.

The two founding populations (40,80) contained equal numbers of unrelated males and females as shown in table 4. Mortality levels were taken from *Regional Model Life Tables and Stable Populations* (Coale & Demeny 1966) model West Level 10 female schedule. This moderate mortality schedule was paired with the values for reproductive variables shown in table 5. These values would produce moderate fertility, representing slightly higher levels of fecundity and pregnancy wastage than that observed for historic European populations (Henry 1972, pp. 51–62). The fertility of the simulated populations would fall short of this level if women either marry late or remain unmarried. In this experiment both men and women were allowed to remarry immediately following the death of a spouse, so any reduction in fertility due to the dissolution of marriage would be due solely to the lack of available mates.

Results

The full results from the 120 runs of ISLAND produced a large primary data file which was stored on magnetic tape. This primary file was reduced to more manageable proportions using an editing routine. This routine reduced the five variables reported by year (births, deaths, population, unwed females, unwed males) to four variables reported by decade (population, average growth rate, unwed females, unwed males). A new file was created using these new variables, the existing decade summaries (child dependency ratio, juvenile/adult

Table 6. *Highest factor loadings for variables over time*

Decade	Growth rate	Population	Unmarried females	Unmarried males	Child dependency ratio	Juvenile /adult ratio	Divergence from stable population
1	9	1	1	1	9	1	1
2	1	1	1	1	1	1	1
3	23	1	6	17	1/23	9	1
4	18	1	6	17	18/1	1/9	1
5	4	1	6	17	21/6	1	1
6	1	1	6	17	16/6	18	1
7	15	1	6	17/6	15/4	1	1
8	19	1	12	2	19	21	1
9	3	1	12	2	3	1/4	1
10	14	1	12	2	14	10/15/19	1
11	7	1	12	2	7	3/19	1
12	18	1	8	22/2	16	14/3/15	1
13	4	1	8	22	16	14	1
14	24	1	8	22	24	16/1	1
15	20	1	8	5/22	4	16	1/4
16	4	1	5	5	4	24	1/4
17	10	1	11	5/13	10	24	1
18	19	1	11	13	10/19	4	1
19	19	1	11	13	19	24/4/10	1
20	3	1	11	13	3/10	10	1

ratio, divergence from stable population), and the three overall estimates for parity, female age at marriage, and male age at marriage. This file of 143 variables provides the basis for the analysis which follows.

The first question to be asked of the simulation result is: which variables are best at predicting the future behaviour of the populations? This question was approached by treating the entire set of simulation runs as a sample of 120 and subjecting the 143 measured variables to factor analysis. A principal factor analysis with Varimax rotation was performed on the data set using the program BMD08M (Dixon 1973, pp. 255–68). The data set provides several different measures of the population at a single point in time, and the same measure of the population over time. It was anticipated that variables which are consistent predictors of future population behaviour would produce consistently high loadings on a single factor for the time span over which they are measured. Variables which are poor predictors of future behaviour would exhibit high loadings on different factors over time. The original set of 143 variables was reduced to 24 factors which accounted for 88% of the total variance. The results of the analysis are not presented in detail here, but a simplified picture may be obtained by showing the factor (or factors if no loadings are particularly high) on which each variable has the highest loading, as in table 6. It is clear that population size and divergence from stable population are quite stable predictors of future behaviour. Growth rate, child dependency ratio, and juvenile/adult

ratio all show no consistent loadings over time and are poor predictors of future behaviour. The numbers of unwed males and females show an intermediate pattern of internal consistency for up to 4 decades.

The second question to be asked of the simulation results is: what effect do the various treatment effects have on the survival of the populations? A multivariate analysis of variance (MANOVAR) was performed by the program TEDDYBEAR (Wilson 1976) on the 24 factor scores for each case produced by BMD08M. These 24 new variables form a reduced rank model of the original 143 variables, and were expected to give an overall picture of the simulation results. The analysis showed that the only significant factor was N (founding population size). However, this result may be misleading. The inclusion of extraneous or redundant variables in a multivariate analysis may erode the power of any tests of significance (Kowalski 1972). Given the previous discussion of short term variation in some variables, it seems likely that the inclusion of these variables would decrease the power of the analysis. This notion was tested in MANOVAR applied to three variables: parity (P), female age at marriage (F), and male age at marriage (M). The MANOVAR results are presented in table 7. TEDDYBEAR also performs a canonical discriminant analysis (Cooley & Lohnes 1971) on each of the factors, and table 8 includes discriminant loadings for the original variables on the discriminant functions which maximise the between-effect differences. These discriminant loadings represent the correlations between the original

Table 7. *Multivariate analysis of variance on 3 variables (parity, female age at marriage, male age at marriage)*

Source of variation[a]	Multivariate F ratio	Degrees of freedom	Significance level
Main effects			
N	7.526	3 , 106	0.000 130
I	1.644	6 , 212	0.136 301
C	26.412	3 , 106	0.000 000
Two factor interactions			
N I	0.515	6 , 212	0.796 711
N C	8.184	3 , 106	0.000 060
I C	0.258	6 , 212	0.955 585
Three factor interactions			
N I C	0.832	6 , 212	0.546 135

[a] N, founding population size; C, clan exogamy; I, incest prohibition

Table 8. *Canonical discriminant analysis on the significant effects for 3 variables*[a]

Factor N (founding population size)

Means	P	F	M
N4	3.8766	26.440	23.392
N8	4.1228	25.918	24.410

Discriminant loadings	P	F	M
	−0.933 41	0.658 03	−0.759 32

Factor C (clan structure)

Means	P	F	M
C0	4.1110	25.779	25.186
C2	3.8884	26.579	22.616

Discriminant loadings	P	F	M
	0.548 45	−0.615 29	0.985 07

N C interaction

Means	P	F	M
N4 C0	4.0302	25.932	25.388
N4 C2	3.7231	26.947	21.395
N8 C0	4.1917	25.626	24.985
N8 C2	4.0538	26.211	23.836

Discriminant loadings	P	F	M
	0.333 70	−0.270 76	0.977 52

[a] P, parity; F, female age at marriage; M, male age at marriage

variables and the discriminant functions, and provide a means of assessing the importance of different variables in producing differences between treatment effects. The significant results of this analysis may be summarised as follows:

(1) Larger founding population size (factor N) increases parity (P) and male age at marriage (M) while decreasing female age at marriage (F). These variables are all reflected in the differences between treatment effects.

(2) The requirement of clan exogamy (factor C) decreases parity (P) and male age at marriage (M) while increasing female age at marriage (F). All three of the variables are significantly correlated with the differences between treatment effects.

(3) There is a significant interaction effect between factors N and C. Exogamous clan structure ($C2$) has a greater effect in smaller founding populations ($N4$). Parity and female age at marriage have a low discriminant loading for differences between treatment effects. Thus it appears that only male age at marriage demonstrates an interaction effect. Supplementary univariate ANOVA results support this interpretation as neither parity nor female age at marriage show significant interaction effects.

This analysis reveals some expected results and some surprises, as perhaps any experiment should. An increase in parity is taken to be evidence for a more successful population. The decrease in female age at marriage is correlated with the increase in parity ($r = -0.63$, $p = 0.001$), earlier marriage producing a longer reproductive span for females. Thus we may infer that smaller founding populations and clan exogamy both contribute to decreased population growth. Against this result the increase in male age at marriage is anomalous. Under conditions conducive to growth, why should male age at marriage increase? It appears that this effect is a result of the marriage rules used in the simulation model. Females attempt to marry males who are, on average, four years their senior. This criterion for optimal marriage is only met when the pool of mates is sufficiently large. Under adverse conditions the pool of available mates is restricted by low numbers and clan proscriptions, thus females must marry younger males if they are to find mates. This effect is compounded when there are a large number of unmarried females and they compete for males as they become eligible for marriage at age 15. Thus the apparent reversed effect for male age at marriage is in fact consistent with the results for parity and female age at marriage.

In addition to the significant main effects of founding population size (N) and clan structure (C) for all three variables, male age at marriage (M) shows a significant interaction effect between factors N and C. This interaction is clearly shown in fig. 3. The result of imposing clan exogamy ($C2$) on the simulated population is greater in small founding populations ($N = 40$) than in large ($N = 80$). This interaction effect is reasonable given the restricted pool of mates available in a smaller population. Why then does the interaction effect only prove significant in the case of male age at marriage? It would

Table 9. *Analysis of variance on population at year 200*

Source of variation	Sum of squares	Degrees of freedom	Mean square	F ratio	Significance level
Main effects					
N	90 420.30	1	90 420.30	467.2660	0.000 000
I	546.87	2	273.43	1.4130	0.247 869
C	2861.63	1	2861.63	14.7881	0.000 204
Two factor interactions					
N I	171.80	2	85.90	0.4439	0.642 691
N C	192.53	1	192.53	0.9950	0.320 764
I C	154.46	2	77.23	0.3991	0.671 896
Three factor interactions					
N I C	78.06	2	39.03	0.2017	0.817 637
Error term	20 899.00	108	193.51		

seem that in selecting a stochastic means for assigning female age at marriage, the variation introduced may have masked the interaction effect for both achieved female age at marriage and parity. This may then be an example of a sacrifice in precision for a gain in reality.

These MANOVAR results were checked against a univariate ANOVA on population at year 200. The results of this analysis are presented in table 9. Founding population size (*N*) and clan structure (*C*) are the only significant effects and the direction of the changes in mean population size under the different treatment levels are consistent with the MANOVAR on three variables. However, population at year 200 does not show a significant interaction effect.

These successive analyses of the ISLAND model results present yet another picture of the effect of small population size and marriage rules on the success of populations. The analyses undertaken so far also suggest reasons for the differences in the results presented by previous investigators (Hammel & Hutchinson 1974; MacCluer 1974; MacCluer and Dyke 1976; Morgan 1974). The demonstration of a significant interaction effect related to population size suggests that the differences between other published results may be partially due to the differing population sizes used in the studies. The observation that different dependent variables give different answers within this study may also account for the variety of results presented in the literature. In particular, the use of growth rate versus final population size may be expected to produce different results. Finally, the diversity of results may be linked to the implementation of marriage systems in the different simulation models employed.

The marriage system used in ISLAND produced some unexpected side effects. Still it would seem that the dependent variables closely related to the marriage system, for example male age at marriage, are most responsive to changes in the treatment effects. The marriage systems employed in other simulation models use widely differing structures, and it appears that the marriage routines employed are at the heart of the problem. A more sophisticated and realistic model for marriage is clearly required for future work in demography and population biology, but a detailed discussion of this topic would take us further afield from the concerns of archaeologists. It should be sufficient to sound a small warning. Demographic studies are very enticing to archaeologists because they provide numerical answers. These answers are quite often produced by computers, adding to their prestige. Yet the answer received is a function of two things — the data input, and the model used. It has long been clear that we must make a great many questionable assumptions in using demographic data from historical populations in an attempt to understand the dynamics of prehistoric populations (Weiss 1973, 1975*b*). We must now also question the models which we use for the processing of the data. Computers are only too

Fig. 3. Interaction effect for male age at marriage.

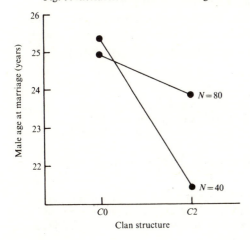

willing to give us lots of numbers, yet we must search further before we accept them as meaningful answers to relevant questions.

Discussion

The evidence from the model ISLAND shows that the imposition of marriage rules in small populations does have an effect on population growth. The imposition of an exogamous clan structure within the model ISLAND results in a 5% decrease in parity and an overall reduction of 16% in population size after 200 years. Will an effect of this magnitude decrease the likelihood of survival for populations on small atolls? It would appear that given the size of historic populations resident on the Outlier islands (Bayard 1976) the reduction of population growth due to mating restrictions would not place established populations at risk of extinction. Yet this result extends only to what we might refer to as ordinary circumstances. There remain a number of extraordinary events which might place a population at risk of extinction.

Vayda (1959) has reviewed a number of unusual events, including cyclones, hurricanes and drought, which have placed atoll populations at risk of extinction. Willis and Booth (1968) document such a population reduction on Tauu. Uninhabited islands which show signs of prehistoric occupation (Levison *et al.* 1973, pp. 52–3) also testify to the reality of local extinction. These extraordinary conditions are important but rare events, and of low predictability. If we cannot tell when they are likely to occur, is their occurrence in the prehistory of a given Outlier also unpredictable? It does appear that if we seek merely to be particularistic culture historians and describe the prehistory of one atoll, we cannot allow for the extreme uncertainty of unique events. Yet as MacArthur and Wilson (1967) have demonstrated, at a higher level of generality we can make useful predictions about the results of a number of unique and historical evolutionary processes replicated on different islands.

The results of our analysis of extinction probabilities suggest that local extinction is only likely to be a rare event among Outlier communities. As MacArthur and Wilson (1967) assert, a species is not likely to become extinct if rates of immigration are sufficient to balance local extinction. In human terms, this model predicts that population and cultural replacement are only likely if an island is extremely isolated. How isolated is extremely isolated? Unfortunately, we are not yet able to arrive at estimates for rates of extinction or immigration. Nonetheless, Levison *et al.* (1973) and Ward *et al.* (1973) have provided a rank ordering of islands in Melanesia based on the total number of landings from all nine sources in Polynesia. This rank order provides a starting point for discussion.

Ontong Java, Nukumanu, and Taumako are the three highest ranked islands in terms of landings by drift voyages from Polynesia (Ward *et al.* 1973). They would therefore be unlikely to show any evidence of population or cultural replacement, and the limited evidence from Taumako (Black and Green 1977; Davidson 1974) does not refute this hypothesis. At the low end of the rank order are Uvea, Emae, Rennell, and Bellona. These Outliers are most likely to show evidence for population or cultural replacement, and the interpretation offered by Davidson (1974) for Bellona is consistent with this prediction. Yet there are other islands for which the predictions are not clearly supported. Mele and Fila (Garranger 1972; Shutler & Shutler 1968) are ranked low in the number of simulated landings (Ward *et al.* 1973) yet do not show signs of cultural replacement. This may be the result of examining only the islands of western Polynesia as potential source areas for colonists. Bayard (1976, p. 77) suggests that Outliers in the New Hebrides were settled from other Outliers, and presents previously unpublished results from the voyaging simulation studies of Levison, Ward and Webb (1973) using the Outlier Tikopia as a starting point. These new results confirm that further work is needed which includes the likelihood of successful drift voyaging between Outliers.

Anuta (Kirch and Rosendahl 1973a, 1973b, 1976) offers perhaps the best case for population and cultural replacement, but is ranked low in numbers of arrivals. Although this ranking is consistent with the archaeological evidence for cultural replacement, Anuta is near the uninhabited island Fataka (Mitre Is.) which is ranked fourth in numbers of drift arrivals (Ward *et al.* 1973), and used for bird hunting by the people of Anuta (Yen, Kirch & Rosendahl 1973). How would this factor complicate the probability of cultural replacement on Anuta? The present model is inadequate to answer this question.

In its present form an immigration–extinction model is far too simple and naive to explain the prehistory of the Polynesian Outliers with sufficient reality and precision. Yet the model is worthwhile if it provides us with testable hypotheses and allows us to ask more precise questions of the archaeological record. Further refinements in the present model must await more detailed information on such disparate topics as the long-term variability of extreme weather conditions and the frequency and nature of contact between Melanesian populations and the nearby Polynesian Outliers. Terrell (1976) presents a review of some theoretical models being developed in human biogeography which hold much promise for future study. At present, the close interaction between model building and field research remains the essential ingredient in any attempt to explain the prehistory of the Polynesian Outliers.

Acknowledgements

The computer model ISLAND was developed as part of an M.A. thesis in Anthropology submitted to the University of Auckland. I would like to thank my supervisor Dr F.J. Meaney for his support and criticism on the project. The Computer Centre of the University of Auckland provided the computing facilities. ISLAND is written in FORTRAN (Burroughs B6700 Version 2.8) and copies are available from the author.

This manuscript has evolved following reviews by R.C. Green, G.J. Irwin, R.J.S. Cassels and F.J. Meaney, all of the University of Auckland. I remain responsible for its present shortcomings. Finally, I am grateful for the strong support and encouragement of Dr John Terrell, Field Museum of Natural History, Chicago, during my attempts to be a fledgling human biogeographer.

References

Bayard, D.T. (1976) *The Cultural Relationships of the Polynesian Outliers* (Studies in Prehistoric Anthropology, Volume 9), Dept. of Anthropology, University of Otago

Black, S. & Green, R.C. (1977) 'Radiocarbon dates from the Solomon Islands to 1975', *Oceanic Prehistory Records* 4: 1–54

Capell, A. (1962) 'Oceanic linguistics today', *Current Anthropology* 3: 371–428

Chikamori, M. (1975) *The Early Polynesian Settlement on Rennell Island, B.S.I.P. Preliminary Report 1974*, Dept. of Archaeology and Ethnology, Keio University

Churchill, W. (1911) *The Polynesian Wanderings* (Publication No. 134), Carnegie Institute of Washington

Coale, A.J. & Demeny, P. (1966) *Regional Model Life Tables and Stable Populations*, Princeton University Press

Cooley, W.W. & Lohnes, W.R. (1971) *Multivariate Data Analysis*, Wiley

Davidson, J.M. (1970) 'Polynesian Outliers and the problem of culture replacement in small populations' in R.C. Green & M. Kelly (eds.) *Studies in Oceanic Culture History Vol. 1* (Pacific Anthropological Records, No. 11), Bernice P. Bishop Museum

Davidson, J.M. (1971) *Archaeology on Nukuoro Atoll. A Polynesian Outlier in the Eastern Caroline Islands* (Bulletin No. 9), Auckland Institute and Museum

Davidson, J.M. (1974) 'Cultural replacement on small islands: new evidence from Polynesian Outliers', *Mankind* 9: 273–77

Davis, K. & Blake, J. (1956) 'Social structure and fertility: an analytical framework', *Economic Development and Cultural Change* 4: 211–35

Diamond, J.M. (1969) 'Avifaunal equilibria and species turnover rates on the Channel Islands of California', *Proceedings of the National Academy of Sciences* 64: 57–63

Dixon, W.J. (ed.) (1973) *B M D Biomedical Computer Programs*, University of California Press

Dyke, B. (1971) 'Potential mates in a small human population', *Social Biology* 18: 28–39

Dyke, B. & MacCluer, J.W. (eds.) (1974) *Computer Simulation in Human Population Studies*, Academic Press

Garanger, J. (1972) *Archéologie des Nouvelles Hébrides* (Publications de la Société des Océanistes, No. 30), Office de la Recherche Scientifique et Technique Outre-Mer

Golson, J. (1971) 'Lapita ware and its transformations' in R.C. Green & M. Kelly (eds.) *Studies in Oceanic Culture History Vol. 2* (Pacific Anthropological Records, No. 12), Bernice P. Bishop Museum

Green, R.C. (1967) 'The immediate origins of the Polynesians' in Highland, *et al.* (eds.) *Polynesian Culture History* (Special Publication No. 56), Bernice P. Bishop Museum

Green, R.C. (1973) 'Lapita pottery and the origins of Polynesian culture', *Australian Natural History Magazine* 17: 332–37

Green, R.C. (1974) 'Sites with Lapita pottery: importing and voyaging', *Mankind* 9: 253–9

Groube, L.M. (1971) 'Tonga, Lapita pottery, and Polynesian origins', *Journal of the Polynesian Society* 80: 278–316

Hammel, E.A. & Hutchinson, D. (1974) 'Two tests of computer microsimulation: the effect of an incest tabu on population viability and the effect of age differences between spouses on the skewing of consanguineal relationships between them' in Dyke and MacCluer (eds.)

Henry, L. (1972) *On the Measurement of Human Fertility* (Translated and edited by M.C. Sheps & E. Lapierre-Adamcyk), Elsevier Publishing Company

Howells, W.W. (1973) *The Pacific Islanders*, Schribners

Kaplan, Susan (1976) 'Ethnological and biogeographical significance of pottery sherds from Nissan Island, PNG', *Fieldiana Anthropology* 66: 35–89

Kirch, P.V. & Rosendahl, P.H. (1973a) 'A note on carbon dates for pottery-bearing layers on Anuta Island', *Journal of the Polynesian Society* 82: 206–8

Kirch, P.V. & Rosendahl, P.H. (1973b) 'Archaeological investigations of Anuta' in Yen & Gordon (eds.)

Kirch, P.V. & Rosendahl, P.H. (1976) 'Early Anutan settlement and the position of Anuta in the prehistory of the southwest Pacific' in R.C. Green & M.M. Cresswell (eds.) *Southeast Solomon Islands Cultural History. A Preliminary Survey* (Bulletin No. 11), The Royal Society of New Zealand

Kowalski, C.J. (1972) 'A commentary on the use of multivariate statistical methods in anthropometric research', *American Journal of Physical Anthropology* 36: 119–32

Levins, R. (1966) 'The strategy of model building in ecology', *The American Scientist* 54: 421–31

Levins, R. (1968) *Evolution in Changing Environments* (Monographs in Population Biology, No. 2), Princeton University Press

Levison, M., Ward, R.G. & Webb, J.W. (1973) *The Settlement of Polynesia: a computer simulation*, Australian National University Press

MacArthur, R.H. (1972) *Geographical Ecology*, Harper and Row

MacArthur, R. & Wilson, E.O. (1967) *The Theory of Island Biogeography* (Monographs in Population Biology, No. 1), Princeton University Press

MacCluer, J.W. (1973) 'Computer simulation in anthropology and human genetics' in M.H. Crawford & P.L. Workman (eds.) *Methods and Theories of Anthropological Genetics*, University of New Mexico Press

MacCluer, J.W. (1974) 'Avoidance of incest: genetic and demographic consequences' in Dyke & MacCluer (eds.)

MacCluer, J.W. & Dyke, B. (1976) 'On the minimum size of endogamous populations', *Social Biology* 23: 1–12

McArthur, N. (1968) *Island Populations of the Pacific*, Australian National University Press

McArthur, N., Saunders, I.W. & Tweedie, R.L. (1976) 'Small population isolates: a micro-simulation study', *Journal of the Polynesian Society* 85: 307–26

McFarland, D.D. (1970) 'Effects of group size on the availability of marriage partners', *Demography* 7: 411–15

Morgan, K. (1974) 'Computer simulation of incest prohibition and clan proscription rules in closed, finite populations' in Dyke & MacCluer (eds.)

Pawley, A. (1967) 'The relationships of the Polynesian Outlier languages', *Journal of the Polynesian Society* 76: 259–96

Polach, H.A. (1973) 'Outlier archaeology: Bellona. A preliminary report on fieldwork and radiocarbon dates. Part II. Radiocarbon dating of Sikumango Midden sample', *Archaeology and Physical Anthropology in Oceania* 7: 206–14

Poulsen, J.I. (1973) 'Outlier Archaeology: Bellona. A preliminary report on fieldwork and radiocarbon dates. Part I. Archaeology', *Archaeology and Physical Anthropology in Oceania* 7: 184–205

Pressat, R. (1972) *Demographic Analysis*, E. Arnold

Richter-Dyn, N. & Goel, N.S. (1972) 'On the extinction of a colonizing species', *Theoretical Population Biology* 3: 406–33

Schoener, A. (1974) 'Experimental zoogeography: colonization of marine mini-islands', *The American Naturalist* 108: 715–38

Sheps, M.C. & Menken, J.A. (1973) *Mathematical Models of Conception and Birth*, University of Chicago Press

Shutler, R. & Shutler, M.E. (1968) 'A preliminary report of archaeological explorations in the southern New Hebrides', *Asian Perspectives* 9: 157–66

Simberloff, D.S. & Wilson, E.O. (1969) 'Experimental zoogeography of
     Islands. The colonization of empty islands', *Ecology* 50: 278–96
Simberloff, D.S. (1970) 'Experimental zoogeography of islands. A two
     year record of colonization', *Ecology* 51: 934–7
Skolnick, M.H. & Cannings, C. (1974) 'Simulation of small human popu-
     lations', in Dyke & MacCluer (eds.)
Terrell, J.E. (1976) 'Island biogeography and man in Melanesia', *Archae-
     ology and Physical Anthropology in Oceania* 11: 1–17
Terrell, J.E. & Fagen, J. (1975) 'The savage and the innocent: sophisti-
     cated techniques and naive theory in the study of human popu-
     lation genetics in Melanesia', *Yearbook of Physical Anthropology*
     19: 2–18
Vayda, A.P. (1959) 'Polynesian cultural distribution in new perspective',
     American Anthropologist 61: 817–28
Ward, R.G., Webb, J.W. & Levison, M. (1973) 'The settlement of the
     Polynesian Outliers: a computer simulation', *Journal of the
     Polynesian Society* 82: 330–42
Weiss, K.M. (1973) *Demographic Models for Anthropology* (Memoirs
     for the Society for American Archaeology, No. 27), *American
     Antiquity* 38(2) part 2
Weiss, K.M. (1975a) 'The mysterious adventures of Electro sapiens',
     Reviews in Anthropology 2: 183–91
Weiss, K.M. (1975b) 'Demographic disturbance and the use of life tables
     in anthropology' in Alan C. Swedlund (ed.) *Population Studies
     in Archaeology and Biological Anthropology: A Symposium*
     (Memoirs for the Society for American Archaeology, No. 30),
     American Antiquity 40(2) part 2
Willis, M.F. & Booth, P.B. (1968) 'Takuu and Nukumanu atolls,
     Bougainville district, Territory of Papua and New Guinea',
     Archaeology and Physical Anthropology in Oceania 3: 55–63
Wilson, J.B. (1976) *TEDDYBEAR Statistical Program Technical Report
     T5 Edition 2 May 1976*, University of Otago Computing Centre
Yen, D.E., Kirch, P.V. & Rosendahl, P.H. (1973) 'Anuta – an intro-
     duction' in Yen & Gordon (eds.)
Yen, D.E. & Gordon, J. (eds.) (1973) *Anuta: A Polynesian Outlier in
     the Solomon Islands* (Pacific Anthropological Records, No. 21),
     Bernice P. Bishop Museum

PART FOUR

The simulation of exchange processes

Published work on the simulation of exchange processes has followed two rather different paths. In the first, settlements arranged in some sort of linear pattern receive goods from an adjacent village and pass on a fraction of what they receive to the next village 'down the line'. In the second, the objects being exchanged move around according to a random walk procedure, all points on a map being able to 'receive' a good.

Two studies provide examples of the first approach. Ammerman, Matessi and Cavalli-Sforza (1978) examine the exchange of obsidian during the Neolithic in the Mediterranean using a simulation model. Obsidian is passed from a source down a line of villages, each village retains some, drops some into an archaeological context, and passes on a proportion to the next village. Variation in the shape of the fall-off frequency curve away from the source could be examined through time, and some interesting relationships between the parameters of the model were uncovered.

Wright and Zeder (1977) have conducted a similar simulation in order to examine Rappaport's suggestion that 'symbolic' artifacts played a key role in the primitive exchange of essential resources. They considered eight communities arranged in a line. The populations of these communities were allowed to vary according to parameters derived from ethnographic work in central New Guinea but including a stochastic component. The first and eighth village produced one essential commodity each in some fixed ratio to population, and one symbolic commodity. In each 'year' in the simulation, each village took what it needed of the vital commodity and a set fraction of the symbolic commodity and passed the rest on to the next village. Wright and Zeder found that they were only able to produce a system capable of maintaining an equilibrium by introducing regulatory devices dependent on the symbolic commodities.

Both these studies are acknowledged to be unrealistic by their authors. Exchange involves complex networks of individuals rather than linear arrangements of communities. Interaction does not occur only with immediately adjacent villages and it is unrealistic to expect that each community near a source should 'take what it wants' and pass on large volumes of the rest to the next village. This approach to the simulation of exchange processes appears for the moment to be simplistic and to be incapable of approximating to the extreme complexity of primitive exchange.

The second approach allows two-dimensional exchange and perhaps permits a more realistic process to be simulated. In a study published by Hodder and Orton (1976), artifacts spread from a single source following a random walk within specified limits (these limits concerned length of step and number of steps per walk, for example). The frequencies of artifacts in ten distance bands around the source were calculated and plotted as fall-off curves. The aim of this procedure was to determine whether different spatial processes of spread could produce different fall-off curves. It was found that remarkably different dispersal procedures could produce the same shape of fall-off, but that, in general, the spread of objects moving a few short steps could be differentiated from those moving many steps. This difference relates to that found between the archaeological fall-off curves of less 'valuable' and more 'valuable' items (Hodder 1974).

The interest of the above study is limited by the fact that absolute frequencies per distance band were used instead of densities per distance band which is the type of data more likely to be available to the archaeologist. Other limitations of this approach are that only one type of artifact is considered and relative values and demand are not incorporated into the simulation. The value of artifacts might certainly be expected to increase with distance from their source and this type of factor needs to be examined in exchange models. The study which follows introduces additional components into this general class of computer simulation.

References

Ammerman, A., Matessi, C. & Cavalli-Sforza, L.L. (1978) 'Some new approaches to the study of the obsidian trade in the Mediterranean and adjacent areas' in I. Hodder (ed.) *The Spatial Organisation of Culture*, Duckworth, London

Hodder, I. (1974) 'Regression analysis of some trade and marketing patterns', *World Archaeology* 6: 172—89

Hodder, I. & Orton, C. (1976) *Spatial Analysis in Archaeology*, Cambridge University Press

Wright, H. & Zeder, M. (1977) 'The simulation of a linear exchange system under equilibrium conditions' in T.K. Earle & J.E. Ericson (eds.) *Exchange Systems in Prehistory*, Academic Press, New York

Chapter 7

The simulation of Neolithic axe dispersal in Britain
Kevin Elliott, D. Ellman
and Ian Hodder

Introduction

The period of time relevant to this study is the British Neolithic, dated approximately to the later 4th and 3rd millenia BC. Several Neolithic axe-producing sources are known at which roughouts of axes were made. The axes were polished into their final form in settlements in the areas surrounding the sources.

But the finished polished axes from each source are found over much wider areas than the main concentrations of axe roughouts. This chapter is concerned with the types of exchange system which resulted in this wider distribution, and the degree of competition between axes entering a settlement from different sources.

Some form of redistributive exchange whereby axes were taken in bulk to a centre and then redistributed around that area may certainly have occurred — for example in the movement of Group I axes from Cornwall to their main concentration in the southeast of England (Cummins 1974). However, Clark (1965) has noted a system of ceremonial gift exchange in Australasia whereby axes travelled hundreds of miles, being handed on from person to person, without the people actually moving a great distance themselves. It is this form of reciprocal exchange which is to be modelled in this study because of the relatively egalitarian nature of society in Neolithic Britain and the lack of a network of really large-scale economic nodes. If redistribution did occur, for example around causewayed camps (Renfrew 1973), it seems unlikely that this was on a large enough scale for the process and end-results to be distinguishable from the simulated procedures used here. Polishing of the axes near the sources seems to have been a dispersed small-scale activity which does not give the impression of centralised control. But future work of two kinds may be able to identify the relative importance of reciprocal and redistributive exchange. First, if axes are handed on reciprocally from person to person, being reused and re-sharpened on the way, there may be a decrease in length of axes away from their source. The reworking of Group VI axes in East Anglia is noted by Clough and Green (1972, p. 140), while preliminary work has identified a tendency for Group VI axes to reduce in size with distance from the source (S. Pier-point, personal communication). Second, it is possible that detailed spatial analyses of the relative amounts of axes in dif-ferent areas, as more axes are studied and assigned to source, may indicate high points around certain redistributive nodes. Such work remains to be done, and the initial trials reported here have used a reciprocal exchange model for the reasons already stated.

Petrological analysis has been able to identify a large number of Neolithic unperforated axes in Britain as to source. Group I axes had their source near Mounts Bay, Penzance in Cornwall. Macroscopically the stone implements in this group are characterised by medium grain, dark green or greenish blue igneous rocks which generally weather to a rougher surface. The market for these axes in Devon and Cornwall seems to have been poor, probably because of the production of other axes in the same area. The majority of Group I axes are found in southeast England, although a small number have been found as far away as Yorkshire.

Group VI axes had their source at Great Langdale in Westmorland. Macroscopically they were made from a volcanic tuff which weathered to a brownish colour appearing bluish-green on a freshly fractured surface. Axes from this group are more numerous than from any other group, with large quan-tities being found in Yorkshire and Lincolnshire.

The location of the source for Group VII axes is Graig Lwyd, near Penmaenmawr, overlooking the sea in Caernarvon-shire. The axes were made from an augite-granophyre rock having a fine-textured, pale-bluish grey appearance which weathers rapidly to a pale grey colour.

Many other axe sources have now been identified, but only the three mentioned above were studied here since there is some evidence that these were in production at least partly contemporaneously. Reliable dating of the periods in which the sources supplied axes is extremely difficult in view of the small number of stratified and well-dated contexts in which axes have been found. The Cornish axe industry began in a small way in the late 4th millenium BC (Evens, Smith & Wallis 1972) but the main dispersal of Group I axes from Cornwall did not begin much before 2000 BC (ibid.). Cummins and Moore (1973) and Clough and Green (1972) indicate slight evidence for a late Neolithic date for Group I while Moore and

Cummins (1974) suggest that Groups I, VI and VII occur together in the middle and later Neolithic in Derbyshire and Leicestershire. The production of Group VI axes may have begun in about 3300 to 3200 BC, although most contexts and the highest output seem to have been in 2700 to 2500 BC while later Neolithic associations occur (Moore & Cummins 1974, p. 62). Cummins and Moore (1973) note that associ-ations between Group VI and VII axes are suggested at several sites. Group VII seems to have been used only after about 3000 BC.

Thus, the lack of reliable well-dated contexts for the axes means that precise dating is difficult, but there is some evidence that the main period of production of Groups VI and VII may have been rather earlier than Group I. However, Evens et al. (1972, p. 253) note that Groups I and VII are definitely contemporary in the 2000 BC period, while Group VI axes are rare in late Neolithic contexts although these do occur (Moore & Cummins 1974, p. 62). Thus Evens et al. (1972, p. 259) are able to talk of Group I axes 'competing directly . . . with the products of Group VI and VII'. In the absence of more detailed dating evidence, it has had to be assumed in the rest of this study that axes from the three sources were being produced approximately contemporaneously. This problem will be further discussed below.

Fig. 1 shows the raw data used in the analysis. The num-bers of axes which have been identified to Groups I, VI, and VII in each cell for which data are available are shown. The

Fig. 1. The position of the three sources and the observed num-ber of axes from each source showing the grid system used. The figures in the cells indicate the numbers of Group I (upper figures), VI (middle) and VII (lower) axes found.

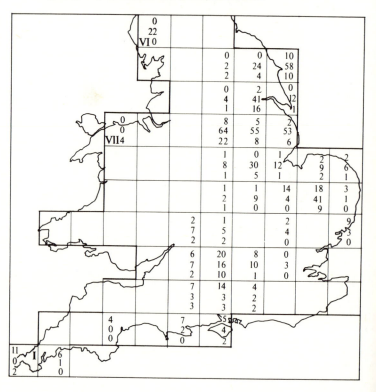

absolute number of axes in each cell depends largely on the amount of work that has been carried out in those areas. To avoid this bias the data were converted into percentages. Thus, when comparing Group I and Group VI axes, the total of these axes in a cell was calculated and the number of Group I axes presented as a percentage of that total, the same being done for Group VI axes. The two values are necessarily interdependent leading often to duplicated results (see, for example, the frequent occurrence of identical results for the pairs of values in tables 2–4).

The computer simulation

The aim of this study is to simulate and experiment with hypothetical processes which could have produced the surviving Neolithic axe distributions. A random walk process is used as the basis of the computer model. This is because it is assumed that the system of exchange involved the axes being transported over large distances via a number of steps and, although each individual exchange was not 'random', the overall exchange patterns can be compared with a random process. In the simulation, axes from any two of the three sources are started on their random walks according to rules which are described below. Their simulated final positions are then compared and contrasted with the actual archaeological data.

In the random walk process an axe starts from an origin – the position of its source. The axe's final position is determined by the values of three variables:

(1)   number of steps allowed per walk,
(2)   length of each step,
(3)   direction taken at each step,

with the direction and perhaps the number and length of steps being random variables. For an explanation of the terms used see fig. 2 and see fig. 3 for examples of simple random walks. If at any stage in a random walk an axe moves into the sea around the British coastline, then that step is invalid and must be retaken. In order to achieve this it is necessary to consider the nature of the archaeological data. These are in the form of lists which contain the find-spot together with the source number of each axe. The find-spots were grouped into squares based on the Ordnance Survey grid system (fig. 1). Only about 800 axes from the three sources studied have been identified in the whole region. It was therefore decided to divide the map into a grid system based on 50 km squares. This gives a grid of size 11 × 11, that is 121 cells. A data-structure representing the map can now be constructed. This is in the form of an 11 × 11 array with

    0 in the cells which are in the sea

    1 in the cells which are inland without data

2 in the cells which are inland with data.

The distinction is made between cells with and without data in order to aid the comparison of simulated results with actual data. Cells without actual data are ignored in the study because the lack of data means that no petrological analysis of axe source has been performed in that area. The simulated results in these cells are also ignored.

A coordinate system with origin at the most southwesterly point follows naturally from the grid. The positions of the three sources with respect to this system (fig. 1) and the number of axes found from each source and used in the simulations are given in table 1.

Table 1. *The position of the sources and the number of axes from each source*

Source	*x* coordinate	*y* coordinate	Number of axes
I	0.7	0.6	168
VI	4.2	10.1	527
VII	3.2	7.5	123

Fig. 3. Example of eight random walks originating from the same source.

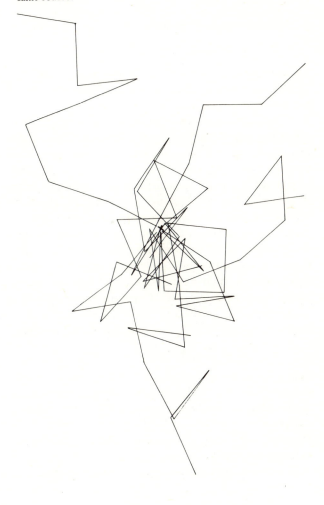

Fig. 2. Explanation of the terms used in the analysis.

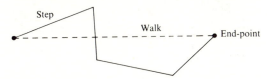

The simulation of the walk process

In each procedure only one pair of axe groups is simulated. The two sources being modelled are assumed contemporaneous and axes are started on their random walks alternately from each source. When the axes from one of the sources are exhausted, the simulation continues with the walks of the remaining axes of the other source.

For each axe, the number of steps N in its walk is first determined. Generally this is fixed for the simulation run, but if it is required to be random a sample from a Poisson distribution is generated. The length and direction of each step and the resulting position are then determined. However, if the resulting position of any step is invalid, then that step is repeated. This is tested as follows. Suppose l_i is the length of the ith step, generally fixed but otherwise generated from a negative exponential distribution, and θ_i gives its direction (this being obtained using $\theta = 2\pi R$ radians where R is a random number in the range $(0,1)$). Then (x_i, y_i), the position of the axe after the ith step with respect to some coordinate system, is given by

$$x_i = x_{i-1} + l_i \cos \theta$$

$$y_i = y_{i-1} + l_i \sin \theta$$

The cell (Ix_i, Iy_i) in which the axe lies after the ith step has coordinates

$$Ix_i = \text{integer part of } (x_i + 1)$$

$$Iy_i = \text{integer part of } (y_i + 1)$$

For example, if (x_i, y_i) is $(4.3, 7.7)$ then (Ix_i, Iy_i) is $(5, 8)$. The data structure representing the map is inspected to see if the cell is at sea, in which case the step is invalid.

A further condition to be satisfied for a valid step is introduced into the simulation. It seems reasonable to assume that the more axes in a particular area, the less the probability of another axe being required in the area. This idea can be interpreted as a means of introducing the concept of competition between the two sources — that is, areas containing one type of axe, perhaps near its source, may be less likely to accept axes from the other source. In order to experiment with this concept, the maximum number of axes (NAXE) allowed in one cell is controllable in the simulation. The probability element was incorporated using a linear function which related P (the probability that an axe is allowed in a cell) to NAXE and TAXE $(0 \leqslant \text{TAXE} \leqslant \text{NAXE})$, the total axes from both sources already in the cell. The relationship used was

$$P(\text{TAXE}) = (\text{NAXE} - \text{TAXE})/\text{NAXE}$$

Thus if TAXE $= 0$, $P = 1$ and the axe is allowed in the cell with certainty. As TAXE increases, P decreases linearly and the likelihood of the axe being allowed into the cell decreases, until TAXE $=$ NAXE when $P = 0$ and the axe is not allowed in the cell. If the axe is not allowed in a cell at any step in the walk that step must be repeated.

Fig. 4 shows the position of the axes obtained in a typi-

cal simulation. Wherever reasonable computer time allowed three separate simulations were run for each set of controlling variables. Means and standard deviations were also obtained for the statistics comparing the actual and the simulated data.

The relative percentage fall-off curves and differences

Although the frequency fall-offs are calculated in the simulations, they are not considered important to the study and are not discussed further. This is because, when comparing two sources, the absolute number of axes found in an area provides little useful information. The actual number of axes manufactured at a source will never be known nor will all the axes in an area be recovered with certainty.

A much more useful exercise is to calculate the relative percentage of each type of axe found in a cell and construct relative percentage fall-off curves. The curves are obtained by calculating the average relative percentage in cells equidistant from a source. These average values are then plotted against the distance of the mid-points of the cells to the source. The resulting curves showing the fall-off in axe percentages with distance away from a source (figs. 6 to 8) are drawn for each simulation and for the actual data in order to allow visual comparison.

The differences between the simulated and actual relative percentages are calculated for each cell as shown in fig. 5. These values can then be averaged for each source. The smaller these overall differences, the better the fit of the simulation, and the results, shown in tables 2 to 4, are discussed in the following section.

Fig. 4. An example of the maps produced by the computer showing the position of the axes from sources VI (+) and VII (*). Some axes occur in the sea because of the differences between the actual coastline and the grid of cells shown in fig. 1.

Discussion of the results

The average differences between the actual and simulated data shown in tables 2 to 4 allow the effect of varying the controlling parameters to be discussed. The first parameter to be considered here is NAXE, the maximum number of axes allowed in a cell. Lowering the value of NAXE from 70 to 40 to 20 changes the behaviour of the model in two ways. (1) Cells nearer a source fill up to their maximum fairly quickly so that later axes have to travel further. The end-result is a less steep fall-off in the frequency of axes with distance from the source. Flatter fall-off curves and lower gradients are found. (2) Competition between axe types is introduced. This is because the presence of large numbers of axes from one source in a cell near that source hinders axes from the other source entering that cell. It cannot, of course, be assumed that competition is a relevant concept in terms of Neolithic society and Neolithic axes. The level of demand for and supply of axes may have been sufficiently small that saturation levels were never approached, while variations in the value of axes may have been insignificant. Sahlins (1972) has demonstrated that the relative 'cost' of goods can play an important role in primitive exchange, but it is also possible that the histories of the axes and their attribution to source were not considered important so that competition between axes from different sources is an irrelevant concept. In any case, the axes were produced over long time periods and it is impossible to know at present the degree of contemporaneity of the production centres. Changes over time may have become blurred into one palimpsest in which any original 'competitive' patterning has been lost. It is, therefore, of interest to examine the effect of

Fig. 5. Relative percentage difference map for source VI (upper figures) and VII (lower figures). Each value indicates the difference between the actual percentage of an axe type in a cell and the simulated percentage.

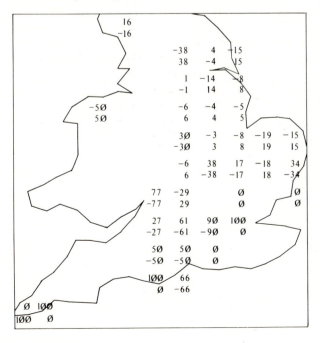

variation of NAXE in the simulations to see whether any competition is discernible in the surviving distributions.

Tables 2 to 4 show that lower NAXE values usually do result in better fits to the actual data. In 19 cases NAXE = 40 provides smaller overall differences between the actual and simulated data, while 7 cases have smaller differences when NAXE = 70. However, most of the latter cases involve very minor differences between the NAXE = 40 and the NAXE = 70 results. If only those differences in the tabulated values are considered which are greater than 10% of each value, then 9 cases provide better fits with NAXE = 40 and only 1 with NAXE = 70. The better fit of the simulated results when NAXE = 40 is seen especially for the results for Group I axes. These axes do have a markedly low gradient when their densities are plotted against distance from source. Since better fits are found when NAXE = 40 with all combinations of step length and number, the NAXE results also suggest that some competition effect is still detectable in the axe distributions. This is so despite all the distorting and blurring factors which have acted. However, the lowest average differences between the actual and simulated data occur consistently for the simulations of Group I against Group VI. These are the most widely spaced sources with least overlap of their distributions. The simulated processes are accounting less well for the distributions in cases where much overlap occurs.

The tables also allow the effects of varying the number and length of steps to be examined, values which were fixed for each simulation. The 'best' results in the tables have been indicated. These occur in the central part of the tables with relatively good results in the areas around the centre and extending to the right-hand side of the tables. The parameter combinations for these better fitting cases involve walks of between 8 and 42 units, with the best results in each table being produced by total walks of between 10 and 24 units — that is 500 to 1200 km. It is important to note that these distances are *not* the straight line distances from source to final position of an axe, but the total 'random walk' distance travelled from source to end-point. This end-point could, of course, be anywhere between 1 km and 500–1200 km from the source. It is likely that the axes from the three sources studied had a relatively high value in the context of Neolithic Britain. These results are therefore not unreasonable.

The smallest differences between the actual and simulated data consistently occur when the number of steps taken per walk is between 5 and 12, and the length of step is between 2 and 3.5 units (100 and 175 km). It is this middle range of values, rather than very large numbers of very small steps or very few very large steps, that provides the better results. It is of interest that a regression analysis of the Neolithic axe data suggested dispersal processes involving more than 7 steps (Hodder 1974). The tables also show that simulations involving Group I axes from Cornwall provide better fits with a step length of 2.0 (100 km) while simulation of Groups VI and VII produces better fits for step lengths of 3.0 and 3.5 (150 and 175 km). It would be of interest if this dif-

Length of step	Number of steps					
	2	4	5	7	12	14
NAXE = 70						
1.0	–	29.64 / 42.53	27.64 / 36.97	26.10 / 26.18	*22.39* / *21.63*	*21.17* / *18.94*
2.0	31.29 / 40.89	*20.92* / *19.53*	**18.92** / **16.60**	**19.31** / **17.81**	**17.86** / **17.86**	20.53 / 20.53
3.0	25.74 / 23.83	20.56 / 20.56	23.26 / 21.07	26.75 / 26.75	26.11 / 26.11	24.28 / 24.28
3.5	–	24.64 / 24.64	24.36 / 24.36	23.64 / 23.64	33.36 / 33.36	–
NAXE = 40						
1.0	–	–	–	24.97 / 25.36	20.66 / 20.25	*17.64* / *17.64*
2.0	–	–	*21.17* / *15.94*	**16.74** / **15.31**	**16.94** / **15.14**	–
3.0	25.56 / 24.12	20.44 / 20.44	25.58 / 23.46	27.58 / 27.58	25.69 / 25.69	–

Table 2. *The average differences between the actual and simulated data for Groups I (upper figures in each pair) and VI (lower figures). The 'better' results are indicated in bold and italic type.*

Length of step	Number of steps					
	2	4	5	6	7	12
NAXE = 70						
1.0	–	–	–	–	51.00 / 30.44	39.45 / 30.82
2.0	61.14 / 31.10	31.51 / 26.39	24.11 / 24.11	24.06 / 20.88	22.78 / 22.78	*18.37* / *20.64*
3.0	43.10 / 31.15	21.33 / 21.33	**15.23** / **15.23**	*21.03* / 18.77	*20.39* / *20.39*	*18.36* / *18.36*
3.5	–	22.08 / 22.08	23.56 / 23.56	25.86 / 25.86	**16.63** / **18.94**	18.03 / 18.03
7.0	62.97 / 41.28	–	–	–	–	–
NAXE = 40						
1.0	–	–	–	–	49.60 / 28.55	32.40 / 28.37
2.0	–	–	25.77 / 22.65	*16.97* / *16.97*	25.03 / 22.89	*17.57* / *19.86*
3.0	44.57 / 32.06	–	20.89 / 18.63	**14.25** / **14.25**	16.83 / 16.83	19.33 / 19.33

Table 3. *The average differences between the actual and simulated data for Groups VI (upper figures in each pair) and VII (lower figures). The 'better' results are indicated in bold and italic type.*

Length of step	Number of steps				
	2	4	5	7	12
NAXE = 70					
1.0	–	–	–	48.75 / 38.50	42.99 / 35.69
2.0	53.98 / 37.21	34.31 / 31.51	–	*32.76* / *27.80*	–
3.0	43.22 / 34.21	–	*30.11* / *30.11*	33.47 / 31.57	–
3.5	–	33.94 / 32.06	–	–	–
NAXE = 40					
1.0	–	–	–	47.79 / 38.16	38.46 / 28.94
2.0	52.91 / 33.90	35.33 / 23.61	–	*30.30* / *26.93*	–
3.0	43.40 / 34.72	–	30.34 / 32.28	–	–
NAXE = 20					
1.0	–	–	–	–	39.91 / 33.30
2.0	–	–	–	28.94 / 28.14	

Table 4. *The average differences between the actual and simulated data for Groups I (upper figures) and VII (lower figures). The 'better' results are indicated in italic type.*

ference could be related to the value attached to the axes. Certainly Group I axes are of medium-grained rock while Groups VI and VII are fine-grained and often show heavier polish and higher quality of finish. Langdale axes may have taken longer to produce because they are fine-grained and more difficult to polish than Group I axes. In addition, Group I was probably slightly later in production than VI and VII. Possibly higher population densities and greater localised wealth in the later period could have resulted in shorter steps being taken.

Figs. 6 to 8 provide some examples of the similarity between the actual and simulated fall-off curves. These curves show the fall-off in the percentages of one axe type with distance away from the source, relative to the other axe type. The curves are especially jagged because distance bands in which there are no data have been plotted on the graphs as zero. The general similarity between the actual and the simulated data is taken here as supporting the view that some form of random walk procedure provides one adequate model for axe dispersal.

In conclusion, the simulation has identified some degree of competition between axes from different sources, and has pointed to the most likely range of numbers and lengths of steps taken in moving from source to destination. That evidence of competition is found, even when the axes were being produced over tremendously long periods of time and only

partly contemporaneously suggests that they had sufficient value for knowledge of their origin to be handed on with them. Thus the 'cost' of an axe, partly related to distance from source, could have produced the apparent competition effect seen in the distributions. This possibility and the evidence for the number and length of steps taken support the view of Clark that Neolithic axe dispersal was comparable to the ceremonial gift exchange of axes in Australasia.

Problems and future work

The work described here is the first stage in an attempt to build a more complex and realistic model of Neolithic axe dispersal. The main changes to the model envisaged at present are perhaps worth describing. It is necessary to examine the effect on the results of the analysis of changing the size and location of the grid of squares on which the whole analysis is based. In addition axe dispersal needs to be allowed from all contemporary sources, not just from pairs of sources. Since different factories were in production at different times, the effect of changing the periods of output needs to be examined. Also, in the procedure described above, axes only 'avoid' other axes by considering the final positions of those axes. This is unrealistic since an axe during its walk needs to consider the position of other axes during, and not only after, their walks. Axes have to be able to move around at the same 'time'. It would also be of value to weight the differences between the

Fig. 6. Actual and simulated percentage fall-off curves for the simulation of Groups I and VI. NAXE = 70, the length of step = 2.0 and the number of steps = 7.

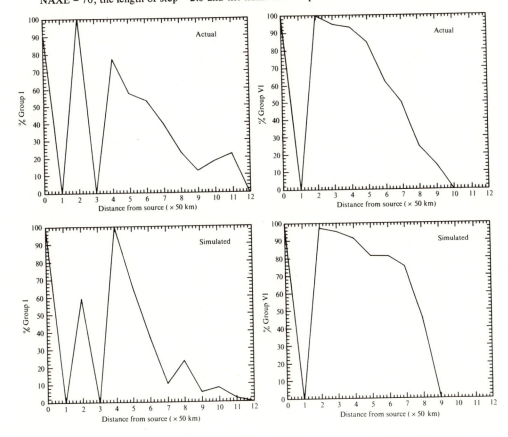

Fig. 7. Actual and simulated fall-off curves for the simulation of Groups VI and VII. NAXE = 40, length of step = 1.0 and number of steps = 12.

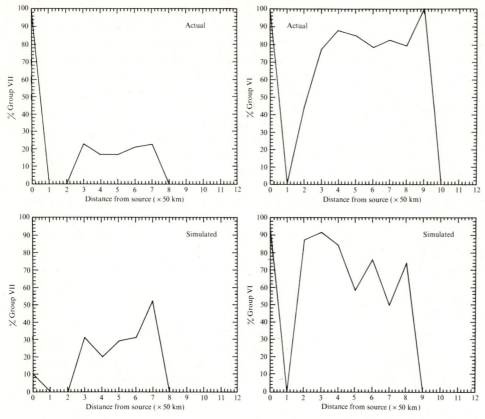

Fig. 8. Actual and simulated fall-off curves for the simulation of Groups I and VII. NAXE = 20, length of step = 2.0 and number of steps = 7.

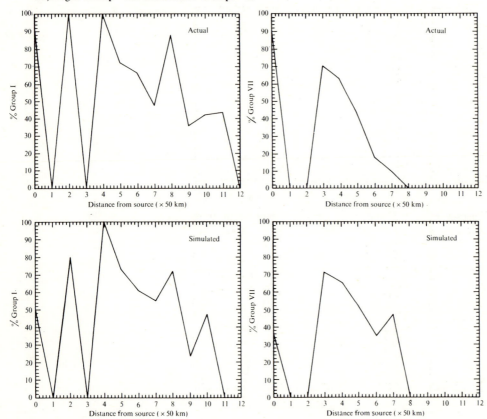

actual and simulated percentages in the grid cells according to the number of axes in those cells. If the simulated percentages for two sources in a cell are 25% and 75%, the actual percentages may be 50% and 50% resulting in a 25%, 25% difference between the simulated and actual values. But these differences are obviously of greater significance if the actual numbers of axes in the cell are, say, 80 and 80 rather than 1 and 1. A weighting could be applied to take this into account.

A further modification will be to describe the data by a number of summary statistics (such as mean and standard deviation of distances of end-points from source). The model procedures will then be simulated a larger number of times in order to obtain the likelihood of obtaining the actual values of the statistics 'by chance' — that is according to the stochastic component within the model.

A final study which has already been mentioned, and which does not involve simulation itself, concerns the relevance of the whole concept of random walks for Neolithic axe dispersal. It remains possible that axes were not handed on from person to person but were sent in shipments to distant localities within Britain, from which they were then dispersed. It is also possible that axes were obtained by making special purpose long distance trips to the source. The relevance of localised, reciprocal exchange for Neolithic axe distribution needs to be checked independently, and the value of examining the sizes of the axes in relation to distance from the source has already been indicated. It is only as checks such as this are carried out that more detailed simulation work can be placed on a sound footing.

References

Clark, G. (1965) 'Traffic in stone axe and adze blades', *Economic History Review* 18: 1—28

Clough, T.H. & Green, B. (1972) 'The petrological identification of stone implements from East Anglia', *Proceedings of the Prehistoric Society* 38: 108—55

Cummins, W.A. (1974) 'The Neolithic stone axe trade in Britain', *Antiquity* 48: 201—5

Cummins, W.A. & Moore, C.N. (1973) 'Petrological identification of stone implements from Lincolnshire, Nottinghamshire and Rutland', *Proceedings of the Prehistoric Society* 39: 219—55

Evens, E.D., Smith, I.F. & Wallis, F.S. (1972) 'The petrological identification of stone implements from South-Western England. Fifth report of the sub-committee of the South-Western Federation of Museums and Art Galleries', *Proceedings of the Prehistoric Society* 38: 235—75

Hodder, I. (1974) 'Regression analysis of some trade and marketing patterns', *World Archaeology* 6: 172—89

Moore, C.N. & Cummins, W.A. (1974) 'Petrological identification of stone implements from Derbyshire and Leicestershire', *Proceedings of the Prehistoric Society* 40: 59—78

Renfrew, C. (1973) 'Monuments, mobilization and social organisation in Neolithic Wessex' in C. Renfrew (ed.) *The Explanation of Culture Change*, Duckworth, London

Sahlins, M.D. (1972) *Stone Age Economics*, Aldine, Chicago

PART FIVE

Simulation trials for methods and techniques

As was noted above (p. 67), when mathematical problems become extremely complex simulation is an alternative approach. Rather than continue with the mathematics, it may often be easier to simulate a particular situation a large number of times and determine empirically the required measurements and relationships from the simulated results. For illustrative purposes take a simple case where the mathematics are, in fact, fairly straightforward. Consider someone playing dice and trying to work out the probability of throwing a double six. The result could be arrived at either by mathematical reasoning or by throwing the die a large number of times (say 1000) to obtain an empirical estimate of the probability. Similarly, the empirical approach of simulation can often be used as an alternative to mathematical analysis. In particular, when mathematical problems become intractible, simulation may offer the only way forward. Some examples of this are given in the following chapters.

A related concept is that of randomisation. The nature of archaeological data often prevents the application of standard statistical tests of significance. The assumptions underlying these tests can seldom be justified in archaeology. In such cases, then, how is one to test the significance of quantitative analysis? For example, one might want to know the significance of a particular correlation coefficient value for the similarity between a set of objects and the distances between them. In other words, is the similarity between pairs of objects significantly correlated with the distance between them? If one feels unjustified in using standard significance tests, one alternative would be to randomise the data. For example, the similarity values could be randomly shuffled so that they became associated with different distance values. The correlation coefficient could then be reassessed and compared with the original correlation coefficient. Doing this a large number of times would provide some idea of the 'significance' of the original values.

Simulation is also of value when the performance of a new statistic or a new method of analysis is being tested. One may want to assess the efficiency of a new statistic in different types of situations. For example, in chapter 9 the performance of a measure of association between distributions is tested. This is done by simulating different types of distributions, applying the measure of association and seeing how able it is to detect the different patterns. Similarly Zubrow and Harbaugh (chapter 10) use non-computer simulation to construct situations against which they can assess the abilities of a particular method of spatial analysis.

In this section simulation is used as an adjunct to the development of quantitative and statistical methods in spatial analysis in archaeology. It is used as an experimental testing ground.

Chapter 8

**Simulations to determine the
variance and edge effect
of total nearest-neighbour distance**
Kevin P. Donnelly

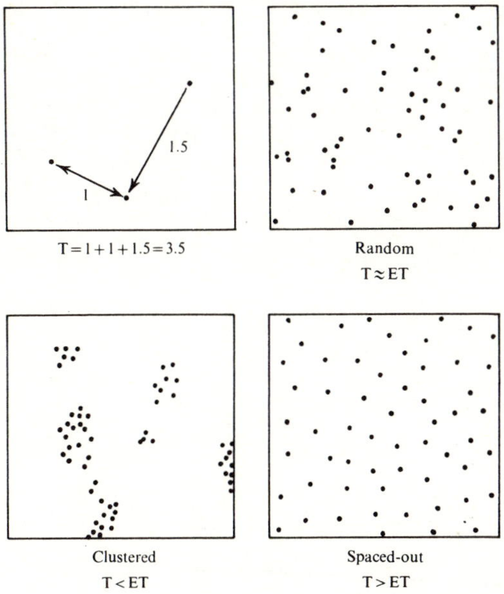

Introduction

Given a sample $u_1, \ldots u_n$ of n points, the 'total nearest-neighbour distance' (TNND) is defined to be the sum of the distances from each point to its nearest neighbour (NN). It will be denoted by the symbol T. In mathematical notation

$$T = \sum_{i=1}^{n} \min_{j \neq i} d(u_i, u_j)$$

where $d(u_i, u_j)$ is the distance between u_i and u_j. Thus in the first part of fig. 1, where NN distances are represented by arrows, $T = 3.5$.

T can be used as a statistic to test the null hypothesis that the points are random – more precisely, that they are independently uniformly distributed over the region in question – against the alternatives that they are clustered or spaced-out.

Nearest-neighbour analysis was first used by ecologists and foresters (Clark & Evans 1954; Holgate 1965) who, however, measured NN distances only from a thin sample drawn from a large number of points. In this case, since the chosen points are likely to be widely separated, their NN distances can be assumed to be independent, and the variance of TNND is easy to calculate. Edge effects are also negligible since the chosen points are likely to be a long way from the edge of the region. When NN distances are measured from all points, neither of these simplifications any longer holds. The necess-

Fig. 1

T = 1 + 1 + 1.5 = 3.5

Random
T ≈ ET

Clustered
T < ET

Spaced-out
T > ET

ary modifications to the method are the subject of this chapter.

It should be noted that previous authors have used the mean of the NN distances T/n as a statistic, whereas I use their total T, since this makes the working and formulas slightly simpler. This makes no essential difference to the statistical method.

Recently TNND has been used in other disciplines, notably archaeology and geography (Hodder & Orton 1976; De Vos 1973). Hodder and Orton give numerous references. People seem to have used the incorrect variance obtained by assuming the NN distances to be independent. P.J. Diggle points out, in an appendix to Hodder and Orton, that the error which this causes appears, from computer simulations, to be negligible in the two-dimensional case. In the following section I present the results of sufficiently many simulations to obtain a good estimate of the correct variance of T for large n. The points are chosen on the surface of a sphere to avoid edge effects.

Simulations of points on a sphere

We have a choice of definitions of 'distance' between points on the surface of a sphere.

TNND will be denoted by T when distances are measured along the surface (along great circles).

TNND will be denoted by $\tilde{T}$ when distances are measured along a chord.

For n random points on the surface of a sphere of radius 1, we can obtain the means of T and $\tilde{T}$ analytically:

$$E(T) = n\, B(\tfrac{1}{2}, n - \tfrac{1}{2})$$

$$E(\tilde{T}) = n\, B(\tfrac{1}{2}, n)$$

where E denotes expectation or mean, and B denotes the Beta function.

The variance appears quite intractable theoretically. Between 10^4 and 10^5 simulations were performed for various values of n between 3 and 40. The results are presented in fig. 2. The following polynomial model was fitted by least squares.

$$\text{var } T = c_0 + \frac{c_1}{n} + \frac{c_2}{n^2} + \frac{c_3}{n^3}$$

$$\text{var } \tilde{T} = c_0 + \frac{\tilde{c}_1}{n} + \frac{\tilde{c}_2}{n^2} + \frac{\tilde{c}_3}{n^3}$$

The model was found to fit the data adequately. Estimates of the parameters were

Fig. 2. Variance of TNND for k random points on a sphere.

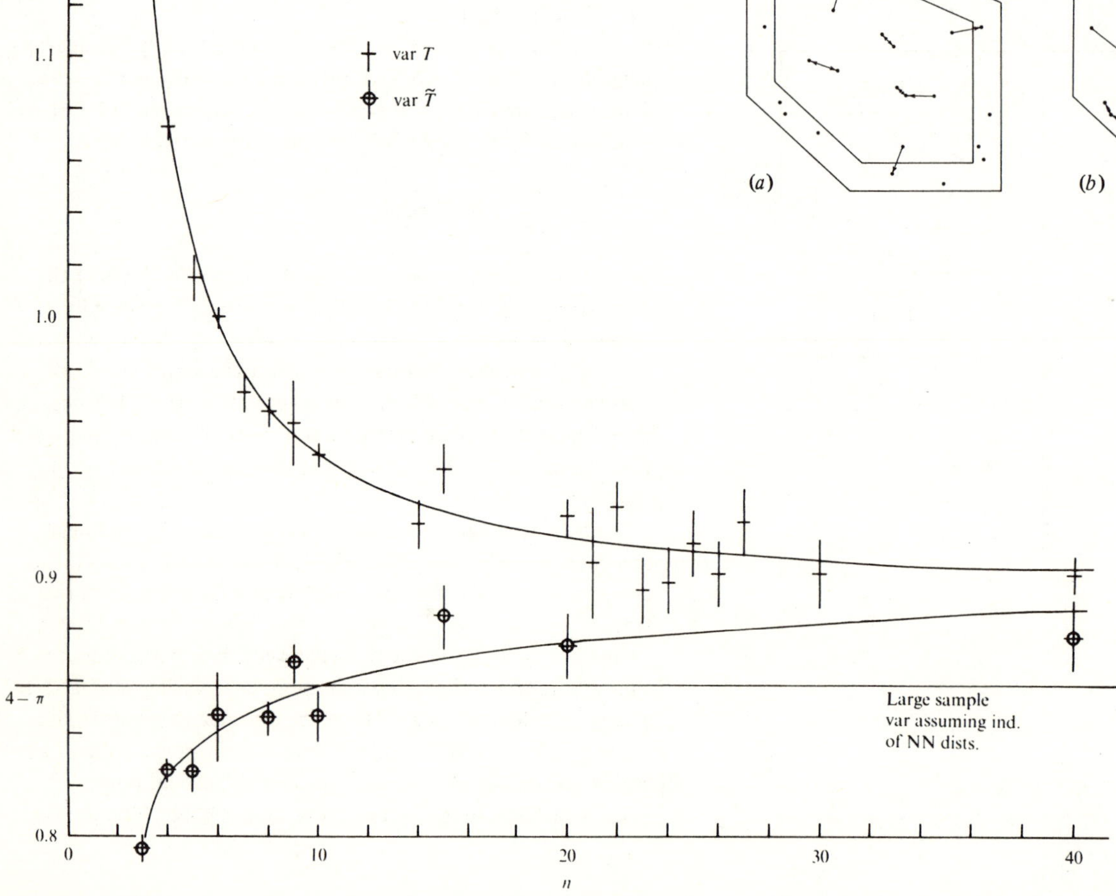

Fig. 3. (*a*) Use of a buffer zone to eliminate edge effects. (*b*) TNND without a buffer zone. Arrows indicate NN distances.

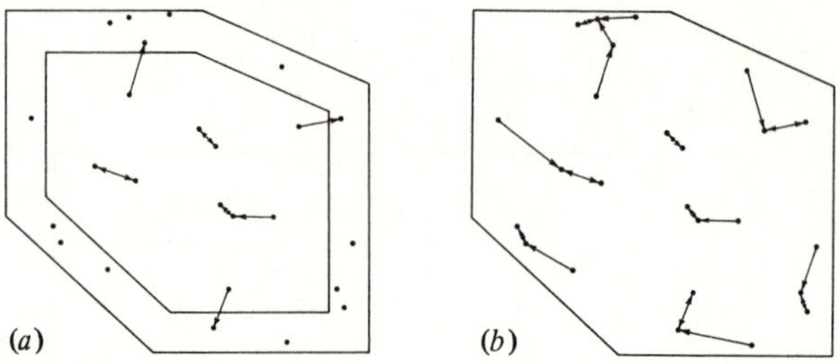

$$c_0 = 0.8915 \pm 0.0067$$

$$c_1 = 0.430 \pm 0.155 \qquad \bar{c}_1 = -0.432 \pm 0.162$$

$$c_2 = 1.37 \pm 0.95 \qquad \bar{c}_2 = 1.18 \pm 1.11$$

$$c_3 = -0.77 \pm 1.68 \qquad \bar{c}_3 = -2.2 \pm 2.1$$

TNND on the sphere may be of some practical use in itself, but its main interest for us is that c_0 gives the variance, for large n, of TNND in the plane. For a large number n of random points in a region of area A on the plane

$$\text{var } T = \frac{c_0}{4\pi} A = c' A$$

where the constant c' is approximately $0.070\,94 \pm 0.000\,53$. All errors quoted are standard errors. By contrast, the constant in the formula given by Clark and Evans, assuming independence of the NN distances, is $0.068\,31$.

Edge effect corrections

A major difficulty in the application of nearest-neighbour analysis has been that the theory applies only to an unbounded region, whereas in practice study must be limited to a finite number of points in a bounded region. The expected NN distance for a point near the boundary will be greater than for a point well inside the region.

One method which has been commonly used to avoid edge effects is the use of the part of the study region within a certain distance of the boundary as a buffer zone, ignoring the NN distances of points in the buffer zone. However, this may mean discarding a lot of information. For instance, in the example illustrated in fig. 3 15 of the 25 points lie in the buffer zone. Moreover, one can never be sure that the buffer zone has been made wide enough.

If TNND is evaluated without a buffer zone, the mean and variance will depend on the shape of the region and on the number of points. In any particular example they may be evaluated by simulation, but this spoils one of the major advantages of TNND: that it is a statistic which may be quickly and easily evaluated by hand.

It might be hoped that the edge effect corrections to the mean and variance of TNND could be approximated well by

Fig. 4. Edge effects on var T. Simulations of TNND for random points in various shapes of region in the plane. Number of points (n) given adjacent to points on the graph.

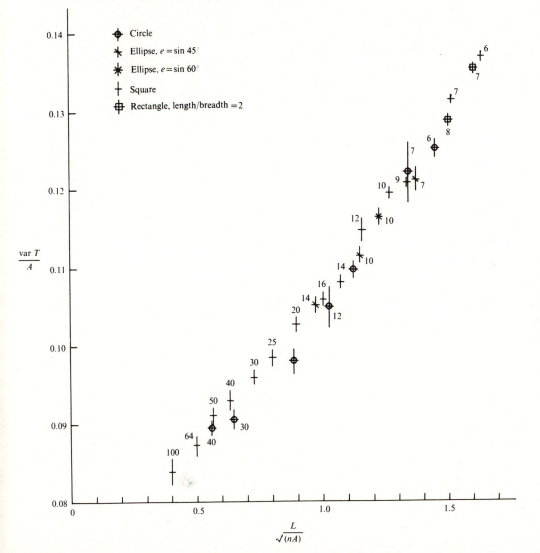

an additional term proportional to the length of the edge and dependent on the density n/A of points, but otherwise independent of the shape of the region or of the number of points. From dimensional considerations we obtain the formulae

$$E(T) = \tfrac{1}{2}\sqrt{(nA)} + c_L L$$
$$\text{var } T = c'A + bL\sqrt{(A/n)}$$

where A is the area of the region and L is the length of the edge. The correction terms are $c_L L$ and $bL\sqrt{(A/n)}$. c_L and b are unknown constants. $\tfrac{1}{2}\sqrt{(nA)}$ is the value of the expectation obtained by Clark and Evans, ignoring edge effects.

Between 6000 and 100 000 simulations were performed of TNND for between 5 and 64 random points in various shapes of region, including circles, ellipses, squares and rectangles. (var T)/A is plotted against $L/\sqrt{(nA)}$ in fig. 4. As was hoped, the graph is nearly a straight line. c' and b may be esti-

mated from the intersect on the axis and the slope. We obtain the approximate formula

$$\text{var } T = 0.07\,A + 0.037\,L\,\sqrt{(A/n)}$$

The value obtained for c' agrees to within experimental error with that obtained in the last section. The constant c_L was evaluated from

$$c_L = \frac{E(T) - \tfrac{1}{2}\sqrt{(nA)}}{L}$$

In fact c_L turned out not to be a constant as supposed above, but to depend on n. However, it was independent of the shape of the region and tended to a limit for large n. In fig. 5 c_L is plotted against $1/\sqrt{n}$. The graph is approximately a straight line. Thus we obtain the approximate formula

$$E(T) = \tfrac{1}{2}\sqrt{(nA)} + \left(0.051 + \frac{0.041}{\sqrt{n}}\right) L.$$

Fig. 5. Edge effects on E(T). Notation as for fig. 4.

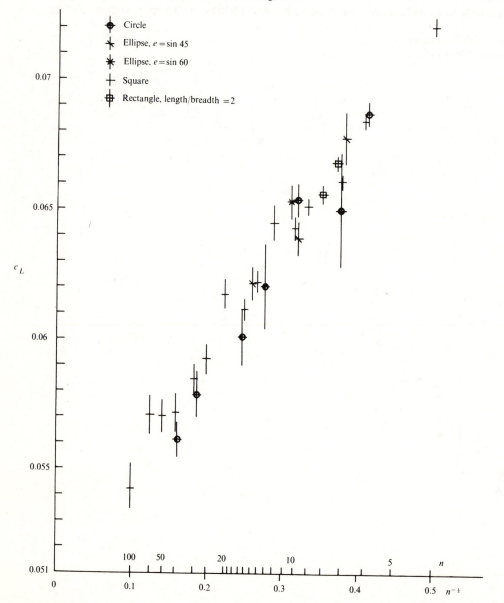

These empirical formulae are sufficiently accurate for more than about 7 points in any region with a reasonably smooth boundary. For example the shapes in fig. 6 have reasonably smooth boundaries but those in fig. 7 do not.
However, when the number of points is fairly large the formulae should work even for regions with fairly unsmooth boundaries.

The method of correcting for edge effects could no doubt be extended to statistics other than TNND, to hypotheses other than the null hypothesis of randomness, and to more than two dimensions.

Example

Hodder and Orton (1976) give on page 42 an example of 19 random points in a square (the inner square in their diagram). Taking the side of this square to be one unit, we have $A = 1$, and $L = 4$. Hence

$$E(T) = \tfrac{1}{2}\sqrt{19} + \left(0.051 + \frac{0.041}{\sqrt{19}}\right) \times 4$$

$$= 2421$$

$$\text{var } T = 0.07 + 0.037 \times \frac{4}{\sqrt{19}}$$

$$= 0.1040$$

T is found to be 2.724. Hence

$$\frac{T - E(T)}{\sqrt{(\text{var } T)}} = 0.940$$

This is neither greater than 1.96 nor less than −1.96, so the hypothesis that the points are random is not rejected.

By contrast, if we do not correct for edge effects and use the Clark and Evans variance, we obtain 2.0847, which is significant.

Conclusion

Total nearest-neighbour distance (TNND) is defined for a set of points to be the sum of the distances from each point to its nearest neighbour. Simulations were performed of n random points on the surface of a sphere in order to produce an empirical formula for the variance of TNND. Extrapolation gives the variance of TNND for a large number of points in a region on the plane.

Simulations were performed of n random points in various shapes of region in the plane, such as circles, ellipses and squares. It was found that the mean and variance of TNND could each be approximated well by the large sample value plus an edge effect correction, proportional to the length of the perimeter of the region.

Postscript

Since completing the manuscript of this chapter I have determined the constant c' by a combination of analytic methods and numerical integration to be 0.0703. The constant given as 0.051 in the formula for $E(T)$ has been determined more accurately as 0.051 368. This provides a cross-check on the values obtained by simulation, which are, however, sufficiently accurate for practical purposes.

References

Clark, P.J. & Evans, F.C. (1954) 'Distance to nearest neighbour as a measure of spatial relationships in populations', *Ecology* 35: 445–53

De Vos, S. (1973) 'The use of nearest neighbour methods', *Tijschrift voor Economshe en Social Geografie* 64: 307–19

Hodder, I.R. & Orton, C.R. (1976) *Spatial analysis in archaeology*, Cambridge University Press

Holgate, P. (1965) 'Tests of randomness based on distance measures', *Biometrika* 52: 345–53

Fig. 6

Fig. 7

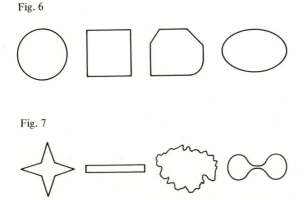

Chapter 9

An index for assessing the association between distributions of points in archaeology
Ian Hodder and Eric Okell

Introduction

Three characteristics of existing methods for assessing the association between distributions of points can be noted (Hodder & Orton 1976). First, they are scale dependent. Quadrat methods depend very much on the size of quadrat used. Nearest-neighbour methods depend on how many neighbours are included. If only first nearest neighbours are used, the analysis is only sensitive to close association.

Secondly, existing methods involve some simplification of the data, or the use of a restricted amount of information. For example, nearest-neighbour methods consider a limited number of links between points, and the Runs test and its variations involve simplifying a two-dimensional pattern into one dimension.

Thirdly, coefficients such as Pielou's (1961) S coefficient of segregation provide very little information about the type of association or segregation. For example, nothing is learnt about the relative sizes of areas covered by the two distributions (their relative dispersions).

The proposed coefficient

An alternative method of assessing the association between distributions which is not scale dependent, which makes fuller use of the available data, and which provides more information about the distributions, can be suggested. If there are distributions of two types of points (A and B), there are three types of linkages which can be measured – links between A points, links between B points, and links between A and B points. If individual points $i = 1, \ldots, n$ are of type A, while $i = n+1, \ldots, n+m$ are of type B, let r_{ij} denote the distance between points i and j, and define

$$\bar{r}_{AA} = \sum_{i=1}^{n} \sum_{\substack{j=1 \\ j \neq i}}^{n} r_{ij}/n(n-1) \tag{1}$$

$$\bar{r}_{BB} = \sum_{i=n+1}^{n+m} \sum_{\substack{j=n+1 \\ j \neq i}}^{n+m} r_{ij}/m(m-1) \tag{2}$$

$$\bar{r}_{AB} = \sum_{i=1}^{n} \sum_{j=n+1}^{n+m} r_{ij}/nm \tag{3}$$

Thus, first take one A point and measure the distance (r) to all other A points, then take another A point and do the same, and so on. Sum all these distances, divide by the total number of links $(n(n-1))$, and so obtain the average distance between A points $(\bar{r}_{AA})$. The average distances between B points $(\bar{r}_{BB})$, and A and B points $(\bar{r}_{AB})$ are obtained in a similar manner. The proposed measure of association can then be defined as

$$A = \bar{r}_{AA}\, \bar{r}_{BB} \,/\, (\bar{r}_{AB})^2 \tag{4}$$

In this formulation, the summations for $\bar{r}_{AA}$ and $\bar{r}_{BB}$ include each measurement twice. If the summations are modified and the devisors changed to $\frac{1}{2}n(n-1)$ and $\frac{1}{2}m(m-1)$ the results are unaltered, so the choice may be considered one of convention. Similarly, in some cases it may be thought preferable, for theoretical reasons, to work with squared distances.

The performance of the A measure of association will be examined in detail below, but it is expected that, if A and B points are well intermingled, the value of A will be close to 1.0. A will approach zero, on the other hand, as the two distributions become more separated and tightly packed. Values of A above 1.0 indicate isolated pairs or clusters of A and B points.

Properties of the A index

The method used to examine the performance of the A measure has been to simulate or randomly generate pairs of distributions, assess the A index for each pair of distributions, and examine the frequency distribution of A values for any one series of simulations. This approach has been preferred to a purely statistical or theoretical discussion since little is known of the complex pattern of correlations among the various recorded distances.

It is important that the null hypothesis being considered (the hypothesis of randomly intermingled distributions) is clear, and that the null hypothesis should have some relevance to archaeological data. Different null hypotheses will be examined which might be used in reference to an observed distribution of A and B points. In all the initial simulations the points were randomly generated from uniform distributions.

As a first attempt at simulating what may be appropriate distributions for two object types, A and B, which may have originated in different regions, two squares were taken side by side. The A points were generated as follows. With probability p a point is uniformly distributed over the left-hand square (and with probability $1-p$ it is placed in the right-hand square, being distributed uniformly over the square). In a similar fashion the B points are generated with an associated probability q of being placed in the right-hand square and $1-q$ of being placed in the left-hand square.

By altering the values of p and q we are able to simulate different degrees of overlap between the two populations. The choice $p = 1$, $q = 1$ gives complete separation of the two populations. All A points are in the left-hand square and all B points in the right-hand square. For values of p close to 1, 'most' of the A points will tend to be in the left-hand square and a few points will have been transported to the right-hand square. The choice $p = 0.5$ corresponds to the situation when A points are distributed uniformly over the total area. The case $p = 0.5$, $q = 0.5$ represents complete overlap in the sense that both A and B points are uniformly distributed over the whole rectangular region.

In each series of simulations for constant values of m, n, p and q, the simulation was repeated 200 times, and the A index for each of these simulations was noted. From the frequency distribution of these A values the 90% limits (the upper and lower 5% levels) were estimated. These are the two values given at each entry in the tables. The values in table 1a are for the case when $p = 0.5$, $q = 0.5$. It is expected that for these given p and q values 90% of the A values will be between these two numbers. The 95% limits for these p and q values are given in table 2a (based on 500 simulations for each entry). The shape of the enclosing area was found to have no marked effect on these results.

Table 3a gives the values for the simulations when $p = 0.75$, $q = 0.5$. Table 4a gives the values for the same p and q but at 95% limits and with 500 simulations for each pair of values instead of 200. To indicate how the A index is altered by a change in the p and q values, tables 5a to 7a give the 90% limits on the A index for a few selected values of m, n, p and q. It should perhaps be noted that rerunning the simulations using different random numbers produced acceptably similar results to all the published tables.

If the tables are used carefully, therefore, it is possible to use their values to construct tests of hypotheses. When testing, for example, $p = q = 0.5$, if the observed A value lies outside the 90% limits (table 1a), then the hypothesis may be rejected. It is not possible to make exact statements concerning the 'power' of such tests. By 'power' here is meant the performance of the test when the null hypothesis is false. However, we may expect a reasonable performance especially in the cases of testing two simple hypotheses. For example, given $m = 10$, $n = 15$, suppose we wish to test H_0 (the null hypothesis; $p = q = 0.5$) versus the hypothesis H_1 ($p = 0.75$, $q = 0.75$). If H_0 is true then by the construction of these limits we should expect to reject H_0 'one in ten times'. However, if H_1 is true, we would like the probability of rejecting H_1 also to be small. H_1 is rejected if H_0 is accepted – that is if the A index lies between 0.801 and 1.119. From a consideration of the complete list of values obtained for the simulation when $p = 0.75$, $q = 0.75$, the probability of rejecting H_1 if H_1 is true is estimated at (approximately) 7/20. By a similar consideration, when testing H_0: $p = q = 0.5$ versus H_1: $p = 0.75$, $q = 1.0$, the same probability is estimated at less than 1/40.

A second type of null hypothesis was also considered. A and B points were located independently of each other in a bounded area within a larger population of A and B points. The aim of this procedure is to avoid the 'edge effects' of nearest neighbour analysis (Donnelly, chapter 8 above). Simulations were carried out which generated a total *population* of A and B points. Within this population an area was defined which contained a *sample* of A and B points. In assessing the degree of association between A points, measurements were made from A points in the sample area to *all* other A points, whether these were in the sample area or in the total population. The same was done for B points and for the assessment of $\bar{r}_{AB}$ and $\bar{r}_{BA}$.

As for the first null hypothesis, 200 pairs of distributions were generated for different values of m and n, and the values of A were examined. The results showed that the 95% ranges of the A values were considerably smaller than those for the first null hypothesis. In addition, the frequency distributions were less skewed around 1.0, although the modal points for the A frequency distributions were still usually in the 1.04 to 1.06 range.

The second hypothesis provides a more exact and rigorous test than the first hypothesis. However, in many archaeological situations the placing of a bounded area well within the total population of A and B points will severely limit the number of points that can be considered. With small samples it is often necessary to consider the total population (as in the first null hypothesis).

Assessment of the A index

It is important, when presenting a new index, to assess its sensitivity to those types of non-random patterning which may be of interest to the archaeologist. A comparison with similar measures is also appropriate.

The type of association in which the archaeologist is interested concerns two distributions distributed over areas by some spatial process. For example, are two types of object distributed within two distinct cultural areas? Are objects distributed over different parts of an archaeological site? Processes of this general type have been further approximated here by allowing points to move by random walks from two separate origins. The walks for each of the points involve moving 5 steps from the origins (fig. 1). The direction moved at each step of fixed length is chosen at random. The ability of the A index to identify the difference between the two distributions resulting from such a procedure can then be examined, using the first null hypothesis discussed above.

It is also possible to examine the ability of other indices to detect non-random patterns of association in the same generated distributions. This allows the relative sensitivity of the A index to be assessed. A number of measures of association are based on quadrat counts (Hodder & Orton 1976). The area being analysed is partitioned into quadrats and the presence or absence of each type of object in each quadrat is noted. One serious problem associated with tests based on this type of information is that the size of the quadrats used has a great effect on the results of the analysis (Greig-Smith 1964, p. 110). Many of the most valuable measures of this type are also greatly affected by the amount of area in which neither

Fig. 1. An example of the random walk of A points (continuous lines) and B points (dashed lines) from two origins.

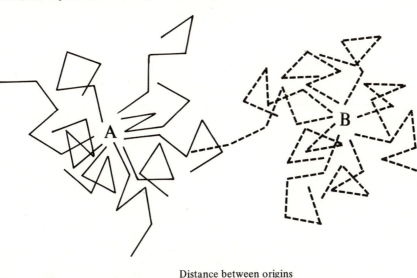

Distance between origins

Table 1. *Empirical 90% limits for (a) the A index and (b) the dispersion ratio for two distributions of points randomly distributed over a rectangle, p = q = 0.5*

		n								
		2	4	6	8	10	15	20	30	40
	2	0.07 1.99	0.20 1.82	0.24 1.64	0.29 1.64	0.17 1.62	0.22 1.56	0.17 1.59	0.17 1.54	0.23 1.59
	4		0.45 1.39	0.46 1.35	0.48 1.29	0.53 1.29	0.60 1.26	0.63 1.23	0.61 1.23	0.57 1.22
	6			0.62 1.27	0.65 1.22	0.71 1.19	0.69 1.16	0.65 1.17	0.72 1.14	0.77 1.13
	8				0.68 1.18	0.67 1.16	0.68 1.14	0.75 1.12	0.82 1.11	0.84 1.11
m	10					0.76 1.14	0.80 1.11	0.77 1.11	0.84 1.09	0.81 1.08
	15						0.82 1.09	0.06 1.08	0.88 1.07	0.89 1.06
	20							0.86 1.07	0.87 1.05	0.91 1.05
	30								0.92 1.04	0.91 1.04
	40									0.95 1.03

(a)

		n								
		2	4	6	8	10	15	20	30	40
	2	0.18 5.21	0.29 2.31	0.25 1.88	0.25 2.08	0.18 1.99	0.21 1.99	0.20 1.99	0.15 2.06	0.24 2.05
	4		0.49 1.77	0.49 1.55	0.52 1.59	0.54 1.49	0.55 1.48	0.58 1.56	0.56 1.48	0.54 1.46
	6			0.62 1.47	0.68 1.47	0.65 1.40	0.68 1.35	0.65 1.38	0.61 1.36	0.65 1.30
	8				0.67 1.45	0.69 1.41	0.68 1.30	0.68 1.32	0.74 1.28	0.72 1.25
m	10					0.73 1.36	0.72 1.29	0.74 1.29	0.74 1.26	0.73 1.28
	15						0.78 1.27	0.78 1.21	0.81 1.16	0.82 1.21
	20							0.82 1.25	0.81 1.19	0.84 1.20
	30								0.83 1.20	0.83 1.17
	40									0.86 1.15

(b)

Table 2. *Empirical 95% limits for (a) the A index (b) the dispersion ratio for two distributions of points randomly distributed over a rectangle, p = q = 0.5*

(a)

m \ n	4	5	6	7	8	9	10	11	12	13	14	15
4	0.38 1.47	0.42 1.42	0.43 1.36	0.40 1.32	0.39 1.32	0.45 1.32	0.42 1.29	0.48 1.30	0.42 1.29	0.41 1.27	0.44 1.28	0.48 1.28
5		0.44 1.33	0.48 1.31	0.51 1.29	0.51 1.27	0.56 1.25	0.54 1.25	0.51 1.23	0.53 1.23	0.61 1.23	0.54 1.22	0.51 1.22
6			0.51 1.26	0.51 1.24	0.59 1.25	0.52 1.22	0.61 1.21	0.61 1.21	0.56 1.20	0.61 1.18	0.59 1.19	0.58 1.49
7				0.57 1.22	0.61 1.22	0.63 1.21	0.56 1.19	0.66 1.18	0.65 1.17	0.65 1.18	0.67 1.16	0.66 1.16
8					0.59 1.20	0.63 1.19	0.64 1.17	0.62 1.16	0.69 1.15	0.68 1.15	0.63 1.16	0.72 1.14
9						0.64 1.17	0.71 1.16	0.72 1.15	0.58 1.15	0.59 1.13	0.64 1.14	0.66 1.14
10							0.73 1.16	0.65 1.15	0.72 1.14	0.72 1.13	0.70 1.12	0.70 1.12
11								0.71 1.14	0.74 1.13	0.70 1.13	0.71 1.12	0.75 1.12
12									0.70 1.13	0.74 1.13	0.75 1.12	0.76 1.11
13										0.72 1.11	0.73 1.11	0.78 1.10
14											0.79 1.10	0.77 1.10
15												0.76 1.10

(b)

m \ n	4	5	6	7	8	9	10	11	12	13	14	15
4	0.47 2.29	0.46 2.02	0.48 1.88	0.46 1.76	0.48 1.85	0.49 1.72	0.46 1.69	0.45 1.66	0.47 1.63	0.45 1.66	0.42 1.52	0.46 1.61
5		0.53 1.93	0.52 1.88	0.52 1.69	0.55 1.67	0.52 1.56	0.58 1.58	0.53 1.52	0.56 1.60	0.53 1.54	0.55 1.49	0.53 1.52
6			0.54 1.81	0.58 1.66	0.57 1.61	0.55 1.64	0.57 1.58	0.57 1.52	0.58 1.54	0.60 1.48	0.59 1.48	0.58 1.49
7				0.61 1.69	0.61 1.63	0.62 1.53	0.63 1.61	0.63 1.63	0.60 1.47	0.65 1.47	0.63 1.46	0.64 1.46
8					0.64 1.62	0.66 1.56	0.66 1.47	0.59 1.47	0.66 1.49	0.69 1.40	0.66 1.47	0.63 1.43
9						0.62 1.61	0.66 1.45	0.65 1.42	0.66 1.45	0.68 1.42	0.67 1.36	0.65 1.38
10							0.69 1.50	0.68 1.44	0.69 1.43	0.71 1.42	0.70 1.39	0.69 1.39
11								0.69 1.41	0.71 1.40	0.70 1.38	0.73 1.36	0.72 1.39
12									0.69 1.46	0.71 1.39	0.72 1.39	0.70 1.38
13										0.68 1.43	0.72 1.34	0.73 1.37
14											0.73 1.33	0.73 1.40
15												0.74 1.36

Table 3. *Empirical 90% limits for (a) the A index and (b) the dispersion ratio when the points are distributed over two squares. The m A points have probabilities 0.75, 0.25 of being in either square, and the n B points have probabilities 0.50, 0.50 of being in either square*

		n								
		2	4	6	8	10	15	20	30	40
	2	0.11 2.21	0.14 1.74	0.16 1.69	0.19 1.62	0.21 1.60	0.14 1.52	0.13 1.57	0.19 1.55	0.16 1.53
	4		0.41 1.42	0.38 1.32	0.41 1.26	0.49 1.28	0.38 1.22	0.47 1.20	0.48 1.20	0.44 1.21
	6			0.42 1.20	0.49 1.19	0.53 1.16	0.48 1.15	0.56 1.14	0.52 1.13	0.61 1.12
	8				0.57 1.16	0.56 1.14	0.56 1.11	0.55 1.12	0.58 1.10	0.65 1.09
m	10					0.59 1.13	0.57 1.10	0.62 1.09	0.67 1.07	0.63 1.07
	15						0.70 1.08	0.72 1.07	0.73 1.05	0.71 1.05
	20							0.74 1.06	0.67 1.04	0.73 1.03
	30								0.75 1.03	0.71 1.02
	40									0.76 1.02

(a)

		n								
		2	4	6	8	10	15	20	30	40
	2	0.19 3.17	0.13 2.16	0.19 1.93	0.20 2.01	0.22 1.98	0.17 1.87	0.12 1.97	0.18 1.93	0.16 1.86
	4		0.46 1.71	0.42 1.60	0.43 1.58	0.46 1.47	0.50 1.34	0.51 1.44	0.45 1.42	0.47 1.41
	6			0.56 1.62	0.56 1.47	0.59 1.44	0.52 1.33	0.56 1.28	0.54 1.27	0.57 1.24
	8				0.65 1.40	0.58 1.38	0.60 1.27	0.58 1.29	0.64 1.22	0.65 1.20
m	10					0.60 1.30	0.63 1.25	0.62 1.22	0.66 1.21	0.64 1.17
	15						0.66 1.21	0.67 1.17	0.72 1.13	0.69 1.10
	20							0.67 1.16	0.72 1.15	0.72 1.10
	30								0.76 1.10	0.74 1.07
	40									0.76 1.07

(b)

Table 4. *Empirical 95% limits for (a) the A index and (b) the dispersion ratio for two distributions of points randomly distributed over a rectangle, p = 0.75, q = 0.50*

m \ n	4	5	6	7	8	9	10	11	12	13	14	15
4	0.26 1.44	0.28 1.40	0.29 1.36	0.35 1.34	0.35 1.33	0.37 1.30	0.37 1.29	0.29 1.28	0.41 1.27	0.35 1.27	0.36 1.26	0.36 1.26
5	0.26 1.41	0.32 1.33	0.34 1.30	0.32 1.27	0.38 1.27	0.41 1.26	0.39 1.23	0.43 1.22	0.42 1.23	0.43 1.22	0.42 1.22	0.42 1.21
6	0.29 1.36	0.37 1.29	0.40 1.25	0.44 1.24	0.37 1.23	0.48 1.22	0.39 1.19	0.47 1.19	0.44 1.18	0.45 1.18	0.48 1.18	0.46 1.18
7	0.32 1.31	0.40 1.27	0.40 1.24	0.44 1.22	0.45 1.20	0.41 1.18	0.45 1.18	0.51 1.17	0.45 1.16	0.46 1.17	0.50 1.15	0.44 1.15
8	0.34 1.32	0.40 1.26	0.45 1.23	0.41 1.19	0.51 1.19	0.45 1.17	0.47 1.16	0.56 1.16	0.51 1.15	0.50 1.15	0.56 1.13	0.50 1.14
9	0.35 1.30	0.41 1.24	0.43 1.21	0.49 1.19	0.47 1.18	0.47 1.17	0.47 1.15	0.51 1.15	0.52 1.13	0.51 1.13	0.55 1.13	0.47 1.12
10	0.32 1.29	0.33 1.23	0.46 1.19	0.44 1.18	0.46 1.17	0.53 1.15	0.47 1.15	0.53 1.13	0.56 1.13	0.50 1.12	0.54 1.12	0.57 1.11
11	0.36 1.27	0.39 1.22	0.47 1.20	0.46 1.17	0.49 1.16	0.52 1.15	0.55 1.13	0.54 1.12	0.53 1.12	0.53 1.11	0.52 1.10	0.55 1.11
12	0.37 1.26	0.49 1.22	0.48 1.19	0.41 1.16	0.45 1.16	0.55 1.13	0.53 1.12	0.55 1.12	0.55 1.11	0.52 1.11	0.56 1.10	0.54 1.10
13	0.39 1.27	0.38 1.21	0.43 1.18	0.45 1.16	0.50 1.14	0.52 1.14	0.56 1.11	0.55 1.11	0.53 1.11	0.62 1.10	0.53 1.10	0.57 1.10
14	0.35 1.27	0.42 1.20	0.48 1.17	0.50 1.16	0.48 1.14	0.47 1.13	0.55 1.12	0.56 1.11	0.56 1.11	0.55 1.10	0.59 1.10	0.57 1.09
15	0.37 1.26	0.43 1.21	0.49 1.17	0.47 1.16	0.56 1.14	0.54 1.13	0.58 1.12	0.59 1.11	0.54 1.10	0.62 1.10	0.60 1.09	0.59 1.09

(a)

m \ n	4	5	6	7	8	9	10	11	12	13	14	15
4	0.39 2.23	0.41 2.05	0.41 1.81	0.40 1.75	0.41 1.73	0.39 1.68	0.43 1.55	0.42 1.55	0.42 1.58	0.41 1.51	0.43 1.59	0.41 1.54
5	0.40 2.07	0.44 1.95	0.46 1.80	0.43 1.73	0.41 1.59	0.43 1.54	0.47 1.51	0.43 1.43	0.42 1.45	0.47 1.49	0.48 1.44	0.47 1.44
6	0.46 2.10	0.46 1.82	0.45 1.54	0.48 1.55	0.45 1.55	0.54 1.56	0.50 1.47	0.47 1.58	0.54 1.45	0.51 1.44	0.51 1.35	0.50 1.41
7	0.45 2.13	0.50 1.82	0.50 1.57	0.51 1.63	0.52 1.53	0.53 1.49	0.47 1.46	0.53 1.45	0.53 1.43	0.51 1.31	0.55 1.39	0.53 1.45
8	0.47 2.03	0.53 1.96	0.52 1.59	0.53 1.47	0.55 1.50	0.52 1.42	0.56 1.49	0.53 1.40	0.52 1.45	0.58 1.38	0.57 1.33	0.54 1.40
9	0.50 1.78	0.53 1.74	0.57 1.55	0.56 1.51	0.54 1.56	0.54 1.39	0.57 1.36	0.57 1.34	0.56 1.37	0.59 1.34	0.56 1.31	0.58 1.34
10	0.51 1.77	0.51 1.72	0.56 1.62	0.53 1.49	0.56 1.42	0.60 1.43	0.59 1.40	0.57 1.36	0.60 1.31	0.57 1.35	0.60 1.33	0.61 1.34
11	0.55 1.93	0.53 1.69	0.55 1.59	0.54 1.47	0.59 1.47	0.57 1.38	0.60 1.43	0.58 1.34	0.59 1.33	0.61 1.33	0.59 1.29	0.57 1.31
12	0.54 1.93	0.56 1.55	0.58 1.51	0.58 1.46	0.59 1.53	0.58 1.44	0.60 1.35	0.62 1.36	0.62 1.27	0.59 1.33	0.61 1.30	0.63 1.30
13	0.56 2.00	0.58 1.89	0.57 1.62	0.60 1.54	0.58 1.49	0.59 1.39	0.60 1.38	0.63 1.28	0.60 1.35	0.60 1.31	0.60 1.31	0.61 1.24
14	0.53 2.02	0.58 1.70	0.57 1.54	0.58 1.46	0.64 1.48	0.60 1.35	0.64 1.35	0.64 1.35	0.65 1.29	0.63 1.32	0.62 1.31	0.64 1.27
15	0.57 1.93	0.57 1.94	0.58 1.51	0.62 1.47	0.61 1.47	0.61 1.39	0.62 1.41	0.61 1.36	0.62 1.29	0.63 1.27	0.65 1.29	0.65 1.26

(b)

Table 5. *Empirical 90% limits for (a) the A index and (b) the dispersion ratio for two distributions of points randomly distributed over a rectangle. m = 10, n = 15*

		q			
		0.50	0.75	1.00	
	0.50	0.80	0.59	0.39	
		1.12	1.11	0.96	
p	0.75	0.58	0.38	0.22	(a)
		1.10	1.03	0.71	
	1.00	0.47	0.25	0.15	
		0.89	0.68	0.34	

		q			
		0.50	0.75	1.00	
	0.50	0.75	0.76	1.17	
		1.28	1.46	2.03	
p	0.75	0.62	0.68	0.99	(b)
		1.21	1.39	1.84	
	1.00	0.50	0.53	0.78	
		0.83	0.98	1.31	

Table 6. *Empirical 90% limits for (a) the A index and (b) the dispersion ratio. m = 8, n = 10*

		q			
		0.50	0.75	1.00	
	0.50	0.68	0.59	0.31	
		1.17	1.16	1.02	
p	0.75	0.53	0.33	0.19	(a)
		1.13	1.09	0.73	
	1.00	0.37	0.22	0.14	
		0.97	0.75	0.36	

		q			
		0.50	0.75	1.00	
	0.50	0.72	0.79	0.97	
		1.42	1.55	2.11	
p	0.75	0.62	0.61	0.86	(b)
		1.30	1.52	1.98	
	1.00	0.47	0.52	0.71	
		0.90	1.02	1.37	

Table 7. *Empirical 90% limits for (a) the A index and (b) the dispersion ratio. m = 15, n = 20*

		q			
		0.50	0.75	1.00	
	0.50	0.86	0.71	0.44	
		1.08	1.07	0.89	
p	0.75	0.63	0.45	0.25	(a)
		1.06	0.98	0.62	
	1.00	0.43	0.25	0.16	
		0.90	0.65	0.31	

		q			
		0.50	0.75	1.00	
	0.50	0.80	0.85	1.27	
		1.23	1.44	1.89	
p	0.75	0.66	0.71	1.04	(b)
		1.12	1.31	1.79	
	1.00	0.53	0.56	0.82	
		0.78	0.93	1.19	

type of point occurs but which is included in the analysis (Pielou 1969, p. 176).

In view of these difficulties, indices based on distance measurements appear, for the moment, to be most relevant in archaeology. One such index is Pielou's (1961) S coefficient of segregation. S varies from +1.0 when the two distributions are completely segregated, to −1.0 when A and B points are associated in isolated pairs made up of one A and one B (corresponding to values of A above 1.0). S equals 0.0 when the two types of point are randomly intermingled. The chi-squared test can be used in conjunction with a 2 × 2 contingency table to assess the significance of the segregation. It is this index and associated chi-squared test that have been applied to the randomly generated distributions in order to provide a comparison with the A index.

Table 8 summarises the results of applying the A and S indices to pairs of distributions generated by random walks. The distance between the origins in each series of simulations is shown, as is the length of step moved at each stage of the walks. For the 20 simulations of line (h), for example, the A coefficient indicates segregation between the two distributions 12 times (at the 95% level), whilst the S coefficient identifies significant segregation only 2 times. In many cases the A index is shown clearly to be more sensitive to the fact that the two distributions are being generated from separate sources.

Table 9 summarises the results of a similar series of simulations in which the origin for both A and B points is identical. But, in moving five steps from the origin, A points move shorter distances than B points. For example, in the first series of simulations in table 9, each A point has moved 5 steps of 0.5 cm length, while each B point has moved 5 steps of 10.0 cm length. The A coefficient is generally more able than the S coefficient to detect differences between the distributions.

Comparisons were also made with other indices using figs. 2 and 3 (see also Hodder & Orton 1976, pp. 205 and 207). For the distributions of types 76 and 67 (fig. 2), the A index is 0.25 and the dispersion ratio (see below) 0.27. From the tables these are both significant at the 95% level. However, there is no significant difference between the distributions if the S coefficient, the Runs test and the 'circular' version of it (Hodder & Orton 1976, p. 210) are used. Similarly, when comparing types 76 and 128 (fig. 3) the A index of 0.27 is

Table 8. *Results of simulations designed to test performance of S and A coefficients. Random walks of points from two origins always involve 5 steps taken at each walk*

	Number of A points	Number of B points	Distance between origins (cm)	Length of steps (cm)	Number of trials	Number of times significant segregation indicated by	
						S	A
(a)	20	20	5	5	20	1	5
(b)	5	5	10	5	40	1	2
(c)	5	15	10	5	40	3	3
(d)	10	10	10	5	20	3	12
(e)	20	10	10	5	40	6	27
(f)	20	20	10	5	20	5	18
(g)	20	20	10	10	20	1	5
(h)	20	20	15	10	20	2	12

Table 9. *The association between distributions of A and B points after simulations of random walks from the same origin but with different lengths of moves*

	Number of A points	Number of B points	Length of A steps (cm)	Length of B steps (cm)	Number of trials	Number of times significant segregation indicated by		Dispersion ratio significant
						S	A	
(a)	20	20	0.5	10	14	14	14	14
(b)	20	20	2.5	10	27	25	27	27
(c)	20	20	5.0	10	27	5	20	27
(d)	20	20	7.5	10	27	0	0	17

significant, but the *S* coefficient is not and the Runs test only suggests a significant difference between the two distributions on one axis. For types 76 and 69 the *A* index is not significant at the 95% level. Neither the Runs test nor the *S* coefficient provide significant results. For the distributions of types 67 and 69 the *A* index of 0.96 is not significant, but the dispersion ratio of 1.44 is. The Runs test produced non-significant results. In these cases then, and especially in the case of the distributions in fig. 3, the results obtained from the *A* index seem more reasonable when compared with a visual assessment. Added to the results of the simulation tests described above, these are favourable findings for the index being suggested here.

Discussion

It is necessary to outline the way in which the *A* index might be used in practice. Such an outline is appropriate because the nature of archaeological data rules out the usual procedure of setting up hypotheses based on one set of evidence and testing it on other 'samples' collected from the same 'population'. Rarely is the collection of further data immediately possible in archaeology. In view of this difficulty, the *A* index can be used in two main ways. First, it can be used as a measure for the comparison of the associations between pairs of large numbers of distributions. In Bergmann's (1970) study of the Early Bronze Age in northwest Germany, 112 distributions of different artifact types were obtained from one phase. The *A* index could be used as a relative measure to see which pairs of distributions were more or less segregated.

A second use of the *A* index concerns the null hypothesis that two distributions are located independently. In this case, it would be possible to begin with the general hypothesis that the A and B points had an equal (0.5) chance of locating in either of two regions. If it proves impossible to reject this general null hypothesis, then it may be felt that no further analysis along these lines is justified. But if the null hypothesis is rejected, then it may be of interest to set up alternative hypotheses. These hypotheses could be based on one category of the data, and tested on other categories. For example, in the Early Bronze Age example mentioned above, 75% of each specific weapon type might be observed to fall in one or other of two adjacent regions. Based on these data, the null hypothesis could be set up that cultural and distance constraints resulted in a 0.75 probability that any particular artifact type would be found in one region, and a 0.25 probability that it would be found in the other region. This hypothesis could then be tested against other artifact types (for example, ornaments, pottery types) to see whether similar patterning occurred. This type of approach is necessary because the alternative, of setting up hypotheses based on one set of data and then testing them against the same data, does not provide an independent test. The use of the chi-squared test to compare observed and predicted values in the two regions would also be less satisfactory because this would be a non-spatial test.

The *A* index thus provides a method for examining different hypotheses about spatial association patterns. In particular, the facts that the A coefficient is not scale dependent, and that it makes greater use of the information available than, for example, the *S* coefficient, result in a greater sensitivity to distinctions between distributions of points which originate from different sources. The *A* coefficient would thus seem particularly valuable for testing the types of hypothesis in which the archaeologist is often interested, and for dealing with the usually sparse archaeological data. Indeed, the main value of this index for the archaeologist, is that it has been developed specifically for archaeological situations and for problems particular to archaeology.

Fig. 2. The distributions of Bronze Age artifact types in the Middle Danube area of southeast Europe. Types 76 (○), 67 (●) and 69 (▽). Source: Hänsel 1968.

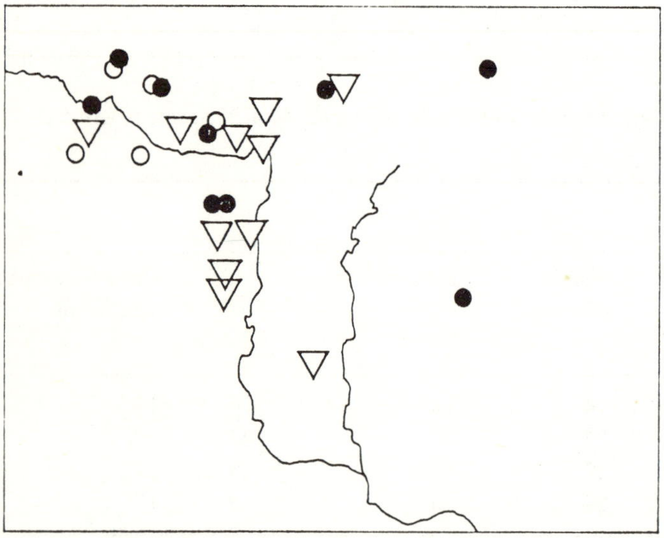

Fig. 3. The distribution of types 128 (●) and 76 (○). Source: Hänsel 1968.

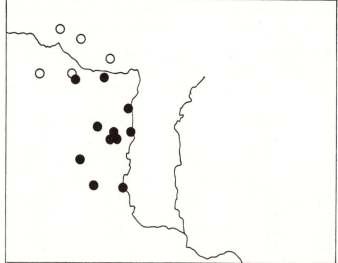

A further advantage of the *A* coefficient is that the data collected in its calculation allow further study of the distributions. For example, it is possible to examine the ratio between $\bar{r}_{AA}$ and $\bar{r}_{BB}$. For two randomly generated distributions within the same area, $\bar{r}_{AA}/\bar{r}_{BB}$ should approximate 1. Tables 1*b* to 7*b* show the degree to which this *dispersion ratio* varies from 1.0 for simulations conducted at different values of *m* and *n*. The simulations are the same as those used for the calculation of tables 1*a* to 7*a*. The limits, within which 90% and 95% of the simulated results occur are given. The dispersion ratio provides an additional way of examining the difference between two distributions. For the simulated distributions summarised in table 9, the dispersion ratio is efficient at recognising a difference between distributions resulting from different spatial processes.

The information needed to assess the *A* index might be used for yet further study of the distributions. The average distance from any one A site, for example, to all other A sites is calculated. Those A sites with greatest average distances to other sites are, in one sense, more isolated than the others. This type of information may provide a useful comparison with data on the cultural similarity between sites, and may help to explain why some sites are less or more similar to the others in terms of their cultural make-up.

Perhaps the main disadvantage of the *A* index is that its calculation is fairly time consuming. Use of a computer may be necessary when many distributions of large numbers of points are being compared. It should also be noted that significance levels for the index have been assessed empirically and have no theoretical basis. Thus the tables are only provided to illustrate the behaviour of the index. Irregular runs of figures often occur in the tables, so that if great precision is demanded the tables should be used with some care. It may frequently be thought preferable to carry out additional simulations in order to ascertain the likelihood of obtaining the observed values of the index.

Acknowledgements
We should like to thank Phil Rees, Peter Diggle and Clive Orton for discussing this work in its early stages.

References

Bergmann, J. (1970) *Die ältere Bronzezeit Nordwestdeutschlands*, Elwert, Marburg

Greig-Smith, P. (1964) *Quantitative Plant Ecology*, Methuen, London

Hänsel, B. (1968) *Beitrage zur Chronologie der mittleren Bronzezeit im Karpathenbecken* (Beitrage zur Ur- und Fruhgeschischtichen Archaologie des Mittelmeer-Kulturraumes, Nos. 7 and 8), Rudolf Habelt, Bonn

Hodder, I. & Orton, C. (1976) *Spatial analysis in archaeology*, Cambridge University Press

Pielou, E.C. (1961) 'Segregation and symmetry in two species populations as studied by nearest neighbour methods', *Journal of Ecology* 49: 255–69

Pielou, E.C. (1969) *An Introduction to Mathematical Ecology*, Wiley, New York

Chapter 10

**Archaeological prospecting:
kriging and simulation**
Ezra B. W. Zubrow and
John W. Harbaugh

Introduction

Archaeological exploration can conveniently be classified into two contrasting categories, namely, sampling and
prospecting. There has been a tendency to sample systematically but to prospect intuitively. The literature on archaeological sampling methodology is voluminous. In recent years
attention has been given to improving surveying and excavation
techniques. Books (Heizer & Graham 1967) as well as numerous articles (Sjoberg 1976; Steponatis & Brain 1976) have been
written on field techniques. Today, virtually all archaeologists
are aware of various systematic sampling techniques, even if
they do not use them. Not only are there technical pro-
fessional discussions (Mueller 1974) but information on
sampling strategies is an integral part of elementary courses
in archaeology (Redman 1974; Watson, LeBlanc & Redman
1971; Fagan 1974; and Hole & Heizer 1973). On the other
hand, archaeological prospecting has been almost totally
ignored in the scholarly literature, while it probably makes up
the vast majority of the practice. Instead, one finds popular
articles in general magazines about ways to find archaeological
sites.

To be clear about the terminology let us contrast archaeological sampling with archaeological prospecting. Sampling
may be defined as occurring when we survey or excavate part
of a region or a site according to a specific sampling design.
Our rationale for sampling may be that the area or site is too

large or expensive to survey or excavate in its entirety. Thus, sampling strategies are motivated by the wish to maximise the information obtained, while minimising the labour and cost expended. In other words, one of the criteria is the so-called 'efficiency criterion'. A second criterion consists of our desire to obtain a representative sample of the entire population which we may describe as the 'totality concept'.

By contrast, we shall define archaeological prospecting as the search for a desired archaeological goal, such as a particular site, a particular culture or a particular set of artifacts. We hope to 'strike it rich' and find a new 'Troy' or 'Pyramid of the Sun'. In archaeological prospecting the efficiency criterion also holds for we generally will not wish to survey or excavate an entire area or site. But, the totality criterion is irrelevant. We are not looking for a representative sample of the total. Rather, we may seek only the oldest, the latest, the biggest, the most important or quintessential example of our quest with a minimum of effort.

Although archaeologists are looking for the archaeological 'motherlode' and wish to hit 'the big strike', archaeological prospecting is still at the intuitive level. Most of us are no more sophisticated than the old grizzled, sourdough prospector complete with burro, picks, shovel and grubstake. We follow 'local information', tradition, and our 'archaeological noses' after leads and hunches. Prospecting, however, can take advantage of search strategies which have been developed by mining companies where there are strong economic incentives. On the other hand, we should not forget that prospecting methodology has been a conservative field in which innovations have been more often rejected than accepted. Nor should we forget that the wildcat oil speculators drilling on hunch alone have discovered a significant proportion of oil fields in the United States, and that many important archaeological sites have been found by luck and intuition. What is new should not be accepted simply because it is new, Kriging methodology included.

This chapter explores the application of Kriging methodology in archaeological prospecting strategy using both simulated data and real data as illustrations. In the past decade a branch of statistical methodology known as 'regionalised variable' theory has developed. 'Kriging' is an aspect of this theory. Regionalised variable theory received much of its early impetus in the work of D.G. Krige of Johannesburg, South Africa. Krige's work involved methods of statistically forecasting gold values in the gold-bearing conglomerates of the Witwatersrand mining district which surrounds Johannesburg. Matheron (1965, 1969, 1970, 1971) and his associates in France have generalised and extended the theory of regionalised variables in a series of classic and difficult papers, which have diffused only slowly to the English speaking world. The name Kriging was applied to the family of techniques to honour Krige. Blais and Carlier (1968) extended the technique to changes in ore content in a mineralised ore body and Huijbregts and Matheron (1971) treated porosity within a petroleum reservoir. In the 1970s work in the United States has been centred at the Kansas Geological Survey, where optimal mapping techniques have been applied to petroleum geology (Olea & Davis 1977).

Various computer programs for Kriging have been developed, including Delfiner's 'BLUEPACK', Olea's 'SEMIVAR' and Sampson's 'SURFACE II'. Kriging, coupled with computerised contouring, is timely for adaptation to problems that involve estimation or interpolation of values between data points. For example, at Stanford University Professor Paul Switzer, a statistician, is applying Kriging to problems of air pollution, Professor L. Cavalli-Sforza to gene maps, and we to archaeological prospecting. Kriging involves the estimation or interpolation of values between data points. It can be adapted as a prospecting technique in which data obtained in an initial phase of exploration are interpolated or extrapolated to areas in which exploration has not taken place.

Review of Kriging
Kriging is a method of interpolation employing moving averages and involves estimation of the values of a spatially distributed variable as well as assessment of the error associated with the estimates. In turn, Kriging involves the measurement of the degree of interdependence of a random variable as distributed over a geographic region.

Such a variable is termed a regionalised variable. It varies from geographic location to geographic location with apparent continuity, but its changes cannot be totally represented by a deterministic mathematical function. Furthermore, because of its geographic dependence and the spatial relationships of the sample observation on the variable, replicated experiments are not feasible because every outcome is unique. As Olea (1972) points out, a regionalised variable may be characterised as exhibiting (1) values that are partially dependent upon geographic location, (2) an average spatial continuity (see note 1), (3) a random or stochastic component which has no spatial continuity.

Regionalised variable theory can be applied to natural phenomena as diverse as the thickness of Alaskan coal seams, the amount of gold per ton of ore, and wheat production per acre. It can also be applied to cultural phenomena such as the number of archaeological sites per square kilometre, and thickness variations of cultural deposits in archaeological sites. Indeed many archaeological variables can be expressed as regionalised variables. Examples include variations in the number of sites per square mile, the number of artifacts per quadrat within a site, and the number of rooms per site. These variables change laterally in a manner which is partially dependent upon their location, but none may be subject to replicable experimentation. The lateral changes in a regionalised variable may be isotropic (i.e. variation is not dependent on particular directions) or may be anisotropic, showing pronounced differences in different directions. For example, certain middens or tells may be isotropic, as a result of the cultural conditions of deposition as well as a result of their topographic and geologic location. But the density of cliff houses or fishing sites in a given region may be strongly anisotropic, reflecting the elongated nature of canyons, rivers, or beaches.

Kriging theory

The concept of Kriging can be best understood if we have a series of points on a regular grid, and have measured a regionalised variable at each point. Later, we shall relax the requirement of a regular grid but for the moment let the points be denoted by X_i and the values at the points by Y_i. We can imagine that the value at any point on the grid is related to the values at other points, but that the influence of points nearby is greater than points at a distance. Furthermore, this 'spatial' influence may be different in different directions (i.e., anisotropic). To express this relationship, we can define vectors, **h**, which have specific directions, for example, east—west, or north—south. The relationship between points at a specified distance apart along a vector can be expressed by a measure of covariance.

It can be argued that a measure of covariance exists at all distances along the direction of vector **h**. But, we are limited to data from our grid points. If the observations are regularly spaced, we compute not only the covariance for all the adjacent points, but also from the points separated by some regular multiple of the grid spacing. For example, if test pits are placed every 100 feet we can compute the covariance between points separated by whole multiples of 100 feet.

Since we denoted the value of Y at point X_i by Y_i, the new point will be $X_i + j$ and the new value $Y_i + j$, where the interval j is some whole multiple of $\triangle j$, the interval between immediately adjacent points (e.g. 100 feet in our archaeological example).

We can compute the 'semivariance' $\gamma(\mathbf{h})$ which is defined as half the variance of the difference, $(Y_{i+j} - Y_i)$ in the direction **h**.

$$\gamma(\mathbf{h}) = 1/(2n) \sum_{i=1}^{n} (Y_{i+j} - Y_i)^2$$

where n is the number of pairs of points treated in this manner. Variance may be defined in the usual manner as the sum of the squared deviations from the mean divided by the number of observations, less one.

The semivariance will generally range from zero, when **h** is equal to zero, up to a maximum value equal to the variance of the overall set of data. These relationships may be graphed as a semivariogram. For a regionalised variable this is thus an empirical function and is obtained by plotting the semivariance values that correspond to different spacings of points. The distances between points along **h** in the grid are whole multiples of $\triangle j$. Fig. 1 is a hypothetical semivariogram. As **h** increases, the semivariance increases until it plateaus as it approaches the overall variance, at **L**. Beyond **L** the difference, ϵ, between the semivariance and the variance is negligible.

If it is difficult to visualise how a semivariogram is constructed, the following illustrations should help. Consider a grid of points, two rows of which are shown in fig. 2a. The

values of the semivariance for a particular direction, **h**, can be calculated, using the above expression. First, we sum the squared differences between all pairs of observed values which are adjacent along **h**. We calculate the semivariance for that particular distance increment in that particular direction. Then we increase the distance increment in that direction, and repeat the process (fig. 2c, d). Thus, for the specific direction there will be a series of values of the semivariance, $\gamma(\mathbf{h})$, for different values of **h**.

Even though the regionalised variable is continuous, we cannot conveniently compute semivariance at all points along the semivariogram, and must settle for points of regular increments of distance. By graphing them, however, we obtain the form of the continuous semivariogram. We should note, however, that there is a boundary problem at the ends of each row of the grid. Values from some points cannot be used (fig. 2e). When the regularity assumption of the grid is dropped and one has irregularly spaced observations, a search procedure and a grouping procedure are used to collect observations at equivalent distances from each other in order to calculate the semivariance.

A semivariogram can be computed for observations arranged in a regular sequence along a single row or traverse. If a rectangular grid of sample points is available, semivariograms can be calculated readily in four directions, as shown in fig. 3. The incremental distance values, $\triangle j$, will differ with the orientation. With a square grid, the $\triangle j$ in the two diagonal directions will be $\sqrt{2}$ times the value parallel to the edges of the squares. The distribution of values of $\gamma(\mathbf{h})$ in the semivariogram will be affected as illustrated in fig. 4. If the regionalised variable is isotropic, the semivariogram will have the same form regardless of direction, and if it is anisotropic, the semivariogram will differ according to direction.

Fig. 1. Semivariogram, or graph of semivariance, $\gamma(\mathbf{h})$, versus distance along **h**. L is the vector beyond which the difference, ϵ, between semivariance and variance (horizontal dashed line) is negligible. (After Olea 1972)

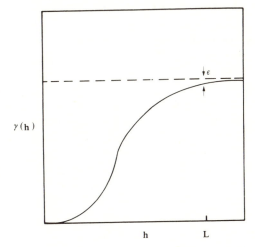

Fig. 2. Calculations for constructing a semivariogram. (*a*) The grid system, **h** horizontal; (*b*)–(*d*) calculating the squared differences between successive pairs of observed values with (*b*) $j = \triangle j$: $(b - a)^2$, $(c - b)^2$, $(d - c)^2$, ...; (*c*) $j = 2\triangle j$: $(c - a)^2$, $(d - b)^2$, $(e - c)^2$, ...; (*d*) $j = 3\triangle j$: $(d - a)^2$, $(e - b)^2$, $(f - c)^2$, ...; (*e*) dropping points at the end of a row: with $j = 3\triangle j$ $(i - f)^2$ is the last difference which can be calculated for the first row.

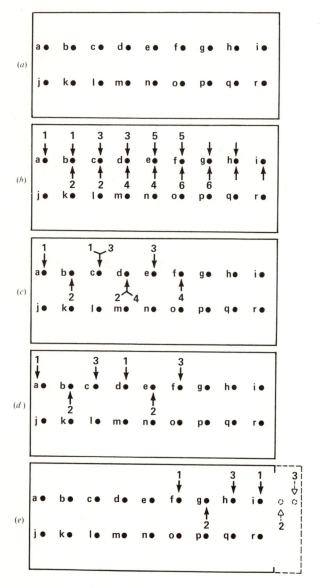

Fig. 3. Example of a grid which readily yields semivariograms in four directions.

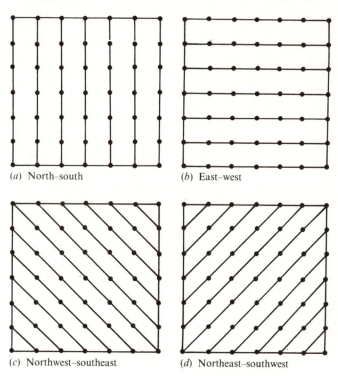

(*a*) North–south   (*b*) East–west

(*c*) Northwest–southeast   (*d*) Northeast–southwest

Fig. 4. Hypothetical semivariograms for two directions at 45° with respect to each other. The regionalised variable is slightly anisotropic. Though the regionalised variable is continuous, the semivariance can be calculated and plotted conveniently only at regular intervals.

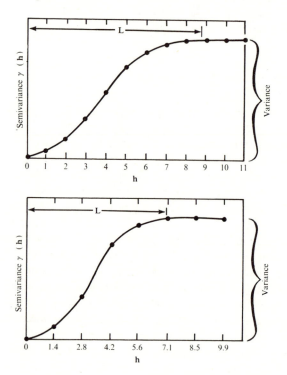

Interpreting semivariograms

A semivariogram describes the behaviour of a regionalised variable. It shows the influence about the sample points and in turn the continuity of the variable through space. For example, let us assume that a semivariogram has been plotted and that the regionalised variable is isotropic. From a sample at a particular point, the values in adjacent areas can be forecast statistically. Radiating away from the particular point our ability to forecast the values will decrease as the semivariance increases. Finally, at distance **L**, our ability to predict the values is no longer influenced by the specific value at a known point (or points). Instead, our predictions depend solely upon the overall variance.

If the regionalised variable is anisotropic, as is the case in many cultural deposits, the anisotropy can be represented by a family of semivariograms for different directions (fig. 5). Fig. 5b shows two hypothetical semivariograms that exhibit slight anisotropy. Although the shapes of the two semivariograms differ, they plateau at the same variance. Thus, they reflect the properties of a regionalised variable that is anisotropic in certain respects, but is isotropic with respect to its overall variance.

Semivariograms provide sensitive measures of the spatial variability of a regionalised variable. Fig. 6 contrasts a variety of hypothetical semivariograms. Fig. 6a illustrates a regionalised variable that exhibits a high degree of continuity, and a strong correlation at distances close to a sample point. In other words, the semivariance is low locally, but it increases rapidly at intermediate distances, as indicated by the increasingly steep slope of the curve until an inflection point is reached, beyond which the semivariance approaches the variance. Fig. 6b is a semivariogram in which the semivariance increases almost linearly with distance from a sample point, with only a gradual decline in the rate of increase of the semivariance with distance. As in fig. 6a, however, the regionalised variable is

continuous. These semivariograms might typify variables such as thickness of cultural deposits or density of artifacts in middens, activity areas, or early man sites.

Fig. 6c is a semivariogram of a discontinuous regionalised variable. The fact that the semivariance is not zero at the origin (i.e. immediately adjacent to the sample points) is an indication of its discontinuous nature. Cultural deposits may be discontinuous. For example, if we assume that the correlations from test pit to test pit are discontinuous, some cultural deposits that are highly lenticular would yield semivariograms that exhibit discontinuity and might be similar to that of fig. 6c.

Regions with spatially discontinuous sites or sites with discontinuous structures, such as temples or marketplaces, should also yield semivariograms similar to that of fig. 6c, unless the variable is regarded as a continuous regionalised variable. Fig. 6d is a theoretical extreme, illustrating a variable that has no lateral continuity. For example if fig. 6d was the semivariogram of an actual cultural deposit's thickness, it would signify that the deposit's thickness could be predicted only as a random variable. While its mean and variance might be specified, the presence or absence of specific test-pit data would not be useful in forecasting thicknesses at other locations, regardless of their proximity to existing test pits.

Fig. 6e is a semivariogram of a regionalised variable whose semivariance rises steeply from zero at zero distance, and then abruptly plateaus. An archaeological example of a variable whose behaviour is similar to fig. 6e may be provided by examining the density of domestic artifacts within a house (the area that is sharply defined geographically) and the density of domestic artifacts outside the house.

Regional drift

As seen above, continuity and the degree of anisotropism are characteristics displayed by semivariograms. A third

Fig. 5. Semivariograms that reflect anisotropic regionalized variables.
(a) strongly anisotropic regionalised variable in which the variances differ according to direction;
(b) mildly anisotropic regionalized variable in which overall variance does not differ with direction. (After Olea 1972)

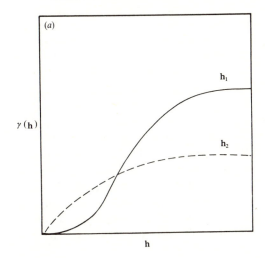

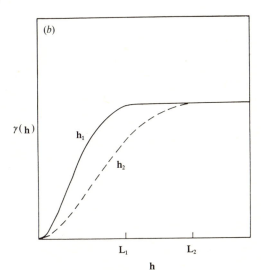

characteristic which must be considered for Kriging and for semivariograms is that of 'regional drift'. There are two parts to a regionalised variable, the 'drift' or regional tendency, and the residuals or local variation. Drift consists of the broad smooth changes over the field of the regional variable, or the wide, gross variation rather than local variation. It is the regional trend whose geographic expanse is much greater than the expanse, **L**, of the semivariogram.

Drift is to be expected in the variation of some archaeological sites. Local variations will often be superimposed on the larger regional trend. This is the case particularly for large archaeological sites which are large towns or small cities. For example, we would expect the density of structures to decrease toward the margins of an urban site. Drift may be removed by well-established methods, such as fitting a low-degree polynomial regression surface (popularly known as a trend surface) to the data employing the least-squares criterion.

Kriging and SURFACE II

Kriging incorporates the assumption of spatial autocorrelation, as it involves estimating the value of the regionalised variable at a location from its values at adjacent locations. The simplest form is called punctual Kriging and requires that the data be (1) collected on a regularly spaced grid, (2) stationary (i.e. the residuals are used after the drift has been

taken out). In addition to punctual Kriging there are two more general forms of Kriging. The most important comparative attributes of the three types are shown below in table 1.

Table 1. *Attributes of different forms of Kriging*

Type of Kriging	Data necessarily collected on regularly spaced grid	Data must show stationarity
Punctual Kriging	yes	yes
Kriging	no	yes
Universal Kriging	no	no

In this chapter we will use universal Kriging. It will produce the most accurate possible estimates of the regionalised variable. From irregularly spaced points the predicted values of the variable are generated at the nodes of a regular grid which makes up a surface. These surfaces are then mapped as optimal predictions. One of the weaknesses of Kriging is that an experienced observer may be able to eyeball several variables interfering with the homogeneity and distance rules more efficiently and effectively than the technique. In practice Kriging requires the proper selection of several parameters, including the slope of the semivariogram as well as increasing computational complexity. However, even with naive estimates it can do no worse than other estimating techniques such as trend analysis. According to Walden the Kriging algorithm consistently gives the highest surface correlations and the lowest error measures of any method. After the drift has been removed, a weighted moving average equation is designed to estimate the true real values of the regionalised variable at successive points on a grid. It uses the semivariance to do part of the weighting and to minimise the potential effect of the relatively high variance of sample values.

Imagine we have to estimate for a point on a map surrounded by other points with known values. Archaeologists might think of a partially excavated building where some rooms have been excavated and some have not. They know the number of artifacts in the excavated rooms and wish to estimate the number of artifacts in a room which has not been excavated. Probably most of us have even used a simple distance-weighted average to develop an estimate for the unexcavated room. We simply divided the number of artifacts in each known room by the distance of that room from the room to be estimated, averaged the values, and multiplied by the average distance of the rooms from the unexcavated room. We will use the appropriate semivariance values for different vectors **h** to help weight the values. Paraphrasing Davis (1973), if we are given n points around a grid point Z to be estimated,

Fig. 6. Different types of semivariograms. See text for explanation. (After Olea 1972)

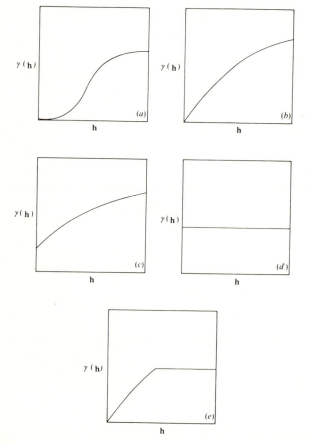

the weights attached to points are determined by solving the system of equations of the form:

$$\sum_{j=1}^{n} a_j \gamma_{(X_i - X_j)} = \gamma_{(X_i - Z)} - \lambda$$

where $\gamma_{(X_i - X_j)}$ represents the semivariance at a given displacement **h**, the distance and direction from X_i to X_j. $\gamma_{(X_i - Z)}$ is the semivariance between a point X_i and the point to be estimated Z. There are n such equations and they can be transformed into matrix form. There is an additional equation which simply states that the weights a_j must sum to 1. The regionalised variable is then estimated by the moving average equation with the recently derived weights. Clearly, as one increases the number of dimensions (usually two (Davis 1973) and often three (Clark 1977)), relaxes the regularity constraints (Olea 1972), and moves from punctual to universal Kriging, the mathematics become considerably more complex.

Until recently Kriging and automatic contouring have been far too difficult a programming problem to tempt the occasional user into actually contemplating its use. This has recently been changed by the development of SURFACE II. This is a graphics package written by Sampson for the creation, analysis and display of spatially distributed data. It makes Kriging a potential tool for the typical archaeologist who has reasonable computer facilities at his disposal. One could justifiably say that SURFACE II is the Social Science Statistics Package (SPSS) and Biomedical Computer Programs (BMD) of computer graphics for the earth sciences (see note 2).

Simulations of archaeological prospecting: synthetic and real data

The theoretical arguments on simulation have already been debated in this volume and will not be discussed here except to indicate briefly our rationale for simulating prospecting strategies. Simulation is the process of conducting experiments on a model of reality in lieu of either (1) direct experimentation with reality itself or (2) direct analytical solutions. Simulators rationalise its use because of the complexity of the problems and data manipulation, the costs of actual experimentation, and the difficulty of formulating validity tests.

We will simulate because we cannot experiment with reality, for archaeological sites are not replicable nor do we expect to be able to find a single analytical solution to prospecting problems. Experimentation on reality may not only cause site damage, it is too expensive. There are numerous complexities which we also wish to avoid. These include, to name only a few examples, problems in the definition of a site, problems in areal and cultural equivalence and problems in the quality of field work. Our simulations will be simulations in the broadest sense of the word. We will pretend to prospect on synthetic and real models of data in order to ascertain the utility of our prospecting strategy.

To simulate real problems of archaeological prospecting, we will ask an imaginary archaeologist to make prospecting decisions about surveying different synthetic and real areas on small amounts of data and compare the results with reality. Although we have limited ourselves to archaeological survey, the same techniques are applicable to site excavation. The differences as previously mentioned are primarily a question of scale.

We will consider four areas — two synthetic and two real. The two synthetic areas are each 64 km^2. This size was chosen because an area of 8 km by 8 km is well within the range expected to be considered by a small to medium size expedition over a three to four summer field effort. In the first area we have created a stream which meanders through the area in two slow turns. Archaeological sites are actually located along the banks of the stream in a haphazard, but not random pattern. This, however, is not known to the archaeologist prior to the survey. The second synthetic area is a uniform, almost undifferentiated plateau in which there are two distributions of archaeological sites. One follows a random, the other a systematic, geographic pattern. These patterns are also not known to the archaeologist.

The two real areas are the archaeological zone in Guanajuato, Mexico called Cañada del Alfaro and the Hay Hollow valley in east-central Arizona. Zubrow directed an archaeological expedition to Mexico during the summers of 1972 and 1973. Cañada del Alfaro is a large zone containing 72 site-structures in 24.5 km^2 which date from approximately AD 350. It is located on the 'northern frontier' of the major Mesoamerican cultures and temporally is at the transition, AD 200–400 between the pre-classic and the classic periods (Zubrow & Willard 1974). The sites were distributed as shown in fig. 7.

Fig. 7. The distribution of archaeological sites in the Cañada del Alfaro zone. A, altar; B, modern building; P, plaza; E ecological sample; numbers are site locations (there are no numbers 70 and 72).

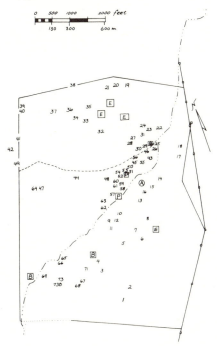

Zubrow (1975) also worked in the Hay Hollow valley between 1967 and 1971 holding positions ranging from field foreman to associate director of the Southwestern Archaeological Expedition. An area 13.5 km^2 was surveyed in 1967. This survey which also covered 100% of the area made up what was called the central survey and was shaped in the form of a snubbed nose triangle (fig. 8). 277 sites were found of which 198 were datable using diagnostic ceramics and radiocarbon dating. The valley was located in the Mogollon culture area and contained sites ranging from 1000 BC to AD 1450.

Let us consider one of the synthetic areas, the two real areas, and then return to the other synthetic area. Our archaeologist has some information about the first area. He has a topographic map, a general idea of the cultures, and of the types of sites which may occur. For example, he knows that most sites range in size from 9 m^2 to 7000 m^2. His first step in applying Kriging to prospecting is to lay a grid over his survey area. The size of the grid can be arbitrary but recognising the size of the sites, he decides on a square grid of 6400 cells. This is sufficiently large that most sites will fit into the

area and sufficiently small that it allows for a reasonable degree of locational resolution.

The simulation begins with our archaeologist following the usual surveying procedure. He collects local leads, examines what he believes are likely places, covers the areas *en route* to his chosen location. After a single field season, he collects the survey data then plots the known sites as well as the areas in which he knows there are no sites on his grid. Let us assume that he has covered 12.5% of the total area but not in a regular or systematic fashion. Using Sampson's (1975) SURFACE II programs for the Kriging computation and our own parameter estimates, we can Krige the data to simulate the prospecting strategy. Fig. 9 shows the output from this analysis consisting of a three-dimensional representation of a contour map with the altitude contour lines indicating the expected number of sites per unit area. A two-dimensional contour map may also be the output.

Our archaeologist's optimal prospecting strategy is to look at the areas where there are indications of a large number of sites in a small area — high density areas. In fig. 9 the *x* and

Fig. 8. The distribution of archaeological sites in Hay Hollow valley.

Microhabitats

I	Top of mesa
II	Sides of mesa
III	Alluvial fans
IV	Second sandstone terrace
V	First sandstone terrace
VI	Bottomlands
☐	Ecological quadrats
•	Sites

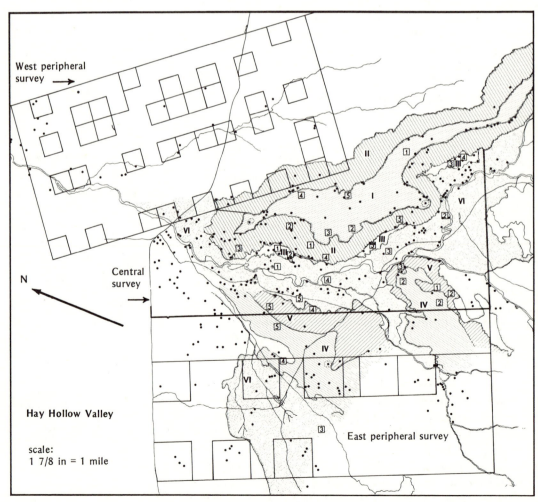

West peripheral survey →

Central survey →

N

Hay Hollow Valley

scale:
1 7/8 in = 1 mile

East peripheral survey

y axes are the geographic axes corresponding to our grid system, while the *z*, or vertical, axis represents the expected number of sites per unit area. The scales of the three axes can be set independently. (We have set *x* and *y* equal and have scaled *z* so as to accentuate the contours.) The three-dimensional representation gives the prospector an 'at a glance' view of the relative proportions of expected sites over the area. Thus, he can make decisions about survey logistics and strategy. The best prospecting strategy is to look for sites where Kriging indicates an expected high density or, in other words, on 'the contour mountains' and to avoid the 'valleys' where there are relatively few sites.

Let us imagine that instead of surveying 12.5% of the area, the archaeologist surveys 50% and analyses the output which results from Kriging the available data. Fig. 10 is the 50% analysis shown in the three-dimensional representation. Several conclusions are inescapable. First, if we followed the prospecting strategy suggested by the 12.5% analysis, we would find the majority of the sites indicated by the 50% analysis in the early stages of the survey. The 'mountains', or high density areas, are located in the same places. This impression is confirmed by the comparison of sets of predictions with each other and with the real synthetic data. Comparing the 12.5% and the 50% strategies, 79% of the total area has corresponding and corroborating predictions. In other words, only 21% of the area has predictions for sites from one but not the other strategy.

Secondly, if we follow the 12.5% strategy, beginning the prospecting at those localities with high predictions, and subsequently prospecting those with lower predictions, all of the sites are found within the first 22% of the area covered. The actual proportion of area that would need to be covered is between 22% and 34.5% of the total area. The 34.5% figure consists of the 22% necessary to find all of the sites, plus the 12.5% already invested surveying to do the Kriging analysis.

Of course, we might expect that a certain proportion of the archaeologist's pre-Kriging survey, the 12.5%, would also be part of the 22% and thus would not need to be resurveyed. Arbitrarily we may estimate the amount that has been surveyed previously by averaging the initial and the post-Kriging survey. This is equivalent to suggesting that one half of the pre-Kriging survey would on the average be included in the post-Kriging analysis and thus would not need to be repeated. In any case, we would not have to survey more than 34.5% of the total area to find all the sites.

Thirdly, by increasing the proportion of the total area surveyed, the numerical and geographical resolution of the predictions are more refined. By the latter we mean that the predictions are more closely located to a specific geographic unit. If our archaeologist has data from 50% of the area prior to Kriging, he can find all the sites after Kriging by surveying 6% of the total area. The analogous minimal, maximal, and average figures to the previous survey are 50%, 56% and 53%. In fact, as the pre-Kriging area surveyed increases, the resolution provided by the Krige improves faster than the degree of numerical predictive ability. Less area needs to be surveyed to get the positive results indicated by finding a large proportion of the sites. The results of these surveys and the surveys which follow are shown in table 2.

Now let us consider simulating a survey of an actual area near Guanajuato, Mexico. First, however, let us describe the way the area was actually surveyed and then show the simulated prospecting strategies and how they could have affected the surveys if these were to be done after running our series of Kriging analyses. The area near Guanajuato was divided into two geographic subdivisions. During each of the field seasons, a field crew surveyed 100% of the area assigned to it. Each crew consisted of half of the staff (3 or 4 advanced graduate students from the United States and Mexico) and 10 or more hired workmen from the local area with considerable if vari-

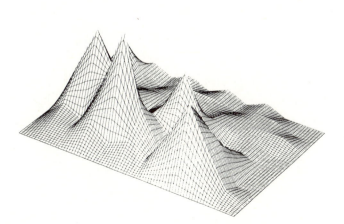

Fig. 9. A three-dimensional representation of the number of sites per unit in the first synthetic area. These simulated prospecting estimates are based on Kriging irregularly collected data from 12.5% of the area. The sites appear to follow the meandering stream.

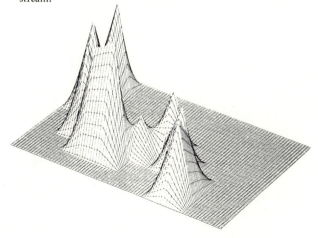

Fig. 10. A three-dimensional representation of the number of sites per unit in the first synthetic area. The simulated prospecting estimates are based on Kriging irregularly collected data from 50% of the area. The sites appear to follow the meandering stream.

Table 2. *A comparison of some simulated prospecting strategies based on a variety of Kriging analyses*

Locale	Area non-systematically covered prior to Kriging %	Area which needs to be surveyed after Kriging to find all sites %	Total area which needs to be surveyed % min.	max.	Average %	Amount of overlap between differing Krige analyses %
Synthetic stream	12.5	22	22	34.5	28.2	
	50	6	50	56	53	79
Guanajuato	12.5	—	—	—	—	
	25	49	49	74	62	
	50	34	50	84	67	82
Hay Hollow	12.5	—	—	—	—	
	37.5	45	45	82.5	63.7	
	50	29	50	79	64.5	89

able archaeological experience. Beginning at the eastern edge of the survey area (fig. 7), they formed a line 55 m long. They began systematically to survey the entire area for archaeological sites. Each time they found a site, its location was plotted using a transit. The location was then recorded on maps and aerial photographs. A systematic sample of surface materials was analysed and a set of site record forms was completed. This effort consumed 720 man days per season and was half of our total labour investment in the project.

Let us now consider three different prospecting strategies based on Kriging simulated at three different points during the field work. The first, fig. 11 is a three-dimensional representation of the Kriging analysis and is based on 12.5% of the survey area. The second and the third are based on 25% (fig. 12) and 50% (fig. 13) of the total areas. None of these surveys needs to be regular or systematic in the sense that they are a regular gridwork or a systematic coverage of the area.

Examining fig. 11 closely, we see that there is not sufficient geographic resolution to give the archaeologist much prospecting help. Almost all of the area is incorporated in the two major 'mountains'. Thus, our Krige predictions suggest that almost everywhere there will be sites. Further, except for the decrease in density of sites towards the sides, there are no significant trends to help in prospecting. However, in figs. 12 and 13, the 25% and 50% strategies, we see major improvements. Visual comparison shows the increasing resolution from fig. 11 through 12 to 13. Comparing fig. 12 with fig. 13, we see that 82% of the area has corresponding and corroborating

predictions — only 18% of the area predicted to have sites by one analysis is not confirmed by the other.

Given that we have actually surveyed both areas, we can calculate the proportion of area to be surveyed using our simulated strategy to find all the sites. Using the 25% strategy (fig. 12), by surveying high density predictions first followed by lower prediction areas, all sites except one would be found in the first 49% of the area surveyed. Using the 50% strategy (fig. 13) all the sites would be found in the first 34% of the area surveyed.

Fig. 11. A three-dimensional representation of the number of sites per unit in Cañada del Alfaro in Guanajuato Mexico. These simulated prospecting estimates are based on Kriging irregularly collected data from 12.5% of the area.

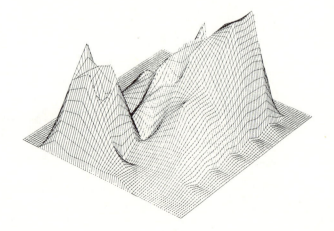

Our actual results are as good as those of the first synthetic example. The 25% strategy requires from 49% to 74% (49 + 25) of the area surveyed to discover 71 of the total 72 sites. Since a total of 1440 man days were required to survey the complete area, given our prospecting strategy we would expect to invest from 706 to 1066 man days on finding all the sites depending upon the amount of survey which is redundant. The best estimate is 886 man days (average), a net saving of 38%. One advantage of Kriging may be the rapidity of success. For example, if one follows the prospecting strategy for 25%, we find 54% of the sites (39) in the first 17% of the area. Taking into account the amount of area which probably already has been surveyed, it is reasonable to expect that more than half of the sites would be found in the first 33% of the area surveyed and at most, it would require no more than 42% of the area. However, this rapidity is not always the case as is shown in table 3 which shows data from some of the surveys on the rapidity of finding sites using Kriging.

We should note that the use of the Kriging analysis of the larger survey area only marginally improves the archaeologist's results. To find all the sites, we need to survey 50 to 84% of the area, depending on the amount of area necessary to resurvey. This requires from 720 to 1210 person days (an average of 965 man days), a net gain of 33%. Although these results may not seem so impressive, a brief reconsideration of exploration strategy demonstrates how significant the improvements are.

When we began our field season in Guanajuato, we decided to divide our time equally between surveying and excavation, for we had no idea initially what the range of sites was and where the sites were located. After part of the first field season, however, we continued the 100% survey for we had no way of knowing whether we had found a small or a large proportion of the archaeological sites. If we could have predicted that we had already surveyed half the sites, we would have deemed that sufficient and would then have put

Table 3. *The rapidity of finding archaeological sites using simulated prospecting strategies based upon Kriging*

Locale	Area surveyed prior to Kriging %	Area surveyed after Kriging assuming no redundancy %	Total sites found %
Guanajuato	25	17	54
Hay Hollow	37	23	50
Synthetic random	50	2	20
		30	40
patterned	12.5	13	23
		29	37

our effort into excavation. Even if we had to survey 74% of the area to get 71 of 72 sites, the saving of 25% of the surveying labour would have allowed us to increase the excavation effort so that we could sample more than one site. In fact, we could have increased our excavation effort by 50%.

The third example involves simulation of three prospecting surveys, in an area called the Hay Hollow valley in east-central Arizona. Kriging analyses, after 12.5%, 37.5% and 50% of the area were covered, are shown in figs. 14, 15 and 16. Again, the figures are similar. By following any of the strategies we could have obtained the majority of the sites with minimal effort. Comparing the 37.5% and the 50% surveys we see that there is a corroborating areal overlap of 89% — only 11% of the area predicted to have sites by one survey is not confirmed by the other. To obtain all the sites with the 37.5% Krige analysis, we need to survey 45% of the total area.

Fig. 12. A three-dimensional representation of the number of sites per unit in Cañada del Alfaro in Guanajuato, Mexico. These simulated prospecting estimates are based upon Kriging irregularly collected data from 25% of the area.

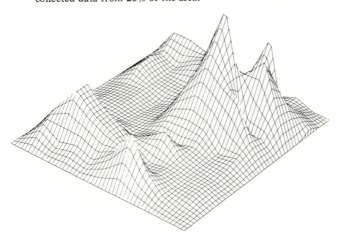

Fig. 13. A three-dimensional representation of the number of sites per unit in Cañada del Alfaro in Guanajuato, Mexico. These simulated prospecting estimates are based upon Kriging irregularly collected data from 50% of the area.

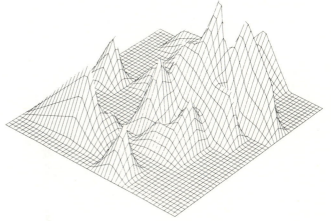

Assuming that the amount already surveyed can be averaged for redundancy, the total area to be surveyed will be about 63.5% (45 + 18.5). The minimum amount would be 45%, 7.5% more than what has already been done. The maximum amount of surveying would be 82%.

If we relax the necessity of finding all the sites, we can survey much smaller proportions of the area. For example, if we need only half of the sites, our 37.5% strategy will provide them in a survey of 23% of the area.

Finally, we shall examine a fourth area which involves synthetic data to show the variations possible with contrasting types of random and patterned behaviour. In this synthetic area imagine two cultures, one a hunting and gathering society in 500 BC. Its site distribution can be modelled by using a limited form of random function (i.e. the function is random within a set of real constraints). The other culture dating at AD 500 is based on a primary agricultural economy and the site distribution of peasant villages demonstrates a slightly distorted Löschian landscape. The hexagonal distribution may be unequally defined across space and incorporate a variety of sites.

Figs. 17 and 18 show the three-dimensional represen-

Fig. 14. A three-dimensional representation of the number of sites per unit in Hay Hollow valley. These simulated prospecting estimates are based upon Kriging irregularly collected data from 12.5% of the area.

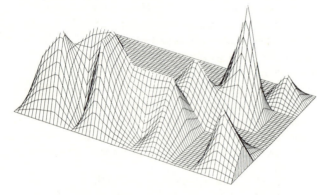

Fig. 15. A three-dimensional representation of the number of sites per unit in the Hay Hollow valley. These simulated prospecting estimates are based upon Kriging irregularly collected data from 37.5% of the area.

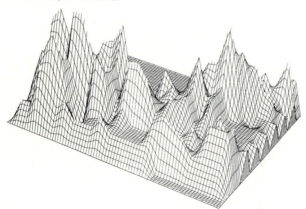

Fig. 16. A three-dimensional representation of the number of sites per unit in the Hay Hollow valley. These simulated prospecting estimates are based upon Kriging irregularly collected data from 50% of the area.

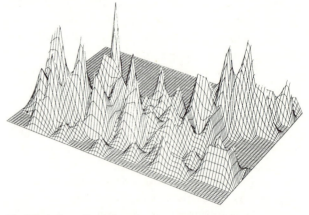

Fig. 17. A three-dimensional representation of the number of sites per unit of a synthetic area with a randomly determined site distribution. These simulated prospecting estimates are based upon Kriging irregularly collected data from 50% of the area.

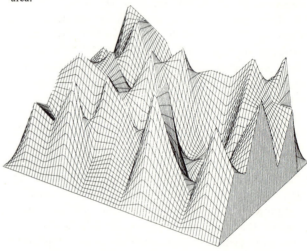

Fig. 18. A three-dimensional representation of the number of sites per unit of a synthetic area with a site distribution which follows a Löschian landscape ($K = 3$). These simulated prospecting estimates are based upon Kriging irregularly collected data from 12.5% of the area.

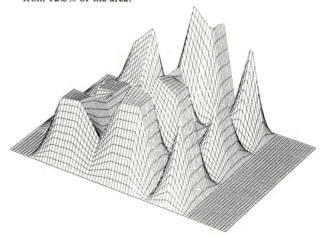

tation of the Kriging analysis for each of these cultures. Fig. 17, the random function, is based upon a 50% survey. Fig. 18, the patterned survey, is based upon a 12.5% survey. What should be noted in both cases is that clear prospecting strategies are appropriately defined.

For the earlier culture we get the first 20%, 98 sites, in the first 2% of the area covered. In order to get the next 20% (97 sites) it requires a survey of 28% after the analysis is run. For the later culture we find similar but better results in that the Kriging is able to make use of the patterning for efficiency. In the first 13% of the area surveyed we found 40 of the 174 sites or 23%. However, to get the next 16% of the sites, 14% of the area would need to be surveyed.

Conclusions

There is a role for improved prospecting strategies, different from sampling strategies, in archaeology. Kriging appears to be such a useful strategy. Prospecting strategies, however, do not provide something for nothing – they increase efficiency. In our examples the simulated prospecting strategies indicate that the archaeologist needed to survey only from 22% to 84% of the total area, and that the saving on the average is approximately 55%. If we can get all of the sites by surveying approximately half the area, there are obvious savings and advantages. Sometimes one will need to survey more – up to 84% – and sometimes less but in these cost intensive times it appears to be a useful and cost efficient strategy. Kriging is very effective if one is willing to settle for less than all the sites, and is most effective in the beginning of the survey. As the amount of sites needed increases the proportion of area to be surveyed becomes larger, but it never reaches 100%. More work will improve the applicability of Kriging to archaeological problems.

Notes

1. One might wish to question whether some archaeological variables show a degree of mathematical continuity. After discussions with several statisticians including Paul Switzer and Bradly Effron we felt justified in making the assumption. As they pointed out all real data are essentially discontinuous, but that what we wish to do is to estimate the empirical fact of discontinuity with an abstraction of continuity. In order to justify this, one's underlying model of the nature of the variable should be indicative of the fact that the phenomenon has a degree of continuity. For example, one could argue that the number of sites in an area, or the density of artifactual material, or the site frequency is continuous. People have been interacting over most of the surface and where material is dropped and preserved is a matter of a variety of probability functions. Thus our model would argue that the density of archaeological materials goes up and down, approaching and even reaching zero at certain locations but that the zero density is as significant for understanding the nature of prehistoric cultures as a positive density (fig. 19). Whether these densities are expressed in units of artifacts per acre, sites per acre, etc. is really irrelevant.

2. We will briefly describe SURFACE II for archaeologists who may wish further information. The package is capable of doing a wide range of operations. These include the input and output of data in standard and matrix form. The matrix may be modified by such operations as gridding (a variety of distance weighting averages), trend (an estimated trend surface or two dimensional polynomial regression fitted

to coordinates of the sample data points), matrix multiply and divide, filter (a weighted two dimensional moving average filter), smoothing (arithmetic averaging of adjacent values), near (a nearest-neighbour search system), and krig (an estimation of the grid matrix by universal Kriging). Output capabilities include contour mapping, three-dimensional perspective mapping, scattergrams, and histograms, to name only a few.

References

Blais, R.A. & Carlier, P.A. (1968) *Applications of Geostatistics in Ore Evaluation* (Canadian Institute of Mining and Metallurgy, Ore Reserve Estimation and Grade Control, Special Volume, No. 9), Montreal, Quebec

Clark, I. (1977) 'Practical Kriging in three dimensions', *Computers and Geosciences: An International Journal* 3(1): 173–80

Davis, J.C. (1973) *Statistics and Data Analysis in Geology*, Wiley, New York

Fagan, B. (1974) *In the Beginning*, Little & Brown, Boston

Heizer, R.H. & Graham, J.A. (1967) *A Guide to Field Methods in Archaeology*, National Press, Palo Alto

Hole, F. & Heizer, R.F. (1973) *An Introduction to Prehistoric Archaeology*, 3rd edn, Holt, Rinehart & Winston, New York

Huijbregts, C. & Matheron, G. (1971) *Universal Kriging (an Optimal Method for Estimating and Contouring in Trend Surface Analysis)* (Canadian Institute of Mining and Metallurgy, Decision Making in the Mineral Industry, Special Volume, No. 12), Montreal, Quebec

Matheron, G. (1965) *Les Variables Regionalisees at leur Estimation. Une Application de la Theorie des Fonctions Aleatoires aux Sciences de la Nature*, Masson, Paris

Matheron, G. (1969) *Le Krigeage Universal: les Cahiers du Centre de Morphologie Mathematique de Fontaineblue*, l'Ecole Nationale Superieure des Mines de Paris

Matheron, G. (1970) 'Random functions and their applications to geology' in D.F. Merriam (ed.) *Geostatistics, a Colloquium*, Plenum, New York

Matheron, G. (1971) *The Theory of Regionalised Variables and its Applications* (Les Cahiers du Centre de Morphologie Mathematique de Fontaineblue, Fascicule 5), l'Ecole Nationale Superieure des Mines de Paris

Mueller, J.W. (1974) *The Uses of Sampling in Archaeological Survey. Memoir of the Society for American Archaeology*, No. 28

Olea, R.A. (1972) *Application of Regionalized Variable Theory in Automatic Contouring* (Special Report to the American Petroleum Institute Research Project, No. 131), Kansas Geological Survey, University of Kansas Center for Research, Lawrence, Kansas

Olea, R.A. (1974) 'Optimal contour mapping using universal Kriging', *Journal of Geophysical Research* 79(5): 695–702

Fig. 19. The density of archaeological materials by distance.

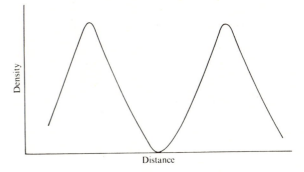

Olea, R.A. (1975) *Optimum Mapping Techniques Using Regionalized Variable Theory* (Kansas Geological Survey, Series on Spatial Analysis, No. 2), University of Kansas, Lawrence, Kansas

Olea, R.A. (1977) *Measuring Spatial Dependence with Semivariograms* (Kansas Geological Survey, Series on Spatial Analysis, No. 3), University of Kansas, Lawrence, Kansas

Olea, R.A. & Davis, J.C. (1977) 'Regionalized variables for evaluation of petroleum accumulation in Magellen Basin, South America', *Bulletin of American Association of Petroleum Geologists* 61(4)

Redman, C. (1974) *Archaeological Sampling Strategies* (Addison-Wesley Module in Anthropology, No. 55), Addison-Wesley, Reading, Massachusetts

Sampson, R.J. (1975) *Surface II Graphics System* (Kansas Geological Survey, Series on Spatial Analysis, No. 1), University of Kansas, Lawrence, Kansas

Sjoberg, A. (1976) 'Phosphate analysis of anthropic soils', *Journal of Field Archaeology* 3(4): 447–54

Steponatis, V. & Brain, J. (1976) 'A portable differential proton magnetometer', *Journal of Field Archaeology* 3(4): 455–63

Watson, P.J., LeBlanc, S. & Redman, C. (1971) *Explanation in Archaeology*, Columbia University Press, New York

Zubrow, E.B.W. (1975) *Prehistoric Carrying Capacity: a Model*, Cummings, Menlo Park

Zubrow, E.B.W. & Willard, A. (1974) *Models and Innovations: Archaeological and Regional Approaches to Guanajuato, Mexico*, Department of Anthropology, Stanford University

Chapter 11

**Towards an evaluation of
sampling strategies:
simulated excavations of a
Kenyan pastoralist site**
Albert J. Ammerman,
Diane P. Gifford and Albertus Voorrips

Problems of estimation and sampling go hand in hand. As more emphasis is placed in archaeology on framing questions about the past in quantitative terms, the need for a closer evaluation of the strategies used in the excavation of sites becomes increasingly apparent. At the same time, questions about the relative efficiency of different strategies in economic terms are also starting to be asked. Sampling is a ghost which has come to haunt the corridors of archaeology. The Hamlets of our day can be overheard speaking to themselves in the following terms:

I know that random sampling is good and wonderful, but how much of this thirty acre site do I have to sample before I can go home, do my analysis and write up my estimates with some peace of mind? 5%? 10%? If I were to dig up 25% of the site, would my estimates improve all that much?

If what I really want to do here is expose a large contiguous area to get house floors, how much confidence can I have in estimates derived from material recovered in this way as opposed to those obtained through random sampling?

Since Dr Blitz trenched his way right through the middle of Tell Hell, how reliable are his estimates about faunal composition at the site?

Since my students cannot turn around in 1 X 1 metre trenches and fight like cats and dogs in 2 X 2 metre squares, would excavating 5 × 5 metre units have an adverse effect on the reliability of my estimates? Or should I try to find smaller students?

While it can be a matter of some levity, the effect on estimates of such factors as the size of excavation units and the proportion of a site excavated have become matters of concern for many archaeologists. There have been a number of discussions about sampling at the regional level or as it relates to survey work in the recent literature (Redman 1974; Mueller 1975; Plog 1976). Much less attention has been paid to the level of the excavated site. Such questions tend to remain imponderables at this level, since even in retrospect one normally possesses a rather limited knowledge about the numbers of different cultural elements occurring over whole sites and since one usually does not have the chance of trying out and comparing several different sampling strategies at a given site. The application of simulation techniques to information obtained from ethnoarchaeological studies offers, however, one way of attacking this set of problems. Ethnoarchaeological research provides a situation where whole sites can be examined and their material remains comprehensively recorded. Computer simulation operating on such a data set makes it possible to excavate a site in as many ways and as many times as we wish.

Here we would like to present some initial explorations involving the simulated excavation of a Maasai site in Kenya. We have focused our primary attention on the relationship between the relative efficiency of sampling strategies and the reliability of the estimates that they produce. In this chapter we confine our inquiry to one specific problem of estimation: that of the composition of the site's faunal assemblage. We determine the various relative proportions or ratio estimates for the animal taxa represented in our samples and compare these to the values known for the entire faunal assemblage at the site. Ratio estimates, usually expressed as percentages, represent a classical, if not very sophisticated, way of handling prehistoric subsistence data. There are more informative ways of dealing with faunal data — such as minimum number of individuals — but since the main aim here is to compare different sampling strategies, the ratio estimates serve as a convenient and familiar measure in this heuristic study. In order to evaluate the efficiency of different strategies, it is useful to compare estimates over a series of points in time or stages in sampling rather than at some fixed (and in most cases arbitrarily selected) end point of sampling. This can be done as indicated below by computing and plotting the estimates of a simulated excavation in a stepwise manner as new units are sampled. In presenting the 'results' of excavation runs, we have avoided using summary statistics, which are often misinterpreted by those not having a statistical background, and have instead preferred to display the actual estimates arising from individual runs in graphic form. The graphs help to portray in a tangible way the degree of variation that can be observed among those runs carried out according to a given sampling design.

Before proceeding to describe the site and the simulation, some general remarks concerning sampling in archaeology are called for. A point that is often not clearly made in the literature is that nearly all survey and excavation work involves what is technically known as cluster sampling (Cochran 1977). This denotes a scheme in which random numbers operate on a list of *groups* (e.g. spatial units such as grid squares at sites), which contain *elements* (e.g. faunal remains), rather than on a list of elements. Archaeological sampling by means of randomly drawn excavation units is analogous to the demographer's or sociologist's use of city blocks in those cases where a list of all the blocks in a city is drawn up and random numbers are used to select those blocks or units to be sampled. After interviewing all of the people living in households located within the selected blocks, estimates are subsequently made with reference to the population of the city as a whole. This cluster sampling approach would contrast with simple random sampling where random numbers operate directly on a list of elements such as the list of names in a telephone directory. It is perhaps worth adding that the person doing a survey of the population of a city has the possibility of working with either lists of groups (i.e. blocks) or list of elements (i.e. names) and will base his choice between the two on a combination of theoretical and practical considerations. In archaeology, there is really no option: prior to excavation no list of elements can be made. The only way to proceed is through the sampling of spatial units of one kind or another.

One of the main reasons for employing random sampling in most fields of inquiry is the opportunity it offers of computing the variance associated with an estimate, thus providing a measure of its precision (see note 1). In the case of ratio estimates in cluster sampling — where there is likely to be a varying number of elements in each group — the ratio estimate, p, is given by the formula

$$p = \Sigma a_i / \Sigma M_i$$

and the variance, $V(p)$, by the formula (Cochran 1977, p. 247)

$$V(p) = \frac{N-n}{Nn\overline{M}^2} \frac{\sum\limits_{i=1}^{n} M_i^2 (p_i - P)^2}{N-1}$$

where

a_i = the number of elements of class a in sampling unit i
N = the total number of units
n = the number of units in the sample
M_i = the total number of elements in unit i
$\overline{M}$ = the average number of elements per unit (or $\Sigma M_i / N$)
P = the population proportion (in practice the ratio estimate given above)
p_i = the estimate of the population proportion for unit i (a_i / M_i)

Without going into a detailed discussion of the terms in this formula, it is worth recalling here that according to probabilistic sampling theory, there is the expectation that the variance will become smaller as sampling progresses. In other words, the estimates should become more reliable as the number of sampled units increases. This is something that can be seen, for example, in fig. 2 where the estimates for a given set of runs are sequentially displayed. It is also worth commenting that an idea of the variance associated with different levels of sampling is provided in graphic form in fig. 2 by the degree of dispersion among the plotted estimates for a particular set of runs.

The site

Site 2001 is a small Maasai pastoralist settlement located about 85 km southwest of Nairobi, Kenya, which was studied by Diane Gifford during her ethnoarchaeological research in Kenya. It lies about 25 m west of the road to Lake Magadi in an area of southern Kenya that is located about 19 km from the prehistoric site of Olorgesailie. The settlement is situated on relatively level ground, at the edge of a narrow river valley, and immediately at the base of a steep rocky hill that is some 200 m high. It was deserted in September 1974, when Gifford and Mr Kanyugi Ikenywa undertook a complete registration of the structures and debris at the site. All items were identified in the field, recorded on the field map, and left in place. Bone and debris were plotted to a distance of about 5 m from the outer fences of the site, where densities fell off sharply.

The most recent inhabitants of the site were not located and interviewed.

Site 2001 is typical in plan of most Maasai settlements, consisting of several single-family dwellings aligned along the internal perimeter of a post and thorn brush fence that entirely encloses a roughly circular kraal or stock pen (fig. 1). This enclosure contains the combined herds of the inhabitants; in the case of site 2001, it measured some 80 by 60 m and enclosed an area of about 4000 m^2. Within the major enclosure lay several smaller pens, which contained the inhabitants' flocks of sheep and goats.

The houses (averaging 6 X 3 X 1.5m in dimension) are nonportable structures of wattle and daub. The major constituent of the plaster is cow dung, which is found in plentiful supply at such settlements. A settlement may be abandoned and reoccupied several times, although not necessarily by the same group of families. A major factor in the abandonment of such a settlement is actually the depth of accumulated manure in the enclosure, which is not swept up or disposed of in any way. Sites are reoccupied when the dung has dried and is somewhat compacted.

The spatial relationships of the houses and the number of gates into the enclosure reflect social relations of the people who originally constructed them. However, with reoccupation by groups of different composition, structures may be added

Fig. 1. Plan of site 2001, a Maasai settlement located near Lake Magadi in Kenya, with the 5 metre grid superimposed.

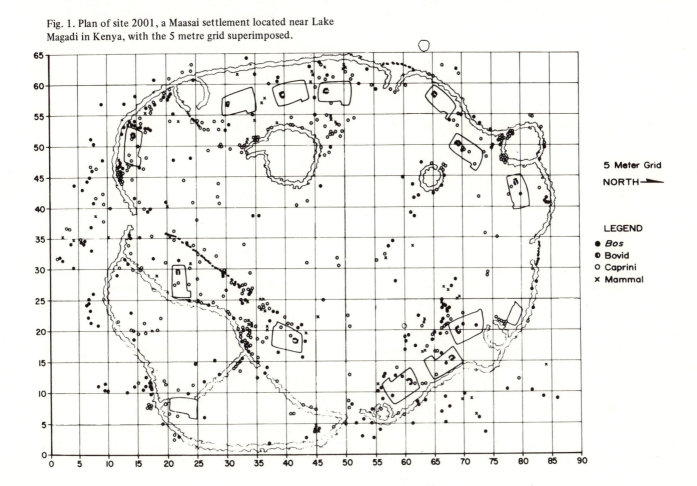

to accomodate new families or may be used as pens for immature stock. The house at the lower left of fig. 1 was probably added after the initial construction of the settlement and had most recently been used as a stock pen at the time that the mapping was done.

Debris was concentrated within the enclosing walls of the site and along the outer perimeter as well, especially the more level eastern and southern sides. A dense scatter of cow bones was also found about 8 m upslope of the palisade on the northwest side. The scatter, representing at least four individuals, was probably a large animal butchery associated with the site. For the purposes of our simulation, it was not included in the site map.

Some 734 pieces of bone were recorded which amount to about 68% of the cultural debris. With the exception of one giraffe metapodial, all identifiable bone derived from either caprines or *Bos taurus*. Although the local people kept donkeys, no remains attributable to equids were found at the site. In recording the pieces of bone, a detailed description was made of the body part involved (Gifford & Crader 1977) and four categories (leaving aside the giraffe element) were used for taxonomic classification: (1) caprine; (2) *Bos taurus*; (3) bovid (certain fragmentary pieces of intermediate size which could not be aged and assigned more definite identifications); (4) mammal (fragments not otherwise identifiable). Normally, Maasai people do not eat wild ungulates and so probably almost all of the pieces in the last two categories derive from caprines or *Bos*.

Artifactual material accounts for the remaining 32% of the total inventory. The remains here included: hearthstones, empty food tins, metal scrap, glass sherds, bits of plastic sheeting, rubber, leather, paper, cloth and basketry as well as damaged cups, bowls and cooking pots. The local people have ready access to a number of small general stores, as well as larger trading centres further afield. Although obtaining their animal protein from their herds in the traditional way, Maasai people in the region today acquire carbohydrates in preprocessed form from the general stores, purchasing maize meal, sugar and tinned vegetables. The evidence for the consumption of such foods lies in the food tins and scraps of paper flour sacks.

Simulated excavations: random cluster sampling

The first two excavation strategies to be considered involve random cluster sampling. These provide in effect a baseline for comparison with other strategies. The simulation procedure employed was straightforward. A 5 metre grid was superimposed on the site and random numbers were then used to determine the order in which the squares were to be excavated. When a square was sampled, the remains recorded as occurring within the spatial coordinates of the square were entered in an excavation inventory. The actual sampling was done in a stepwise fashion: one square or excavation unit was drawn at a time with its remains being added to the totals of previously excavated material. The faunal composition esti-

mates were recomputed and displayed with the addition of each new unit. Sampling (without replacement) continued until 125 squares — equivalent to 50% of the site area — had been excavated. Twenty separate runs were carried out following this procedure. The choice of twenty simulation runs represented a trade off between having a sufficient number of runs to reflect the patterns of variation associated with a given sampling design and at the same time a convenient number for the plotting of estimates (the main problem is one of crowding on the right-hand side of the graphs). In order to control for possible effects due to the size of the excavation unit, a second set of twenty runs was made in the same fashion but using a 2.5 m grid (having squares one-quarter of the area of the squares used in the first set of runs), drawing a total of 128 units (equivalent to 12% of the site area).

The results of the two simulations are presented in fig. 2. For our present purposes, we shall only look at the estimates for the most abundant animal taxa, the caprines (sheep and goats). The parametric value (i.e. the population value based on the mapping of finds in the field) for the relative proportion of Caprini among the faunal remains is 0.50. In fig. 2, the parametric value for the caprines lies in the middle of the vertical axis and the number of squares that have been sampled is indicated along the horizontal axis. Each point represents the ratio estimate obtained for a given number of excavated squares in a given run; open dots are used for those points falling within the 0.40 — 0.60 range, which can be regarded as a zone where estimates are reasonably good. The graphs make it possible to examine patterns in the estimates both with respect to accuracy (the presence of bias in the estimates) and precision (the degree of dispersion of the estimates) at the same time. Perhaps more important, they also permit us to observe the behaviour of estimates over time or as progressively more of the site is sampled. In looking at the graphs, it is worth restating some of the questions that we initially had in mind when we started working on the simulations.

(1)   How many squares do we have to excavate in order to have a good chance of obtaining estimates that are reliable (in terms both of accuracy and precision)?

(2)   What is the pattern of gain or improvement in estimation as an increasing proportion of the site is excavated? Is this the same or different at various points during the excavation? At what point are we confronted with diminishing returns when it comes to sampling further units?

(3)   Does the size of the sampling unit have an appreciable effect on the estimates? If the same proportion of the site area is to be excavated, which size would produce the more reliable estimates?

One of the first things to note is that the chances of obtaining a good estimate are quite low if only a small number of squares are sampled. For example, when eight of the larger (5 X 5 m) squares have been excavated, six out of twenty estimates fall outside the ± 0.20 range and only nine (less than half) fall within the ± 0.10 range. It is only when well over twenty squares (of either size) are excavated that we start to get some reliability in estimation. A second point worth noting is that in terms of accuracy there is little indication of bias in the pattern of the estimates. It can be seen that the estimates converge towards the parametric value with the points being more or less symetrically balanced about this value. In contrast, there is a clear suggestion of bias among the set of prior knowledge runs to be discussed later. Thirdly, it is apparent

that a fairly large number of squares will have to be sampled, if we are to have a good chance — say even three out of five — of obtaining an estimate that falls within the 0.40 to 0.60 range. For the larger squares, at least twenty squares would be required which would entail the excavation of some 500 m^2 or about 8% of the total site area. In the case of the smaller (2.5 × 2.5 m) squares, more than forty squares would have to be excavated, which would involve at least some 250 square

Fig. 2. Plot of the estimates of the relative proportion of the caprines in the faunal assemblage at site 2001 obtained during simulated excavations. The parametric value of the caprines (0.50) is located in the middle of the vertical axis, while the number of squares sampled is indicated along the horizontal axis. The area between 0.40−0.60 is bounded by a dashed line and between 0.30−0.70 by a dotted line. An open dot is used for those estimates falling within the 0.40−0.60 range. The excavation strategies employed — random cluster sampling (*a* and *b*) and prior knowledge (*c*) — are described in the text.

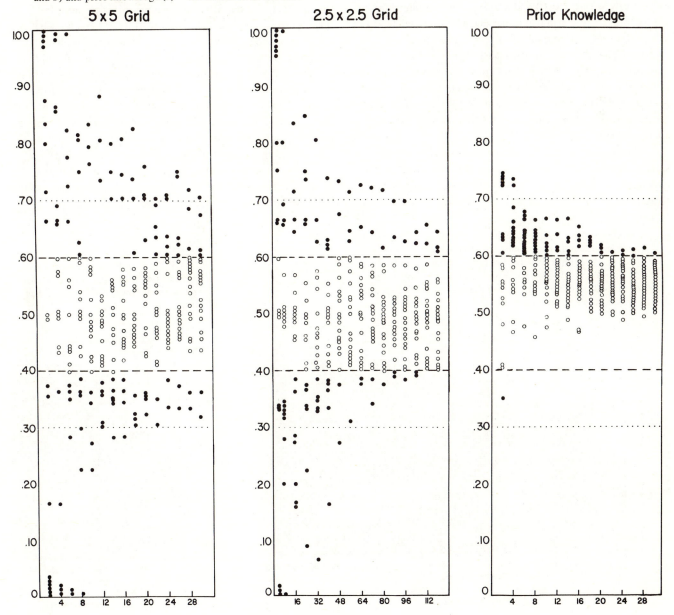

metres or about 4% of the site area. In practical terms, we would be dealing with fairly large-scale excavations in both cases.

Turning to the question of gain in estimation, it can be seen that this tends to decrease over time. There is a rapid improvement in estimation in going from 1% to 5% of the site area. The gain continues, if at a somewhat slower pace, between 5% and 10% of the site area. Above 10% of the site area, the improvement achieved by further sampling appears to be relatively small. This is perhaps shown more clearly in figs. 3–4 where the number of estimates falling respectively within ± 0.20 and ± 0.10 of the parametric value are plotted as 'gain' histograms. There would seem to be only a modest return for each new unit sampled beyond 15%–20% of the site area. It is, however, worth noting that the pattern of gain depends in part on the level of precision in estimation that is set as acceptable. As can be seen in fig. 5 where estimates falling respectively within ± 0.10 and ± 0.05 of the parametric value are plotted, there is still a considerable gain to be made as far as the more refined interval is concerned in going above 20% to 30% of the site area. Another observation that can be made with respect to fig. 5 is that there are still some estimates that fall outside the 0.05 interval when as much as 40% of the site is excavated. This 'resistance' of some estimates to convergence is somewhat surprising and is a point that we shall return to in a later section.

Turning to the third question, it is evident that the smaller squares tend to produce more reliable estimates. The excavation of a smaller proportion of the site area is required to achieve the same level of precision or dispersion among the estimates. This might be expected on the basis of probabilistic sampling theory, since the use of the smaller squares involves the drawing of many more sampling units. In trying to make an assessment of which square size to use in an excavation, a range of factors would need to be considered and the choice would depend in part on how much of the site area we plan to excavate. If we were to excavate either less than 2% or more than 15% of the site, there is not all that much difference in terms of faunal composition estimates between the two square sizes. If we planned to work in the range between 2% and 15% of the site area, the apparent advantage of the smaller squares would become relevant. On the other hand, it is important to bear in mind that the smaller square size may have definite disadvantages from other points of view.

Simulated excavation: central trenching

It is of obvious interest to see what kind of result would be obtained by excavating the site according to more traditional strategies. Such excavation strategies involve what is called nonprobabilistic sampling or judgement sampling in the sampling literature. The example that will be considered here is a classical one: excavating a trench through the centre of a site. The basic strategy to be followed starts with the excavation of two adjacent squares (each 5 × 5 m) placed either in the middle or along one side of the site. In a stepwise fashion, additional adjacent squares are excavated on one side or both sides, forming an expanding trench across the site. Again, as each new square is sampled, its remains are entered in the excavation inventory and the various estimates are recomputed. Ten runs with different starting points were carried out fol-

Fig. 3. Gain histogram for the twenty simulated excavation runs based on a random cluster sampling strategy and 5 × 5 m squares. The number of estimates falling within respectively ± 0.20 and ± 0.10 of the parametric value of the Caprini are indicated for different amounts of the site (number of squares and percentage of the area) sampled.

Fig. 4. Gain histogram for the twenty simulated excavation runs based on a random cluster sampling strategy and 2.5 × 2.5 m squares.

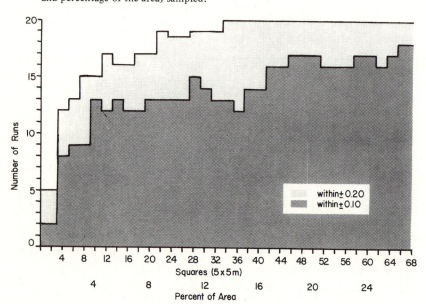

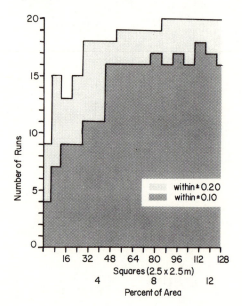

lowing this basic design. The results from these excavations are shown in the form of a gain histogram in fig. 6. It can be seen that a fair number of squares again have to be sampled before we have a good chance of getting a reliable estimate. If a comparison is made with the results from random cluster sampling using the same square size, there does not appear to be all that much difference between the two (see fig. 5). For example, in terms of estimates falling within ± 0.10 of the parametric value, the following can be seen: at ten squares, 6 out of 10 for central trenching versus 12 out of 20 for random cluster sampling; at thirty squares, 7 out of 10 versus 12 out of 20; and at fifty squares, 9 out of 10 versus 17 out of 20. If the ten examples of central trenching are representative of what can be expected from judgement sampling, then neither

of the two different strategies can be regarded as distinctly *better* or *worse* in the estimates that they produce. This would seem to offer little comfort to those advocating either new school or old school approaches to sampling.

Simulated excavation: prior information

There is one common feature of the two strategies considered so far: both are basically naive or operate on the basis of little information about the site except the location of its perimeter. In most situations where excavations are to be made, various kinds of information are available which can be incorporated in sampling strategies. The information can take different forms but probably the most common one consists of material obtained through surface collections at the site. A

Fig. 5. Gain histogram for the twenty simulated excavation runs based on a random cluster sampling strategy and 5 × 5 m squares. The intervals used here are respectively ± 0.10 and ± 0.05.

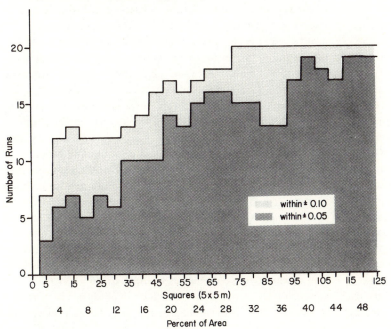
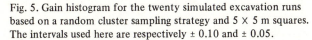

Fig. 6. Gain histogram for the ten simulated excavation runs based on a central trenching strategy and 5 × 5 m squares. Note that the count of estimates is plotted only every five squares here.

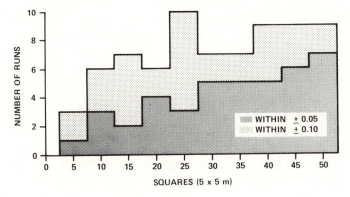

prior information strategy that comes readily to mind would be to excavate those areas of a site where material is found on the surface. If we are interested in the question of faunal composition, we might want to concentrate on those places where bones are present or even abundant among surface collections. In the version of this strategy to be considered here, the actual sequence in which units will be sampled is based on the abundance of surface faunal remains. We start with the richest square and proceed in a stepwise fashion to sample the second richest and so on. In the case of a tie with respect to the abundance of surface remains, random numbers are used to decide on the order among the squares involved. Again, 5 × 5 m squares are used and estimates are recomputed as each new square is excavated. What is, of course, required to carry out this strategy is a set of surface material. Simulation techniques have been used to generate such surface collections. Using the same grid system, surface collections were generated by a Monte Carlo simulation in which the probability of 0.10 was used in determining whether or not any given piece (in the inventory of material recorded in the field) appeared on the site surface. Twenty different sets of surface material were produced in this way. Each of these served, in turn, as the prior information for a simulated excavation conducted along the lines of the strategy described above and with a total of thirty squares being sampled during each run. Before looking at the results, it is worth making two comments. The first is that the prior information provided by the simulated surface collections amounts to an ideal case in many respects. The ratio of surface to sub-surface material is quite high and a 'fair' picture is offered over the whole site area. The second comment is that this sampling strategy can be viewed in some ways as an example of a stratified random cluster sampling design (see note 2). The way in which the prior information is used in effect divides the squares at the site into two strata: those abundant in bones and those with few or no bones. Sampling weight is concentrated in the first of the two, which can be seen as a reasonable practice in retrospect considering how the ratio estimate is calculated (see the formula presented earlier), and the Monte Carlo generated surfaces effectively introduce a randomising procedure in the order in which squares are drawn. The results of the twenty runs are shown in fig. 2c where a much more rapid convergence of the estimates can be seen. Even at the stage of eight squares the dispersion is quite low. But this gain in precision is not obtained without its price. It is clear that the estimates produced by this strategy are biased: initially the parametric value is overestimated by about 0.10 and subsequently the bias subsides at twenty sampled squares to about 0.05. In considering the trade off between precision and accuracy, it is common practice in sampling work not to be overly concerned about bias in estimation procedures if the bias is not large relative to the parametric values involved (Cochran 1977, p. 14). This is particularly so if we possess some knowledge about the direction and magnitude of the bias. There is some irony in the situation at hand, however, since although the long-term bias appears to be reasonably small, the

bias at the start where the prior information strategy would seem to offer a real advantage is relatively large.

Discussion

In looking back over the sampling strategies presented, it should be emphasised that we are dealing with a case study. We are cautioned against generalising to other kinds of sites. This is not such an unfavourable thing as it may first appear: sampling is not an activity that is done in general contexts but rather is in practice case oriented. What would be required for a more general evaluation of excavation strategies is the development of a wide repertoire of such case studies. It is also worth repeating that only a few of the main sampling strategies have been considered here. There are other strategies that would clearly be worth exploring. Another aspect of the study that needs to be stressed is its heuristic nature: for example, the assumption has to be made that the occupation surface observed in 1974 was somehow buried and survived as such until excavated by some future archaeologist. Estimation is treated as a primary concern of sampling (which has not always been the case in the literature on sampling in archaeology) and estimates for one class of material are used as the means of comparison between the different sampling strategies. In excavating a site, we would obviously be interested in developing simultaneously several different lines of information. At the same time, in attempting to make archaeological inferences we shall eventually have to assess how well we are doing or we can expect to do along individual lines of evidence.

It is apparent that no matter which strategy is used, there is little chance of obtaining a reliable estimate for the caprines if only a few squares are excavated. This means that statements about the percentage of different animals in the faunal assemblage in such a case are at best on shaky grounds. It is only in the range between 3% and 10% of the site area that estimates of some reliability start to emerge. If random cluster sampling is to be employed, our chances would seem to improve if we adopt squares of a smaller size, which implies the use of more sampling units. There would also appear to be advantages — as well as some disadvantages such as the bias mentioned above — in trying to incorporate prior information in the sampling strategy. Another observation that can be made is that there may not be much merit in continuing to excavate beyond about 15%–20% of the site area: the gain in estimation for each new unit sampled beyond this point is quite modest. In some respects, the site appears to offer even 'resistance' to estimation. We might have expected a much stronger convergence of estimates toward the parametric value for sample sizes covering more than 20% of the site area (see fig. 5). This cannot be explained by the relative thinness of remains over the site or small sample sizes, since the sample sizes should consist of several hundred bones at the larger sampling levels. It is more likely that the resistance has something to do with the structure of the data itself and may even turn out to be a welcome 'problem'. We are fortunate here in having the chance to look back over the whole site in retrospect. In fig. 7, the frequency distribution of grid squares in terms of the number of bones they contain is shown. The distribution reflects a strong element of heterogeneity and, in fact, resembles a Neyman Type A distribution (Johnson & Kotz 1969, p. 216), which is sometimes used as a model representing heterogeneity. Most of the squares have few or no bones (and sampling them makes relatively little contribution to estimation), while a small proportion of the squares contain most of the bones. It is not surprising then that the prior information sampling strategy produced a much more rapid convergence.

But this is only part of the story. If we examine table 1 where the frequency of estimates within sampling units or squares is given for the richer squares, it can also be seen that there is considerable heterogeneity with respect to the composition of the faunal remains found within any one square.

There are only nine out of 56 squares where the estimate for the sampling unit falls in the 0.41–0.60 range. A situation of this kind – where there is heterogeneity both in terms of the number of elements per group or sampling unit and of the estimates occurring within sampling units – is not a favourable one for random cluster sampling techniques and probably for most judgement sampling strategies as well. If the situation implies difficulties for estimation, it is, however, just the one that the archaeologist interested in the identification of activity-areas and spatial patterns is looking for. The suggestion is that what may be involved is a complex interaction and compromise between two of the major objectives — estimation and the recognition of spatial patterns — of modern archaeological research. This represents a challenging subject for further study.

Table 1. *The frequency of estimates of the relative proportion of caprines within sampling units for squares containing a total count of 5 or more bones*

Relative proportion of caprines	Number of bones per square (5 × 5 m)						
	5–7	8–10	11–13	14–16	17–19	20–22	Total
0.00–0.20	10	2	1	0	0	0	13
0.21–0.40	5	8	0	0	1	0	14
0.41–0.60	4	2	0	1	2	0	9
0.61–0.80	2	3	2	1	0	2	10
0.81–1.00	5	3	0	0	2	0	10
Total	26	18	3	2	5	2	56

Fig. 7. Histogram showing the frequency of 5 × 5 m squares at site 2001 containing different numbers of bones.

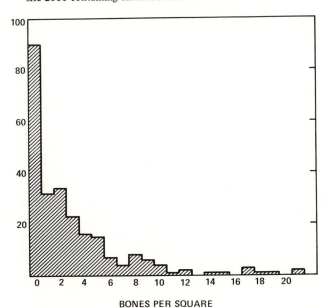

BONES PER SQUARE

Notes

1. The standard deviation, a commonly used measure of dispersion in statistics, is based on the square root of the variance. It is worth noting that the values for the terms $(N - n)/Nn$ in the formula become progressively smaller as more units are sampled. As can be seen in the terms $M_i^2 (p_i - P)^2$, the magnitude of the variance is sensitive, especially for those squares rich in bones, to the pattern of difference between the ratio estimate values for given sampling units and the overall ratio estimate. It is interesting to look at the values shown in table 1 in this context.

2. Most stratified random sampling designs rely in one way or another on information known prior to the start of sampling. The evaluation of stratified random sampling strategies – there is a large family of such designs to consider – involves in part seeing how well a given strategy makes use of the available prior information. One problem that obviously arises in trying to evaluate such designs along the lines of the present study is that the prior information is not known (in the sense of actual surface collections) but is generated by a procedure that we specify. Other procedures could be specified leading to different sets of prior information, where the application of other sampling designs might turn out to be more efficient. There is the dilemma that in cases where we have actual surface collections to start with, we are unlikely to have a comprehensive picture of what is happening below the surface. The study of this class of sampling strategies (including the variant discussed in this chapter) stands at the present time as largely an heuristic exploration. An additional point about stratified random sampling worth making is that the strata, although they have commonly been treated in this way in archaeology, do not have to consist of spatially or geographically contiguous sampling units.

Acknowledgements

This is a revised version of a paper given at the Symposium on Computer Simulation as Archaeological Model Building, Annual Meeting of the Society for American Archaeology, 1977. The computer programs were prepared by Juliana Hwang of the Department of Genetics of Stanford University and the simulation runs were made on the SUMEX Computer Facility of Stanford University. Support for Diane Gifford's research in Kenya was provided by a National Science Foundation Dissertation Grant and a National Defense Education Act Fellowship. The fieldwork was carried out under the permission of the Office of the President of the Republic of Kenya, under the sponsorship of the Trustees of the National Museums of Kenya, and made possible by the cooperation of the local Maasai community and the assistance of Mr Kanygui Ikenywa, then head of the Olorgesailie Prehistoric Monument staff. Support toward the study of the material from the site was also provided by a Regent's Fund Grant of the University of California (Berkeley) and a faculty research grant from the University of California (Santa Cruz). Albertus Voorrip's participation in the study during a visit to Stanford University was made possible by a grant from the Netherlands Organisation for the Advancement of Pure Research (ZWO). We would above all like to thank Professor Glynn Isaac for his role in initiating the fieldwork in Kenya and his continuing interest in the project.

References

Cochran, W.G. (1977) *Sampling Techniques*, third edn, Wiley, New York

Gifford, D.P. & Crader, D.C. (1977) 'A computer coding system for archaeological faunal remains', *American Antiquity* 42: 225–38

Johnson, N.L. & Kotz, S. (1969) *Discrete Distributions*, Wiley, New York

Mueller, J.W. (ed.) (1975) *Sampling in Archaeology*, University of Arizona Press, Tucson

Plog, S. (1976) 'Relative efficiencies of sampling techniques for archaeological surveys' in K.V. Flannery (ed.) *The Early Mesoamerican Village*, Academic Press, New York

Redman, C.L. (1974) *Archaeological Sampling Strategies* (Addison-Wesley Module in Anthropology, No. 55), Addison-Wesley, Reading, Massachusetts

PART SIX

Conclusion and assessment

From the papers in this volume it is clear that simulation is usually taken to mean modelling a process by a similar process (see also Schultz & Sullivan 1972, p. 4). As the term is used by Zubrow and Harbaugh (chapter 10), this does not necessarily involve use of a computer. Indeed the involvement of a computer is not an essential element in the distinctive process called simulation. The distinguishing characteristics of simulation would seem to be as follows. First, the modelling is of non-deterministic processes. Most simulations in archaeology have involved some stochastic element so that exactly the same result is not obtained every time the same input data are used. The underlying idea is that, although individual actions are not in any sense random, the aggregate result of unconstrained human behaviour can be compared with random processes. As Clarke (1972, p. 20) notes, such aggregate situations occur when actions are affected by a great many variable factors.

Secondly, simulation appears to be intimately concerned with change. An example is the study of the processes of change that occurred between the static Middle Helladic and static Late Helladic settlement pattern (Chadwick, chapter 5). Unlike many geographical models, which are concerned with stationary problems, simulation has a fundamental link with time and with explanation in terms of temporal processes.

Thirdly, simulation usually involves attempts at being realistic. A difference when compared with many models is that the researcher is less moving *away* from the data towards simplified generalities, and more moving deductively *towards* the data in an attempt to mimic with greater realism the actual events. On the other hand, simulation must not be too realistic because, if it is, understanding of the processes may not be furthered. Thus, simulation in archaeology lies somewhere between experimental archaeology and mathematical modelling. It combines the realism of the one with the generality and precision of the other to provide a flexible, exciting approach to hypothesis formation and testing.

A further distinguishing characteristic of simulation often appears to be that the ultimate concern is with complete models. This is because the modeller has full control over all variables and he can examine the effects of these variables to a degree impossible in any other form of experimentation. Thus, the idea of modelling 'total societies', or at least highly complex processes, becomes feasible, although dangerous as will be shown below.

Given these main features of simulation in archaeology, it seems that archaeological simulation has been used in two rather different ways. Most work is concerned with 'predicting' a set of actual data. The aim is to find some process that will produce as accurate a copy as possible of the real pattern. Success here is measured in terms of the similarity between two static patterns — the actual and the simulated. This is unfortunate if it directs interest away from the internal processes of the model and their logical consistency. Other work, however, has been concerned primarily with these internal relationships. For example, Black (chapter 6) examines the way in which different factors in the growth and survival of small populations are interconnected. Success here is measured in terms of the amount that is learnt about the factors affecting population growth, rather than in similarity to any particular data set.

In the remaining part of this chapter, an attempt will be made to summarise the value of applying computer simulation in archaeology. The chapters have identified many problems raised by such application. These difficulties and limitations will also be discussed.

Many of the authors in this volume (e.g. Chadwick p. 47, Hamond p. 6, Zimmerman p. 30) have claimed that computer simulation brings clarity, objectivity and precision to hypothesis formation in archaeology (see also Doran 1970, p. 297). A theory is made 'real' (Zimmerman p. 30) so that one's assumptions are exposed and forced into close scrutiny. The attempt to write a computer simulation of a hypothetical process often uncovers aspects of the problem which had not been fully thought out, and inconsistencies and illogical reasoning are often realised. Indeed, it may be this initial self-educative process which is the most fruitful in the simulation procedure (Watt 1968, p. 371). It is certainly possible to be non-rigorous in developing and testing a computer simulation, but some degree of rigour is often claimed (e.g. Zimmerman p. 30) due to the encouragement to be explicit about one's ideas and hypotheses. In addition, many simulations are concerned with trying to output a set of archaeological data — such as a map

of sites or artifacts — as the end-product of a particular process. The encouragement therefore exists to demonstrate explicitly, even if not statistically, the fit of one's hypothesis to the data. Although this may be seen as a move towards rigour, it is often fairly easy to find some procedure which will give a reasonable fit to the data. If rigour is to be introduced, the likelihood of getting the observed degree of fit or the relative fit of a number of different hypotheses should be examined.

Indeed, a further value of the application of the computer simulation of stochastic processes in archaeology is that the likelihood of getting an observed statistic summarising a set of archaeological data can be assessed in a way that is immediately understandable. The speed of computers means that the same stochastic process can be 'run' a large number of times. Obviously each end-result will not be the same because of the random, stochastic component in the model. But it is this variation in the results which is of importance since it allows the likelihood of getting an observed set of data by chance to be assessed — 'by chance' here means 'due to the stochastic component in the model'. For example, imagine that the average distance between sites has been used to describe their distribution. After simulating a particular stochastic process, say, 200 times, it is found that the actual average distance between sites is simulated less than 2 times and has a less than 1% chance of occurring. One can therefore say that it is unlikely that the actual data were produced by the hypothesised process. In fact this type of procedure has been little used in published work and in the examples in this book (see, however, chapters 7 and 9). This is probably partly because of the large amounts of computing time necessary to run complex simulations hundreds of times. However, the approach would seem to be an important one if any sort of statistical rigour is to be developed in simulation studies.

The use of explicit models is now an accepted part of theory and analysis in archaeology. Often these models are mathematically defined. For example, the gravity or regression models are expressed as mathematical equations for which a solution can be found when applied to a set of archaeological data. However, these are extremely simple models, and the gravity model at least has little interpretive value. The search for simple universal models or laws, which was the central theme of much of the 'new archaeology' has been disappointing (Doran & Hodson 1975, p. 299). There are few simple laws of human behaviour which exist and which are more than platitudes. Human behaviour, and the processes which form the archaeological data are much too complex to be described satisfactorily by simple laws and models. It is, therefore, necessary to build complex models in which there are a large number of parameters and interrelated variables. But, as was found by Black (p. 67), it becomes impossible to find direct mathematical solutions for complex and realistic models. Simulation offers an escape from this difficulty. Using simulation, the behaviour of a system can be determined and understood by experiment rather than by mathematical solution.

For many archaeologists who have had little mathematical training, the use of simulation has a further advantage. It is probably considerably easier to understand a well-described simulation than to follow a highly complex mathematical argument. Understanding of, and even involvement in, the building of complex models thus becomes possible for a wider range of archaeologists (although Moore, p. 12, suggests that the archaeologists will probably not be able to get involved in writing programs himself).

Whether computer simulation involves greater rigour in archaeological analysis really depends on the researcher involved. The real value and importance of simulation in archaeology lie in the possibility for coping with the full complexities both of human behaviour and the relationship between that behaviour and the archaeological record. In the latter respect, Ammerman, Matessi and Cavalli-Sforza (1978) have introduced dropping-rates into their simulations of artifact dispersal. The rate at which artifacts are dropped into the ground is incorporated into the model. Hamond (p. 4) has noted the possibility of simulating post-depositional processes. Simulation offers the chance of experimenting or 'playing' with these different types of hypotheses and examining the effects of different variables on the archaeological data. It is this process of experimentation with complex models that leads to new ideas about the data. 'Surprises' may be met (Black p. 21) and new approaches to the field collection of data may become necessary. The successful running of a complex simulation program is an exciting and rewarding experience in which the researcher constantly feels on the brink of discovering something new.

That having been said, computer simulation brings with it as many or more problems than advantages. For example, as noted above, an important function of computer simulation is to allow the building of complex models. This, however, often involves incorporating a vast number of parameters, events and variables into the simulation. This has been well pointed out by Hamond (p. 5, see also Zimmerman p. 36). If the simulation is to be run enough times so that as many combinations of variables are studied as possible, an enormous amount of computer time and resources may be required, never mind the amount of personal time necessary for the writing and 'debugging' of the computer program. In any case, the simulation might become so complex that the results cannot be understood any better than the real processes (Zimmerman p. 30). There is clearly little point in building a model so complex and realistic that comprehension of what is going on is brought no nearer.

Another consequence of the building of complex simulation models is that it may often be possible satisfactorily to mimic the archaeological data by a large number of different combinations of parameter values. One may, then, not apparently be much nearer understanding the processes involved. In any case, if one can produce a good copy of the archaeological data nothing is proved — other unconsidered processes could have been at work. Sometimes it may be possible to carry out independent tests on the relevance of a par-

ticular hypothesis — for example, it was predicted (p. 80) that the relevance of a random-walk procedure for the dispersal of Neolithic axes could be further tested by examining whether there was any decrease in size of the axes with distance from the source. But, in general, simulation can only show what types of processes *could* have produced an observed set of data. It is rather the simulated data which do *not* fit the actual observations that provide most information and are of greatest value.

Many of the papers in this volume end with a section devoted to future changes of the simulation model which are thought necessary. This may be another result of the complexity of modelling human behaviour. It becomes possible endlessly to tinker with the model in an attempt to understand better its functioning or to improve the results. In one sphere particularly, there may be few guidelines for the choice of appropriate parameters so that long term 'playing with' the simulation procedure may be involved. Post-depositional processes — the survival and recovery of the evidence — are obviously important constituents in any complete archaeological simulation. Their relative absence from published work and from the studies presented above may indicate the difficulties of introducing such factors into simulations. There may be so many unknowns in the processes of survival and recovery of, for example, a 6000-year-old settlement pattern, that satisfactory modelling is difficult. Even when the factors affecting post-depositional processes are better understood in general, their impact is only likely to be very predictable in a few particular instances. Extended 'playing with' complex models may thus become a feature of archaeological simulation studies.

Another special difficulty of simulation studies in archaeology is that a complex model may require more data and information than the archaeologist can really supply. Doran and Hodson (1975, p. 305) note that Thomas' (1973) simulation study suffers from the paucity of basic data available to him. The archaeologist is thus forced frequently to substitute approximate data (perhaps derived from modern situations) and make large numbers of assumptions. This point is made by Black (p. 68) in relation to population studies, and assumptions are made explicitly and necessarily by O'Shea (p. 42) when his data are insufficiently detailed. Now, a simulation might work perfectly well and produce good results even though the assumptions are incorrect. Thus, again, the fact that a set of data can be reproduced by using one set of assumptions does not mean that it cannot be mimicked using other sets of assumptions. The more unjustifiable assumptions that have to be made, the more time that must be spent in trying different variables and parameters, and the less satisfactory the simulation. This is a special problem in archaeology where very little is usually known about the processes being examined.

Even if a simulation has been successfully and correctly run on a computer it is still necessary to test the fit of the results to the actual data. Does a particular process account well for a particular set of data and what is meant by 'well'? When a spatial process is being considered, measures and tests of spatial autocorrelation can be used (see Chadwick, p. 53). The differences between the simulated and actual data can be assessed for each site or grid cell on the map. One must then decide whether these differences show any spatial patterning or dependency. If they do, then there remains some spatial organisation in the actual data which the simulation has not accounted for. Generally, however, it is extremely difficult to construct valid tests so that Doran and Hodson (1975, p. 301) suggest that part of the judgement of simulation models might concern their internal coherence and commonsense plausibility. In this author's view, the archaeologist is justified in following two types of 'testing' procedure. First, and as already mentioned (p. 134), he can simulate a stochastic process a large number of times and calculate the likelihood of obtaining a statistic derived from the data 'by chance'. Second, from certain points of view, there is little point in the archaeologist knowing that he has produced one 'good' fit to his data according to some arbitrary significance level. Given the nature of much archaeological data this is probably fairly easy to do at least once. More important, as already noted, is that multiple working hypotheses should be examined and that their *relative* fit should be assessed. Which types of hypotheses give better results than others and what are their salient features? Relative measures of fit may be of more value in *interpreting* the data than *absolute* tests of goodness-of-fit.

The final problem in applying simulation studies in archaeology to be mentioned here is that the development of a simulation program often appears to follow rather a circuitous route. An hypothesis is often derived from a set of archaeological data and is tested against the same data. Unlike other disciplines, there may be no independent check — no other set of data available until further excavation takes place. For example, an important parameter in the simulation of settlement spread is the distance moved by sites as they spread out and change location. The frequency distribution of distances moved is usually derived from an observed set of data. For example, it may be noted that early Neolithic settlements in part of central Europe are spaced about 2 km apart. In simulating the spread of that settlement pattern, sites are not allowed to move less than 2 km, or to a point less than 2 km from another site. It is hardly surprising, then, that the simulated map of settlement is similar to the archaeological map, and little new is learnt by the simulation.

This circular procedure is obviously unsatisfactory. Ideally, the archaeologist's hypotheses should be derived from data (such as modern situations) independent of those he is trying to reproduce in his simulations. Indeed this is the approach used by many of the writers in this volume. O'Shea uses historical and ethnographic references to predict settlement behaviour, and Elliott, Ellman and Hodder use the idea of ceremonial gift exchange derived from other disciplines. Where some degree of circularity does exist in developing a simulation, the interest of the simulation lies more in understanding the relative effect of different variables on the functioning of a system, than in the ability to reproduce accurately the archaeological data.

It is clear, then, that there are as many or more problems posed by simulation in archaeology as there are advantages gained. But the overall view is that simulation will become of major importance in archaeology because it can cope with some of the major problems posed by archaeological data. With sparse, limited data, there will always be numerous hypothetical processes which must be taken into account. Computer simulation offers the chance of dealing with this range of possibilities in an explicit logical manner. It seems likely that computer simulation will play an important part in archaeology for additional reasons. Recent developments in archaeology have been concerned, amongst other things, (*a*) with the use of systems theory, (*b*) with an emphasis on deductive reasoning, and (*c*) with the need to be rigorous and precise. Computer simulation (*a*) is 'the practical equivalent of systems theory' (Doran 1970, p. 296), (*b*) demands an explicitly deductive approach, and (*c*) can be seen as encouraging clarity and precision. In view of this, it seems reasonable to suggest that computer simulation and its further development will remain with a long term central role in archaeological analysis.

References

Ammerman, A.J., Matessi, C. & Cavalli-Sforza, L.L. (1978) ' Some new approaches to the study of the obsidian trade in the Mediterranean and adjacent areas' in I. Hodder (ed.) *The Spatial Organisation of Culture*, Duckworth, London

Clarke, D.L. (1972) 'Models and paradigms in contemporary archaeology' in D.L. Clarke (ed.) *Models in Archaeology*, Methuen, London

Doran, J. (1970 'Systems theory, computer simulations and archaeology', *World Archaeology* 1: 289–98

Doran, J. & Hodson, F.R. (1975) *Mathematics and Computers in Archaeology*, Edinburgh University Press

Schultz, R.L. & Sullivan, E.M. (1972) 'Developments in simulation in social and administrative science' in H. Guetzkow, P. Kotler and R.L. Schultz (eds.) *Simulation in Social and Administrative Science*, Prentice Hall, Englewood Cliffs, New Jersey

Thomas, D.H. (1973) 'An empirical test for Steward's model of Great Basin settlement patterns', *American Antiquity* 38: 155–76

Watt, K.E.F. (1968) *Ecology and Resource Management: a Quantitative Approach*, McGraw-Hill, New York

INDEX